# Soccer Coaching Activities, Session Plans and Assessment for Plus 2 Players (6, 7 & 8 Years Old)

## Coaching for Player Development Series

Written by David Newbery
Contributions by Tony DiCicco

Corporate Office:
1477 Park Street, Suite 13C
Hartford, CT 06106

www.SoccerPlus.org

With thanks to:

Shawn Kelly (cover art)

Val Brown (proofing)

Copyright © 2010 by SoccerPlus FC and David Newbery & Tony DiCicco

ISBN: 1453746366

EAN-13: 9781453746363.

Published by SoccerPlus FC, PO Box 1586 Westerly, RI 02891. All rights reserved. No part of this work may be reproduced or transmitted in any form, for commercial purposes or by any means electronic or mechanical, including photocopying or recording from any information stored in a retrieval system, without permission from the authors.

# About the Authors

## David Newbery

<u>Director of Coach & Player Development, SoccerPlus</u>

For over 20 years David has studied and worked in youth education, soccer development and coaching. A former University Professor and CEO of a Youth Sports Company, David has been fortunate to travel extensively in the USA, meeting with coaches and club officials and learning about their approach to player development and coaching. Experiences from hundreds of clubs have afforded him the opportunity to support and guide youth soccer organizations, endeavoring to develop an educationally sound environment for players, coaches and parents. David regularly contributes to publications and blog discussions on various topics pertaining to youth soccer, and has authored several books and manuals.

## Tony DiCicco

<u>Technical Director & President, SoccerPlus</u>

In addition to developing successful businesses, Tony has established a record in elite soccer making him the most successful coach in USA Soccer history. In 1996, DiCicco led the USA Women's national team to Olympic gold and he followed that triumph with victory over China in the 1999 World Cup Final - the game setting the world record for the highest single game attendance in women's sport (90,185). Tony returned to international soccer in 2008 to lead the USA U20 Women's National Team to World Cup glory in Chile and recorded his third successive world championship. Tony is the Head Coach of the Boston Breakers professional women's team playing in the WPS league in the USA.

# Table of Contents

## Contents

| | |
|---|---|
| Preface | 4 |
| Introduction | 6 |
| **Chapter 1** | 8 |
| Player Development – defining and evaluating your program! | 9 |
|     Curriculum | 9 |
|     Player Development Pathway | 9 |
|     Stages of Development | 10 |
|     Understanding the basics of child development | 11 |
|     Learning focus | 11 |
|     Child/Player Centered | 12 |
|     Vertical vs Horizontal integration | 12 |
|     Long Term Focus | 14 |
|         Horizontal Integration Model for Organizing Player Development | 15 |
|     Ability based | 15 |
|     Player Assessment | 17 |
|     Holistic Approach to learning | 17 |
|     Equal opportunity program | 18 |
| Player Development Self Evaluation | 20 |
| **Chapter 2** | 21 |
| Practice and Game Organization | 21 |
| Practice and Game Organization | 22 |
|     Fundamental Movement Skills (FMS) | 22 |
|     Window of Opportunity | 23 |
|     Playing up and playing down | 24 |
|     Training to game ratios | 25 |
|     A word about 'Winning' | 26 |
|     A word about 'Talent' and Tryouts | 26 |

| | |
|---|---|
| Specialist Position Training | 27 |
| Game Format & Team sizes | 28 |
| Frequency and Duration | 29 |
| Warm-up, Cool down and Stretching | 29 |
| Creating an environment for participation and learning | 30 |
| Selecting appropriate activities and progression | 30 |
| Repetition and Reinforcement (Imprinting) | 31 |

## Chapter 3 — 33

| | |
|---|---|
| Plus 2 Stage of Development | 34 |
| What you need to know about development | 34 |
| Development characteristics helpful to know about 6, 7 & 8 year olds | 35 |
| Translation to Player Development | 36 |
| Player Competencies and Assessment | 37 |
| Plus 2 Competencies Matrix | 38 |
| Coaching Tips - Do's and Don'ts | 43 |
| Do's | 43 |
| Don'ts | 44 |
| Coaching Formula | 45 |
| Plus 1 – Coaching Formula | 46 |
| Plus 2 – Coaching Formula | 47 |
| Skills Challenge Pyramid™ | 48 |
| About the Skills Challenge Pyramid™ | 48 |
| Plus 1 Skills Challenge Pyramid™ | 49 |
| Plus 2 Skills Challenge Pyramid™ | 51 |

## Chapter 4 — 53

| | |
|---|---|
| The Coaching Plan for 8, 10 & 12 Week Seasons | 54 |
| Coaching plan for 8 weeks – 1 session per week | 55 |
| Coaching plan for 8 weeks – 2 sessions per week | 56 |
| Coaching plan for 10 weeks – 1 session per week | 57 |
| Coaching plan for 10 weeks – 2 sessions per week | 58 |

| | |
|---|---|
| Coaching plan for 12 weeks – 1 session per week | 59 |
| Coaching plan for 12 weeks – 2 sessions per week | 60 |
| **Chapter 5** | 61 |
| Coaching Activities & Session Plans | 62 |
| Plus 2 - Early to Mid Stage Activities | 64 |
| Plus 2 - Early to Mid Stage Sessions | 137 |
| Plus 2 - Mid to Late Stage Activities | 156 |
| Plus 2 - Mid to Late Stage Sessions | 202 |
| **Chapter 6** | **214** |
| Player Assessment | 214 |
| Plus 2 Assessment Activities | 217 |
| Appendix | 226 |
| SoccerPlus Big Picture of Curriculum | 227 |
| SoccerPlus Player Development Model | 228 |
| SoccerPlus Y-SAT Club Assessment | 229 |
| Facts about SoccerPlus FC | 230 |

SOCCER COACHING ACTIVITIES, SESSION PLANS AND ASSESSMENT

# Preface

# PLUS 2 COACHING FOR DEVELOPMENT

## **Preface**

Welcome to the SoccerPlus Coaching for Development Series

Great youth soccer coaches have talent to balance *education* and *fun* in creating a positive and rewarding learning environment. In the **Coaching for Development Series**, we outline the blueprint for coaching success. In easy to understand guidebooks, we navigate novice and experienced coaches through the complexities of 'true' player development.

In this manual we address player development for 6, 7 & 8 year old players - connecting development (growth and maturation), performance standards, content, coaching methodology and player assessment.

Features of this manual include:

- Developmentally appropriate activities.
- 24 sessions organized for 8, 10 and 12 week seasons.
- Session plans with graphics.
- Skills and activities progress from session to session.
- Assessment activities.
- 6 different seasonal training schedules to offer maximum flexibility for coaches.
- Performance standards – competency benchmarks (what players need to learn, when to learn it and how to coach to performance expectations).
- Comprehensive player assessment.
- Practical description of player development and a survey to measure the 'player development appropriateness' of a soccer program.
- SoccerPlus Skills Challenge Pyramid™

Manuals in the series:

Plus 1 – 4 & 5 years old

Plus 2 – 6, 7, & 8 years old

Plus 3 – 9, 10 & 11 years old

Plus 4 – 12, 13 & 14 years old

Plus 5 – 15, 16, 17 & 18 years old

'Coach and Player Learn Together' – coaching Pre K players

Goal Keeping – Plus 2 & 3

Goal Keeping – Plus 4 & 5

# SOCCER COACHING ACTIVITIES, SESSION PLANS AND ASSESSMENT

## Introduction

This is the second manual in the 'Coaching for Development Series' written for coaches working with players at the second stage (Plus 2) of development. Player development occurs on a continuum where physical, cognitive, emotional and psychological readiness is more important than the chronological age of the child. To this end, the manual builds on the approach, skills and activities of the first phase of development (Plus 1). Assuming a player had developed at or above expectation; has been exposed to regular coaching sessions (twice a week for a minimum of 25-30 weeks per year); has demonstrated a propensity to practice outside of formal sessions and can adequately perform the pre-requisite skills for Plus 2, the player will be prepared for the challenge of Plus 2. It is expected the majority of players at the stage of development will be aged between 6, 7or 8 years old, although it is not uncommon to have advanced 5 year old and late developing 9-11 years old players at this stage.

The 'SoccerPlus Coaching for Development Series' is written for coaches with varying levels of knowledge, experience and qualification who are responsible for teaching and nurturing youth soccer players. We provide a detailed description of our approach to coaching, namely, 'Player Development' – an education philosophy receiving significant attention, but rarely understood.

For the past three decades Tony DiCicco and I have been working with young players at all levels of the game - recreation to world champions. Most recently our business interests' position us as youth soccer consultants and we regularly engage in educational seminars designed to help organizations adopt a new approach for player and coach development. Much of our time is directed in the USA, where soccer has seen unprecedented growth in the number of registered players and the communities that it is reaching. Soccer has become the sport of choice for more young players than any other sport. Conversely, however, players between the ages of 9-14 year olds seem to be leaving the game in as vast numbers as they entered.

Our research suggests in some cases youth soccer organizations are losing up to 50% of players who started playing in Kindergarten (5 years old) by the time they reach 4th grade (10 years old). There are a number of external causes for attrition such as other sports, hobbies and academic commitments, but what is more concerning is inadequate attention to internal factors such as poor coaching, 'tryout fall out', inappropriate treatment of players, exodus of strong parent coaches to 'premier' club programs and unequal focus on recreation soccer in comparison to competitive soccer.

## PLUS 2 COACHING FOR DEVELOPMENT

Essentially, the critical years for shaping a child's successful participation in soccer are 4-10 years of age. The speed and capacity for pre-adolescent (prior to puberty) players to learn are high and the gains in performance and understanding the most dramatic. It is essential children receive coaching considering the developmental stage of each child and that coaches focus on individuals before the team. Players should be competent in basic soccer skills, e.g. dribbling, turning, creating space and passing; understand the essentials of attacking and defending; be able to perform fundamental movement skills, e.g. running, jogging, jumping, skipping, throwing and catching etc, before graduating to large sided games (8v8+). Elementary skills and techniques not only provide the foundation for soccer, but also provide the basis for participation in most other sports.

Unfortunately, the sophistication of town soccer has not evolved with the growth of the sport and very few programs have adopted a 'true' player development model. We believe firmly the future of soccer and mass participation resides with parent volunteer coaches and non-for-profit clubs. However, town clubs need to start applying more appropriate strategies to stem the tide of attrition.

In this manual we will challenge the reader to make changes and accept new ideas supported by research and practical application. This is truly a program of learning – where every child, regardless of ability, has the opportunity to improve. The learning environment will be 'informed' – and activities and sessions connected to competencies and assessment.

We wish you all the best in your coaching endeavor. We welcome your feedback and wish to hear about your experiences – please leave us a message via our website www.soccerplus.org and we will be sure to respond.

# Chapter 1
# Player Development

PLUS 2 COACHING FOR DEVELOPMENT

# Player Development – defining and evaluating your program!

The term 'Player Development' is now common soccer vernacular. Clubs and coaches all around the globe are using Player Development to convey a more modern and sophisticated approach to coaching young players. Have these programs and coaching methods truly evolved or has 'Player Development' just become a trendy expression used for marketing and promotion?

To address this question please read the following criteria SoccerPlus employs to evaluate the extent to which a youth club is adopting a TRUE Player Development approach. Once you have finished reading, complete the 'Player Development Evaluation'.

## Curriculum

The term 'Curriculum' is most commonly associated with teaching and school education. In general terms, an educational curriculum consists of everything that promotes intellectual, personal, social, and physical development of the participants. When transferred to sport, the term curriculum is usually related to a book of activities and games organized in such a way to aid the coach plan for a practice session. Rarely do these curriculum books engage the reader in a rationale for selecting such activities, or describe how coaching methodology is as important as the activities themselves. Unfortunately this approach usually leads to very low adherence by the coaches – particularly if subsequent coaching sessions do not realize the outcomes suggested in the text.

Activities and session plans are important, but should be selected to realize the outcomes of the program. A club's Player Development Curriculum details the framework, aims, objectives and content and helps to raise standards, performance, and expectations. A curriculum should include approaches to teaching, learning, assessment, and focuses on the quality of relationships between coach, players and parents (see pg. 227 SoccerPlus Big Picture of Curriculum).

## Player Development Pathway

Children entering soccer at aged 4, 5 or 6 will start a 'journey' that should have a clearly defined beginning, middle and end, including multiple assessment points and learning experiences. Some players and parents will choose to end the journey early, but for others who aspire to play soccer into adulthood, the Player Development Model manages every step of the way. For many players and parents understanding the steps to success, expected outcomes and focus on education and training are extremely important factors. True Player Development provides such a pathway, building programs around principles that respect the developmental needs of all children.

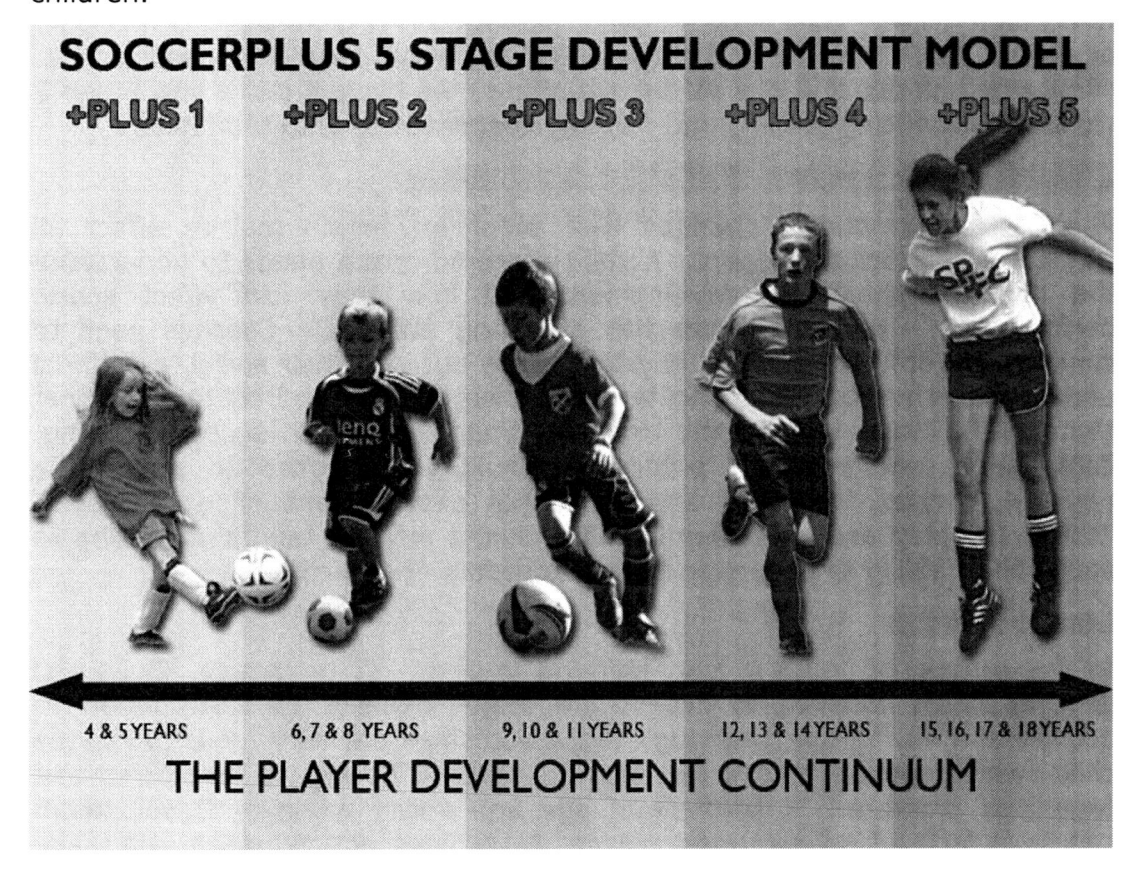

**SOCCERPLUS 5 STAGE DEVELOPMENT MODEL**

+PLUS 1 — 4 & 5 YEARS
+PLUS 2 — 6, 7 & 8 YEARS
+PLUS 3 — 9, 10 & 11 YEARS
+PLUS 4 — 12, 13 & 14 YEARS
+PLUS 5 — 15, 16, 17 & 18 YEARS

**THE PLAYER DEVELOPMENT CONTINUUM**

## Stages of Development

SoccerPlus has developed a five stage development model, a soccer adaptation of the Long Term Athletic Development Model created by Dr. Istvan Balyi (see pg. 228 SoccerPlus Player Development Model). Originally a model for Elite Athlete Development, the model provides a process for development from early childhood through retirement. Plus 1 (4 & 5 year olds), Plus 2 (6-8), Plus 3 (9-11), Plus 4 (12-14) & Plus 5 (15-18). Each stage of the model promotes a different development focus – the interplay between physical, cognitive, emotional, psychological and social variables. For example, when working with four and five year olds consider that players of this age tire easily, need repetition and reinforcement, have short attention span and mostly approach tasks individually.

In terms of soccer participation, we need to ensure the sessions are short, activities change constantly, skills are demonstrated and continually reinforced and information needs to be camouflaged and concealed, such as using cartoon characters and creating a story for a particular activity. Importantly, every child should have a ball at their feet for the vast majority of time. Team play at this stage of development should be restricted to small sided games and one vs one situations. As players move into Stage 2 we start introducing passing and working cooperatively with teammates.

## **Understanding the basics of child development**

Physical and emotional changes that occur as people mature affect all aspects of life including sport. A child centered coach needs to understand the different phases of development and how they can affect sports performance – particularly coaches of young athletes. Coaches need to consider not only the players' physical needs but also their social, emotional and cognitive needs. Adapting teaching methodology and content to meet the players' needs significantly improves their progress in soccer. Training, competition, and recovery programs should be designed to match the physical, mental, cognitive and emotional development of each player. Ethics, fair play and character building should also be taught according to each child's ability to understand these concepts at different ages.

## **Learning focus**

In the context of youth soccer, learning is often left to chance. Clubs and coaches seem satisfied to accept the major benefits of participation as activity and having fun. Although these outcomes are very beneficial to the child, wider ranging results can also be realized through a structured and organized program. Regardless of age and ability a Player Development Coach is focused on nurturing players to achieve end of stage goals and attainment targets.

To this end, SoccerPlus has developed a Player Development Competency Matrix (4-18 years old). Benchmarks for performance are provided at the end of each stage of development. The assessment program measures the players 'competence' – the relationship between skill, selection and application of skills, tactics, strategies and ideas and the readiness of body and mind to cope with the activity.

# SOCCER COACHING ACTIVITIES, SESSION PLANS AND ASSESSMENT

## **Child/Player Centered**

Central to the theme of Player Development is the concept of 'Child-centered' learning. The focus of the SoccerPlus Player Development Curriculum is the need of individual players (child) – first and foremost. The education environment is constructed to focus on the player's, abilities, interests, and learning styles and the coach performs as the facilitator. At each stage of development the player should actively participate in creating learning experiences. Individual performance outcomes should largely direct coaching content and activities. Conversely, 'Coach-centered' approaches have the coach as the central director and players in a passive, receptive role.

Soccer during the first two stages of development should be largely an individual sport. Although players are organized in teams/groups, the vast majority of time dedicated to training children 4-8 should be individual. One ball per player is a good start, but as coaches we need to identify and coach to the personal needs of each player. During activities and small sided games, coaches should provide individuals with instruction and corrective measures to improve their performance. At stage 1 & 2, a minimum of 75% of practice time should be dedicated to one ball per child and individual instruction.

By stage 3 (9 years old) players should have attained a level of individual competence allowing them to learn the basics of team play. Individual focus should still dominate team focus – approximate 60% of a session should be one ball/one player. Stage 4 (12-14) 50% individual and 50% team. Stage 5 (15-18) will be the first time team focus should rule individual focus, but even then players will need plenty of time touching the ball. Individual focus at stages 4 & 5 should be more position specific training – i.e. forward players will train with their back to goal and defenders work on recovery runs.

## **Vertical vs Horizontal integration**

A typical youth soccer program is 'vertically' integrated. Players are organized in age groups usually by school grade or by calendar year (see pg. 13, Vertical Integration Model for Organizing Player Development). This model perpetuates the 'Under Syndrome' – Under 6's for example are most often organized into mixed ability groups and randomly assigned to parent coaches, with an administrative coordinator assigned to the age bracket.

Worryingly, the vertical model adopted by the vast majority of youth soccer organizations and league administrators is causing an issue that most try so passionately to prevent – player attrition. At root cause of player attrition is player engagement, or more appropriately described disengagement (see pg. 15, Ability Based, for more details).

## PLUS 2 COACHING FOR DEVELOPMENT

Horizontal integration model on the other hand organizes players by stages of development (see pg. 15, Horizontal Integration Model for Organizing Player Development). For example, the SoccerPlus Player Development Model has five stages of development - Stage 1 – 4 & 5 year olds, Stage 2 (6-8), Stage 3 (9-11), Stage 4 (12-14) & Stage 5 (15-18). Coordinators in a horizontal model have oversight across two or three age groups making ability/development based decisions easier. Significantly, this model can result in far less attrition by engaging the late developing players. Consequently the player pool increases, teams become more competitive, expectations increase and performance standards rise.

Vertical Integration Model for Organizing Player Development

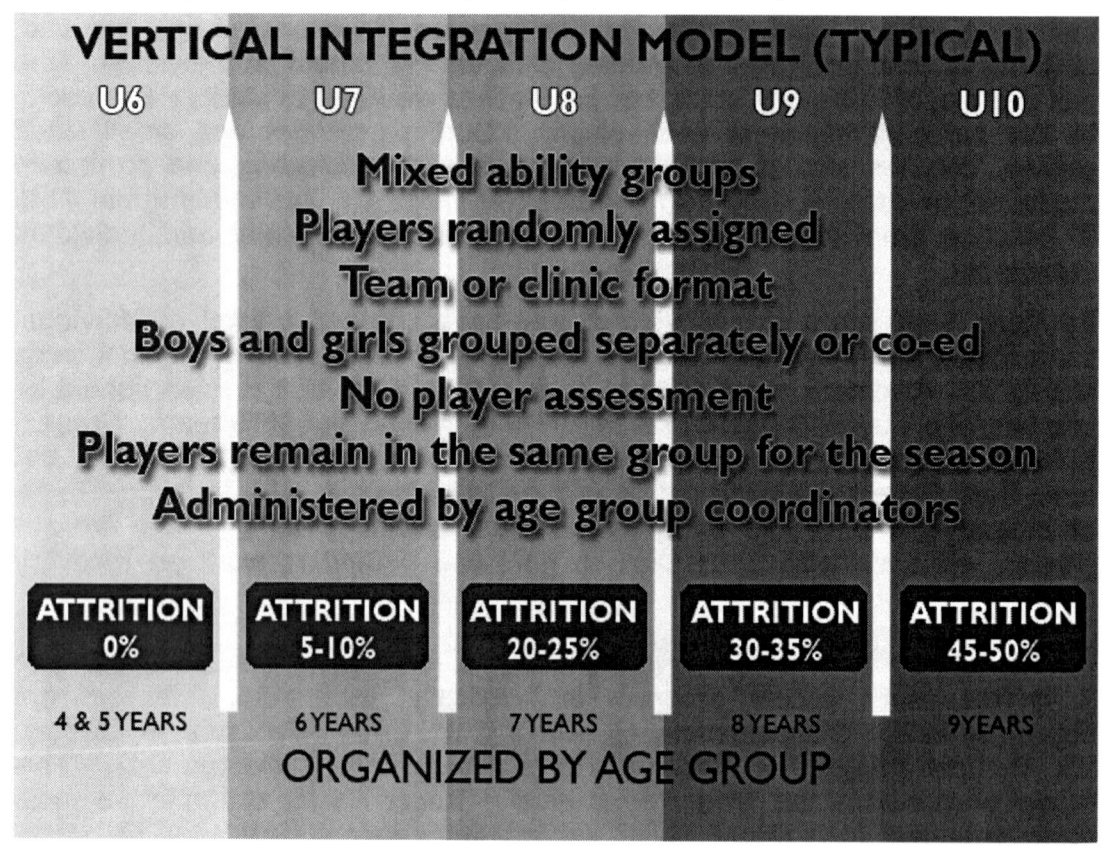

**VERTICAL INTEGRATION MODEL (TYPICAL)**

| U6 | U7 | U8 | U9 | U10 |
|---|---|---|---|---|

Mixed ability groups
Players randomly assigned
Team or clinic format
Boys and girls grouped separately or co-ed
No player assessment
Players remain in the same group for the season
Administered by age group coordinators

| ATTRITION 0% | ATTRITION 5-10% | ATTRITION 20-25% | ATTRITION 30-35% | ATTRITION 45-50% |
|---|---|---|---|---|
| 4 & 5 YEARS | 6 YEARS | 7 YEARS | 8 YEARS | 9 YEARS |

**ORGANIZED BY AGE GROUP**

# SOCCER COACHING ACTIVITIES, SESSION PLANS AND ASSESSMENT

## **Long Term Focus**

"Rome was not built in one day" quote by English Playwright John Heywood (Circa 1550)

Research exists suggesting that becoming an Elite athlete requires dedication of 10,000 hours. Three hours of practice every day for 10 years. Although this elite level of performance outcome is only applicable to a very small percentage of the playing population, this example does illustrate a correlation between time, maturation and achievement. The SoccerPlus Model represents a more realistic perspective of commitment, focusing more on the quality of instruction, ratio of practices to competitive games and self dedicated time, than on the volume of hours. However, becoming a competent performer takes time as the body and mind need to adapt to growth and experience. Unfortunately, in youth soccer a short term perspective is regularly implemented by coaches and parents with an over-emphasis on winning and achieving immediate success – this has been referred to as 'Peaking by Friday' mentality.

Progression is a term used frequently in soccer coaching to represent advancement in training complexity or applying coaching conditions to increase demands on the players. Progression is also used to describe how coaches gradually build learning experiences in stages rather than all at once, coordinating the instruction and content with the player's motivation and developmental phase. In moving too quickly to tactics, formations and positions, coaches will pass over general movement skills and gradual skill progression. This is a significant oversight as failure to become proficient in the fundamentals of the game and in movement will create deficiencies in performance later. For players and parents with aspirations of playing soccer in college or beyond, failure to master the foundations of the game will affect their opportunities in adult sport.

# PLUS 2 COACHING FOR DEVELOPMENT

## Horizontal Integration Model for Organizing Player Development

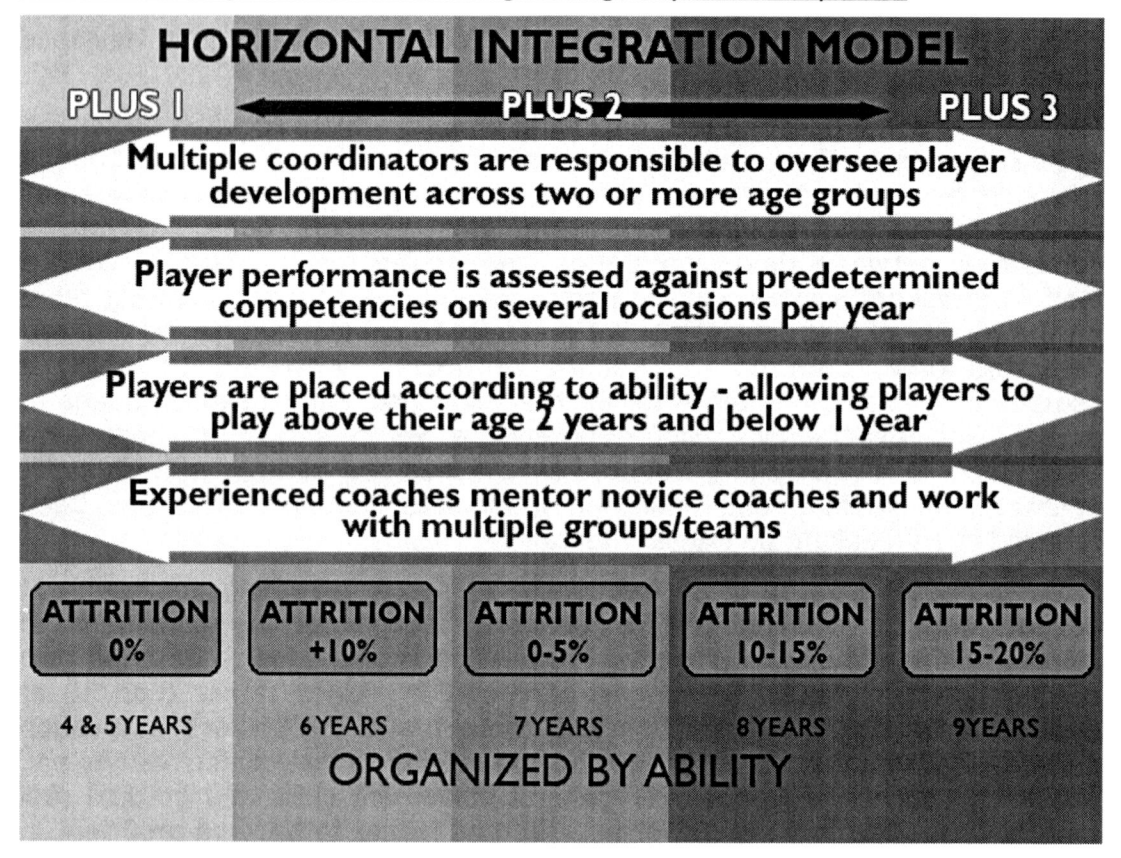

**HORIZONTAL INTEGRATION MODEL**

PLUS 1 ←———— PLUS 2 ————→ PLUS 3

- Multiple coordinators are responsible to oversee player development across two or more age groups
- Player performance is assessed against predetermined competencies on several occasions per year
- Players are placed according to ability - allowing players to play above their age 2 years and below 1 year
- Experienced coaches mentor novice coaches and work with multiple groups/teams

| ATTRITION 0% | ATTRITION +10% | ATTRITION 0-5% | ATTRITION 10-15% | ATTRITION 15-20% |
|---|---|---|---|---|
| 4 & 5 YEARS | 6 YEARS | 7 YEARS | 8 YEARS | 9 YEARS |

**ORGANIZED BY ABILITY**

### Ability based

Player Development philosophy supports the adage "If you are good enough you are old enough" - but it is easier to keep the children within their age group and requires considerably less explanation. Moving fully to developmental coaching would be a significant departure from the norm and would be in conflict with the competitive landscape that exists in youth soccer. Ability based programming provides each player with equal opportunity to reach the highest level of performance success they desire and have the ability to pursue. The benefits of ability based coaching are considerable – especially for the middle/lower talented player who is often a forgotten entity when coaches plan content.

Extensive research by SoccerPlus with town soccer programs has realized a concerning trend – an attrition rate of players from the sport of up to 50% between Kindergarten (5 years) and 4th Grade (9 years). Many external reasons have been offered, but three prevalent issues within the control of the soccer programs are low player engagement by coaches, limited improvement/success and content targeted too high or low for the child's ability. We believe, and research clearly supports, that children of all ages benefit most by learning in an environment that is developmentally appropriate. Children as young as 5 years can vary in cognitive, physical, emotional, and social development by as much as +2 or –2 years (some research suggests even greater variance). To this end significant disparity exists in performance between players of the same chronological age and this is strongly correlated to the child's engagement, enjoyment and participation.

Interestingly, the mid to low level players account for a disproportionate percentage of the 50% dropout. These are the very players town soccer clubs pride themselves on serving and protecting, often going out of the way to distance themselves from promoting 'elite' development. The A (high level players) usually stay with the program as they receive more attention, experience more success, develop quicker, and thoroughly enjoy participation. As well as promoting 'A' player development, an ability based program is designed to offer maximum opportunity for B & C players (mid and low level players). Often early developers will touch the ball 2 to 3 times more than B and C, they will pass the ball to equally gifted players, and they are more likely to continue playing beyond $4^{th}$ grade. Simply, ability based coaching offers B and C players more chance of success and adherence to the sport. Some additional benefits of an ability based program include:

- Players grouped with peers of similar ability allowing greater success and challenge.
- Players engaged throughout the session without dominating or being dominated by others.
- Coaches will find it easier to plan for and coach players of similar standard.
- Coaches can focus on content all players will be able to perform. There is no more difficult coaching assignment than training 5 and 6 year olds in mixed ability groups.

In simple terms, developmentally appropriate coaching offers players the opportunity to play with and against children of similar ability - age is not as important as skill, technique and physical attributes.

# PLUS 2 COACHING FOR DEVELOPMENT

## **Player Assessment**

The concepts of assessment and evaluation regularly cause concern and are prickly topics. This is no truer than in a youth sports environment where assessment is typically associated with selection. In soccer assessment means tryouts. Tryouts are designed to answer one question – are you good enough to play travel soccer?

Assessment has its place … it should be used at every opportunity to make a difference for learning. Assessment should also be fit for purpose – the quantitative and qualitative methods used must be appropriate to the stage of development and also relevant to the skill, knowledge or behavior being tested. Identifying the appropriate level of play for a particular child often provides an organization with a number of sensitivity issues. Talent identification should not be restricted to a once a year occurrence, but needs to be an ongoing process involving coaches, players and parents. Ultimately, the aim of a talent identification program is to ensure that all players have the opportunity to progress at a rate and level that their talent and development allows. Matching the resources and expertise to meet the needs of the player requires both an internal and external perspective.

A progressive assessment process encourages a variety of methods. For example, utilizing several assessors to evaluate players can offer strength to the process, as does the use of video analysis. An assessment program should have clear objectives, such as:

- Determine progress in skill acquisition and performance.
- Evaluate the success of a particular approach to coaching and learning.
- Validate the curriculum.
- Identify issues in assessment and develop corrective actions.

## **Holistic Approach to learning**

Tony DiCicco uses a phrase 'Soccer sessions life lessons' to describe the role soccer should play in developing characteristics such as leadership, team work, commitment and responsibility. Participation in sport and physical activity not only helps to shape character traits but can also contribute to better academic performance.

A strongly held belief by many administrators of town soccer is the perception that fun and learning are mutually exclusive – if we make the environment more conducive to learning (small side activities, ability based, player assessments, individual instruction, shorter and more focused sessions etc) we sacrifice fun. This belief has no scientific foundation and in fact flies in the face of common logic. In cases where programs cite bad experiences in implementing a 'learning environment', we propose the issue is more in the way implementation was approached and communicated, than in the idea itself. In his book 'Good to Great', Jim Collins[1] addresses organizations having an issue in changing when their current approach is seemingly realizing good results. Collins refers to 'good being the enemy of great' and this is certainly applicable to youth soccer. Why change the approach to learning when participation numbers in soccer exceed all other sports in the town?

We must also think of ways to encourage players to learn the sport outside of scheduled practices and games. Taking the ball out in the yard with friends and parents, attending a live game (high school, college or professional) or watching the game on TV are some of the ways we can further engage players and parents in the learning experience. Finally, SoccerPlus believes a Player Development Model should encourage players to play a variety of sports for as long as possible, until such times as the player decides to commit more fully to soccer. Soccer performance can benefit significantly by learning from physical transfers from other sports and vice versa. For example, tactical similarities such as attack and defense in basketball or field hockey - rebounding, quick feet and lateral movements in basketball can greatly enhance explosive movements required in soccer. Playing soccer 3-5 nights per week for a 7 year old child is too much. We do however recommended players participate year round to limit performance regression – developing their competencies in movement and fundamental ball skills.

## **Equal opportunity program**

Although many clubs aim to provide equal opportunity very few truly achieve this aim. Common practice is best described as offering 'equal rights' to participation, meaning each child has the opportunity to practice and play for a similar amount of time. Randomly assigning players to teams is common practice, although this often creates significant equalities – something programs rarely overcome. For example, picture a Kindergarten program with five or six teams playing on a Saturday morning. It is not uncommon to have one Head Coach with previous playing, teaching and coaching experience and the other four or five coaches with little or no experience. For the lucky twelve players assigned to the experienced coach the opportunity to be successful will be significantly better than the players assigned to the parent coaching for the first time.

An equal opportunity program distributes coaching experience, so that all players are exposed to good coaching. This can be achieved in several ways.

---

[1] Jim Collins (2001), Good to Great – Why Some Companies Make the Leap ... and others don't.

## PLUS 2 COACHING FOR DEVELOPMENT

One way is to designate the most experienced coach as a coaching mentor, the person providing oversight and guidance to less experienced coaches and rotating from group to group. Another, is to rotate the groups between 2-4 coaches each session – each coach teaching the same activity/skill to each group.

SOCCER COACHING ACTIVITIES, SESSION PLANS AND ASSESSMENT

# Player Development Self Evaluation

Does your soccer organization adopt a player development approach? Score your youth soccer organization against the SoccerPlus definition and approach. Refer back to the supporting text for the SoccerPlus definition of 'true' player development.

Key: Yes (Y), Somewhat (S) No (N)

|  |  |
|---|---|
| Is there a written curriculum with clearly defined aims, objectives and outcomes? | Y S N |
| Does a comprehensive rationale to player development exist that is taught and disseminated to volunteer/professional coaches? | Y S N |
| Is there a 'player pathway' enabling the seamless transition of players between stages of development and built around principles of child development? | Y S N |
| On the whole, do coaches have a good working understanding of child development and the differences likely to exist between children of the same age? | Y S N |
| Are coaches required to produce/follow a session plan? | Y S N |
| On the main, are coaches able to address the unique needs of individual players within a team training environment? | Y S N |
| Does the organization establish end of stage/season player competencies for determining player and coach progress? | Y S N |
| Is the organization approaching administration and player development horizontally (see vertical vs horizontal integration paragraph)? | Y S N |
| Does the club have a long term perspective in developing players and teams? | Y S N |
| Does ability and not age determine player groupings for training and games? | Y S N |
| Are players formally assessed at several points in the year? | Y S N |
| Is player assessment used for the primary purpose of development? | Y S N |
| Are coaches encouraging players to become students of the game by setting 'soccer homework' and watching high level games on TV or in person? | Y S N |
| Does the organization see a correlation between learning, enjoyment and adherence to the game? | Y S N |
| Does the organization provide equal opportunity for all players? | Y S N |

How many '<u>Yes</u>' answers? Compare your score against our research: **11-15** (Fabulous – in the top 3%), **8-10** (Great – much more than most, top 10%), **4-6** (OK - but program needs review – top 30%), **0-3** (Time for change – 70% of organizations)

Also available online – instant evaluation free – www.soccerplus.org/YSAT

# Chapter 2
# Practice and Game Organization

# SOCCER COACHING ACTIVITIES, SESSION PLANS AND ASSESSMENT

## Practice and Game Organization

### Fundamental Movement Skills (FMS)

As soccer coaches we spend a considerable amount of time and energy planning sessions to develop fundamental soccer skills. This is particularly the case for players in the formative stages of development. However, whether consciously or unconsciously, we all too often overlook the foundation for fundamental soccer skills – fundamental movement skills.

Naturally we should expect parents, pre-school and school systems to provide young players with instruction and exposure to skills such as walking, running, jumping, skipping, kicking, catching and throwing. Unfortunately, evidence suggests many children do not receive suitable movement education and as a result they stay at the elementary stage of skill development. Failure to acquire movement skills by the end of Plus 2 (8 years) has a dramatic effect on the progress potential for children in youth sports programs. In a wider context, children need to develop basic physical skills and a degree of competence to continually participate in physical activity, not just sport. Perceptions about physical activity formed during the first few years of participation provide the key to future motivation and participation. In general, movement skill acquisition leads to confidence and performance successes that in turn result to continuous adherence to a sport or physical activity.

As previously discussed, before progressing on to more complex skills, it is imperative the child can competently perform foundation and basic skills. Fundamental movement skills are the building blocks upon which all sport skills are based and must be mastered before learning more complex, specialized skills like those needed in games, sports and recreational activities. To this end, movement competence is a prerequisite for fundamental soccer skills. That is not to say, however, a soccer ball cannot be introduced into movement skill activities.

# PLUS 2 COACHING FOR DEVELOPMENT

## Fundamental Movement Skills

| Locomotor Skills | Stability Skills | Manipulative Skills |
|---|---|---|
| Crawling, Running, Galloping, Walking, Hopping, Skipping, Dodging, Jumping, Sliding, Galloping, Leaping | Stopping, Bending, Twisting, Landing, Climbing, Balancing, Turning | Throwing, Catching, Striking, Bouncing, Dribbling, Kicking |

**Locomotor** skills involve the body moving in any direction from one point to another.

**Stability** skills involve the body balancing either in one place (static) or while in motion (dynamic).

**Manipulative** skills involve handling and controlling objects with the hand, the foot or an implement (stick, bat or racquet).

## **Window of Opportunity**

It has been fairly well established that the "window" of opportunity for acquiring fundamental movement skills occurs during the first 8 years of life. However, children do not acquire the movement skill competencies by maturation alone. They need sound instruction, a supportive atmosphere, and many opportunities to practice these skills. The SoccerPlus curriculum particularly emphasizes movement skill acquisition in the Plus 1 and Plus 2 stages of development (4-8 years old). If the mature form is not established by age 9, smooth and fluid movement patterns are far more difficult to achieve. Plus 1 and Plus 2 are sensitive periods for learning new skills, when acquisition is more straightforward and faster. If the mature form is not acquired by age 9, players may steer away from activities that require these skills.

It is a misnomer to think we are teaching and practicing movement skills when we play most games. Too often practices heavily emphasize soccer specific skill development and this progression is too advanced for players without movement competence. In general, more time must be dedicated to practice and time during the practice planned for developing movement. In addition, coaches must understand and appreciate the sequence of development. For example, Children learn to skip after they learn to hop.

# SOCCER COACHING ACTIVITIES, SESSION PLANS AND ASSESSMENT

Motor skill progression is similar for all children (although the rate varies). Even within skills there is a progression. Coaches should know the developmental sequences for all skills; intra-task (e.g. when kicking a ball, body weight momentum should be moving forward to keep the ball along the ground) and inter-task (e.g. the technique for shooting is an extension of the technique for passing).

## **Playing up and playing down**

Deciding whether to allow players to play competitively outside of their age group (playing up & playing down) is a dilemma most youth soccer organizations contend with annually. The simple answer to this difficult question is there is not one answer that fits every situation. However, in principle, SoccerPlus supports the assertions by US Soccer that a gifted player benefits from playing-up with players of similar or better ability – from age 9 years upwards.

*"Associations that create rules restricting an individual player's option to play at the appropriate competitive level are in effect impeding that player's opportunity for growth. For development to occur, all players must be exposed to levels of competition commensurate with their skills and must be challenged constantly in training and games in order to aspire to higher levels of play and thus maintain their interest and passion for the game.*

*When it is appropriate for soccer development, the opportunity for the exceptional player to play with older players must be available. If there is a concern regarding the individual situation, the decision must be carefully evaluated by coaches and administrators familiar with the particular player. When faced with making the decision whether the player ought to play up, adult leadership must be prepared with sound rationale to support their decision. Under no circumstance should coaches exploit the situation by holding players back in their quest for winning team championships, nor should parents push their child in an attempt to accelerate their ascension to the top of the soccer pyramid. In addition, playing up under the appropriate circumstances should not preclude a player from playing in his or her own age group when it is evaluated to be in the best interest of the player's development."*

(US Soccer Federation)

A consideration for all youth soccer clubs must be how to make practice sessions more challenging for the gifted player. The opportunity for a player to 'practice-up' is as important to a young player's development as playing-up. For example, if a player practices twice a week, one session could be with their age appropriate team and the second with an older team. Finally, playing down is rarely discussed and is probably more contentious than

# PLUS 2 COACHING FOR DEVELOPMENT

playing-up. However, if we apply similar development logic to playing-down as we do for playing-up, one can argue the late developer can benefit by repeating and reinforcing more basic learning. Anecdotal evidence from academics can attest to the effectiveness of this strategy.

## Player Development Focus

| Technical | Soccer Psychology | Soccer Physiology | Soccer Sociology | Tactical |
|---|---|---|---|---|
| Soccer Intelligence<br><br>Technique (Ball Manipulation)<br><br>Skill Acquisition<br><br>Teamwork<br><br>Understanding | Confidence<br><br>Concentration<br><br>Commitment<br><br>Mental Preparation<br><br>Managing Expectations<br><br>Routines<br><br>Anxiety<br><br>Thinking Clearly Under Pressure | Strength<br><br>Speed & Reaction<br><br>Movement Skills<br><br>Physical Maturity<br><br>Power<br><br>Agility<br><br>Speed Endurance<br><br>Fatigue | Roles & Responsibility<br><br>Coach, Parent, Player Relationship & Interaction<br><br>Ethics<br><br>Morals<br><br>Self Concept<br><br>Team Cohesion<br><br>People Skills | Principles of Defending & Attacking<br><br>Defending as a Team, Unit & Individual<br><br>Attacking as a Team, Unit & Individual<br><br>Systems of Play<br><br>Patterns of Play<br><br>Movements On & Off the Ball<br><br>Creating & Exploiting Space<br><br>Set Plays |

### Training to game ratios

A major criticism of young sport for many years has been an overemphasis on competitive games to the detriment of practices. Ratios of one practice to one (or even two) games are common place. The mere suggestion of telling players and parents the adoption of less games and more practice can cause cold sweats for the Director of Coaching and Coaches alike. Children love to play games and parents like to see their children playing even more!

Thus, somewhat controversially, the SoccerPlus Player Development Model advocates higher practice to game ratios than most clubs are currently implementing. The key is providing a training environment allowing and empowering coaches to develop and correct individual and team performance, and at the same time not creating an exodus of unhappy parents and players. Adopting a true child centered approach, requires doing

# SOCCER COACHING ACTIVITIES, SESSION PLANS AND ASSESSMENT

their utmost to ensure players can competently perform fundamental skills in practice before placing excessive pressures to do so in a competitive game environment.

Typically, fun and enjoyable practices have goals and competition – one team vs another. The purpose of the game of soccer is for one team to attempt to beat (win) an opponent and to resist this purpose would lessen the experience. Striving to win and to better oneself against another is not *the* issue in youth sport – it is often how winning and competition is approached, emphasized and organized by adults that causes concern for many educators. SoccerPlus Player Development Model heavily promotes the inclusion of games and game activities in practice environments. Players, particularly younger players, will receive as much, if not more enjoyment playing 2 v 2 or 3 v 3 with their team mates than in a competitive game manufactured by coaches.

## **A word about 'Winning'**

Winning is <u>not</u> regarded by SoccerPlus as a necessary evil of competition. SoccerPlus believes there are significant values for the player, coach and club when striving to win games, leagues and tournaments. However, 'winning' is not so absolute - it has a broader definition than triumphing over another team. Winning is an appropriate description for players and teams achieving realistic goals, in practice and in games. In this context, winning can be symbolized by learning how to overcome adversity as an individual or team, by employing a new team tactic to great effect or by developing camaraderie as players working together. Player Development places winning in the context of the 'bigger picture' – if players learn and master fundamental skills and movement patterns, the likelihood of winning is greatly increased. In essence, winning becomes a by-product of good practice.

## **A word about 'Talent' and Tryouts**

Selecting players to teams becomes a major task for youth soccer programs and very few people (players, coaches or club officials) enjoy the experience. Typically, one-time-per-year tryout events are hosted prior to the fall season and all players wishing to be considered for the travel program must participate. Players, given a number to encourage objectivity, are required to perform a series of skill activities and play in small sided games in front of the assessors. The assessors, usually coaches in the club, but sometimes independent professionals, are equipped with a clip board, grading sheet and set of instructions and are assigned the unenviable task of selecting the players into the first sixteen, second sixteen and so on. However there are several flaws to this approach:

## PLUS 2 COACHING FOR DEVELOPMENT

- Assessing talent requires time – usually two tryout sessions are not sufficient.
- Objectivity is generally compromised by the team coaches having discretionary powers to select the teams.
- The people assessing the talent are generally not qualified or experienced to do so.
- The assessors rarely receive any assessment training.
- Negative outcomes from the process are often damaging to the reputation of the club and with the engagement and goodwill of the parents.

Talent takes time, a significant amount of effort and regularly emerges later than we hope or expect. Players grow at different rates, hit puberty at different times, possess different work ethics, have varying motivations and receive different instruction. However, many coaching practices perpetuate the belief that talent manifests itself early and does not need nurturing or developing. To this end, if we want the best for our players and we want to allow talent to materialize. The methods used to select players to teams and the treatment of players after selection or rejection needs to change.

Cutting young athletes from a team without the infrastructure that encourages them to adhere to the program and offers them new opportunities to be successful, will result in 'late developers' lost to the game and the competitive stream. Additionally, this approach provides children without the athletic potential to continue playing in a positive educational environment. Children who do not continue to play soccer in high school or beyond are more likely to continue adopting healthy behaviors if their experiences are positive. The SoccerPlus Long Term Player Development Model applies to all players – regardless of potential. Recreational players will learn more skills and have more fun, while elite performers develop the skills required to perform at High School and beyond.

### Specialist Position Training

Some of the world's greatest soccer players play professional soccer in different positions than they played in youth soccer. An integral part of the soccer experience is learning to play multiple positions. Coaches that limit players to a fixed position too early in the development are effectively restricting the chances of a player reaching their full potential. There should be no positional coaching at Plus 1 and Plus 2. Players should receive instruction and experience in all positions – including basic goal keeping. As players enter competitive play at Plus 3, greater emphasis should be on a primary unit (Goal Keeper, Defense, Midfield or Attack) but players should also continue to experience other positions. At Plus 3, goal keepers should receive goal keeper specific coaching and to this end it may be appropriate to

# SOCCER COACHING ACTIVITIES, SESSION PLANS AND ASSESSMENT

narrow the goal keepers to 2-3 players. At Plus 4 and Plus 5 players will certainly have a preferred position, but scenarios in the game may require adjustments leading to positional movements. For example, a defender who wins the majority of balls in the air may be moved forward to win balls for a smaller but quick forward, or a right side full back may be pushed forward to counteract overloading by the opposition in the midfield.

## **Game Format & Team sizes**

SoccerPlus adopts and supports US Soccer Federation's recommendations for game format.

US Soccer Federation Recommendations for Game Format & Team Sizes

| Age | U5 & U6 4 & 5 yrs | U7 & U8 6 & 7 yrs | U9 & U10 8 & 9 yrs | U11 & U12 10 & 11yrs | U13 & U14 12 & 13 yrs | U15-U18 15, 16 & 17 yrs |
|---|---|---|---|---|---|---|
| **Game Form** | 3 v 3 | 4v4 or 5v5 | 7v7 or 6v6 | 9v9 | 11v11 | 11v11 |
| **Duration** | 4 x 8min | 2 x 20min | 2 x 25min | 2 x 30min | 2 x 35min | 2 x 40min or 2 x 45min |
| **Substitution** | Free | Free | Free | Free | No re-entry in half | No re-entry |
| **Goal Keeper** | None | Last defender in 5v5 | Players rotate as GK in game | GK share time in order of priority | GK chosen based on ability | GK chosen based on ability |
| **Field Size (yards)** | 30 x 20 | 5v5 (45 x 30) or 4v4 (40 x 25) | 60 x 40 | 100 x 50 | 110 x 60 (min) | 115 x 70 (min) |
| **Ball size** | 3 | 3 | 4 | 4 | 5 | 5 |

(US Soccer Federation, 2006)

# PLUS 2 COACHING FOR DEVELOPMENT

## Frequency and Duration

There are a number of factors to consider when determining how often (frequency) and how long (duration) to practice. As previously mentioned, the primary consideration should always be what is best for the child. To this end, development characteristics of the players at each stage will significantly influence frequency and duration. For example, 4 and 5 year old players are limited by factors such as energy levels (physical) and attention span (cognitive). A practice session for Plus 1 players should be no more than one hour (45 minutes is ideal), involve 4 or 5 activities lasting no more than 10 minutes each, and the session/activities should be repeated constantly. Two or Three sessions per week in season (spring and fall) and one or two sessions per week out of season (winter and summer) are appropriate.

## Warm-up, Cool down and Stretching

There is mounting research on the topic of warm-ups, cool downs and stretching, offering some conflicting evidence. For many years static stretching, holding a stretch for a few seconds when the muscle reaches a point of tension, was largely regarded as the most effective way to prepare the body for the main exercise and prevent injuries. However, several studies conclude static stretching prior to the main exercise can actually reduce muscle strength and the ability of the player to perform explosive movements.

Lately however, research supports dynamic warm-ups and stretching to optimize performance, body movements gradually increasing the intensity and pliability of the muscles. Dynamic movements are not to be mistaken with ballistic movements, where the purpose is to force the joint beyond the range of motion. Dynamic movements can be performed with or without the ball and are an excellent prelude to the dynamic movements included in the main part of soccer practices. The warm-up should raise body temperature and locate the muscles and joints to be utilized. In general, dynamic movements decrease the risk of injury and increase flexibility.

With that said, children aged 4 & 5 are naturally flexible and do not require stretching activities for the purpose of developing range of motion. Movement patterns resembling dynamic stretches can be included in the training plan.

# SOCCER COACHING ACTIVITIES, SESSION PLANS AND ASSESSMENT

## Creating an environment for participation and learning

Fun should be a given for any youth sport environment. A secure and supportive environment that focuses on participation, enjoyment and learning of movement skills will produce positive outcomes. In establishing this kind of environment, consider the following:

- Establish a positive atmosphere in which children and adults interact in a supportive and enthusiastic way, and positive reinforcement and praise dominate.
- With young players particularly, coaches should become animated and exude enthusiasm – often taking on mannerisms of cartoon/TV characters.
- Maximize participation by limiting line drills (players standing in a line waiting for their turn) and providing access to equipment – i.e. one ball per player.
- Avoiding elimination games – when playing 'knock out' games, eliminated players should start a second game.
- A coach's repertoire should include 'fill in' activities that can be introduced to change the tempo of the session.
- Understand ways to differentiate the practice/activity to cater for different performance abilities - change rules, equipment, grouping, area and demands of the task.
- Ensure children's safety both physically (e.g. equipment, facility) and emotionally (children are comfortable about what they are doing and confident to extend themselves).

## Selecting appropriate activities and progression

For many coaches finding the correct starting point is a challenge. Several variables complicate this matter, including varying abilities of players in the group, little performance knowledge of the players and their abilities, player motivation and previous coaching experiences. The activities and session plans in this manual are designed to account for a variety of development factors, including growth, maturation and cognitive development. It is important to understand that development occurs at varying rates and is related to, but does not depend on the child's age and experience. When children are ready to learn they will have the prerequisite physical, social and cognitive skills and will be interested, keen and motivated. Also children are likely to develop skills in a progressive order, learning simple before complex skills (e.g. walking and hopping are simple movement patterns and combine to create a skip). Finally, children tend to develop control of their body from the centre (trunk) to the more distant parts (arms, hands and feet).

## PLUS 2 COACHING FOR DEVELOPMENT

Coaches must remember the curriculum is a 'Progressive Curriculum' and most activities progress from more basic skills and concepts. Advancing too quickly to more sophisticated activities can affect overall performance and confidence of the players and coaches. Research clearly indicates that players receiving instruction in basic skills, techniques and tactics for a longer period of time are more likely to master and eventually perform advanced activities more competently.

This manual considers skill development as a progressive process – meaning, competency in basic skills must be achieved before progressing to more complex skills. With this in mind, the SoccerPlus Standards of Performance and Assessment Matrix guides coaches when players should be 'Introduced' to a skill and when players should be expected to demonstrate a 'Competency'.

### **Repetition and Reinforcement (Imprinting)**

Coaches have the tendency to move quickly from one skill and activity to another. This is a mistake, as children need to have continuous repetition and reinforcement, particularly at a young age and on more complex tasks. The ability of a child to cognitively process information is far less sophisticated than an adult. Too many coaching points, too complex activities and insufficient time devoted to developing competency are contributory factors as to why players do not reach a level of proficiency needed to move to the next progression.

This does not mean however that a coach needs to repeat the activity ad nauseam or until the player perfects the skill. Tony DiCicco refers to this concept as creating an "Imprint" – performances will improve a little each time with repetition until the objectives are fully achieved. Attempting to perfect the skill can be frustrating for the athletes and coach and may turn fun into drudgery.

In an ideal scenario, players are able to receive some quality soccer coaching year round. Training once or twice per week can enhance muscle memory and neural pathways, enabling the player to perform gross and fine skills more efficiently and automatically.

Skills are performed by linking nerve fibers in the brain and sending signals to the relevant muscles. Repetition of activities increases the amount of 'Myelin' (insulator wrapping around the nerves) aiding the speed of neural transmission and ensuring that fewer electrical impulses escape.

Interestingly, the production of myelin is not a by-product of who you are, but what you do. The implications of this research is quite clear for coaches

## SOCCER COACHING ACTIVITIES, SESSION PLANS AND ASSESSMENT

– given the right dedication and opportunity, coaches should not dismiss a late developing player or dwell on a early developer.

Most adaptations to the body and mind are reversible, so maintaining performance levels during off season periods are important.

# Chapter 3
# Plus 2 Stage of Development

SOCCER COACHING ACTIVITIES, SESSION PLANS AND ASSESSMENT

# Plus 2 Stage of Development

## What you need to know about development

Skill development for players at Plus 2 is best achieved through the combination of quality instruction by qualified and experienced coaches and unstructured play in a safe and challenging environment. A significant emphasis of development should be on the continued emphasis on fundamental movement skills and basic soccer skills. For the sake of the child and the benefit of the soccer player, children should be encouraged to play a variety of sports year round. Players start to demonstrate a strong sense of fairness and to this end they should be introduced to simple rules and ethics of the game. Simple tactics and strategies can also be introduced, such as scoring in one goal and prevent goals being scored in another.

Developing independence from family becomes more important now. Events such as starting school bring children this age into regular contact with other children and adults. Friendships become more and more important. Physical, social, and mental skills develop rapidly at this time. This is a critical time for children to develop confidence and adults need to reinforce good behavior with praise and recognition.

# PLUS 2 COACHING FOR DEVELOPMENT

## Development characteristics helpful to know about 6, 7 & 8 year olds:

| PHYSICALLY | PSYCHOLOGICAL SOCIAL | COGNITIVE/ MENTAL |
|---|---|---|
| • Coordination and body control improving rapidly, as there is slower growth.<br>• Boys and girls have equal ability.<br>• Reaction time slow, but improves as child grows.<br>• Lots of energy as endurance levels increase, but may have fluctuations in energy.<br>• High need for skill development.<br>• Fine motor skills developing.<br>• Visual and hand-eye coordination improving.<br>• Height and weight increasing at a steady rate.<br>• Balance improves with ear developments.<br>• Learns best by being physically active.<br>• Needs to repeat activities that are well known and mastered.<br>• Eye development and ability to track objects in motion improving.<br>• High center of gravity so balance can be difficult. | • Interests often change rapidly.<br>• Enjoys initiating activities.<br>• Enjoys being praised for endeavors from adults.<br>• Players start becoming more independent & attempt to exercise control over own environment.<br>• Players appreciate consistent environment.<br>• Players learn by repetition.<br>• Experimental, exploratory behavior is part of development.<br>• Still egocentric – each player wants a ball.<br>• Peer group becomes increasingly important.<br>• Players are concrete thinkers and find abstract thinking difficult.<br>• Players start to develop powers of reasoning i.e. if you do 'X' the result is 'Y'.<br>• Easily motivated, eager to try something new.<br>• Seek risk and adventure.<br>• Needs guidance and praise from adults to stay on task and to achieve their best performance.<br>• Increasingly self-assured but can be childish and silly at times<br>• Stronger sense of right and wrong.<br>• Growing desire to be liked and accepted<br>• Enthusiastic and impatient | • Imaginative, spontaneous and creative.<br>• Able to stay on task longer due to increased attention span.<br>• Likes to be tested but often dislikes public failure.<br>• Likes to try new activities.<br>• Better able to understand and learn because of growing memory capacity.<br>• Starting to visualize instructions – although demonstrations are much more concrete.<br>• Inconsistent attention span.<br>• Interests can be short and quick changing.<br>• Highly verbal.<br>• Asks fact-oriented questions (e.g., wants to know how, why and when)<br>• Rapid development of mental skills.<br>• Greater ability to describe experiences and talk about thoughts and feelings.<br>• Less focus on one's self – seek social comparison. |

# SOCCER COACHING ACTIVITIES, SESSION PLANS AND ASSESSMENT

## **Translation to Player Development**

Translated to player development, this means:

- Continued involvement of fundamental movement skills – running, jumping, skipping, throwing etc
- Focusing on ball familiarization and dribbling skills – one ball per child.
- Introduction of paired and cooperation activities.
- Help players understand a task by demonstration and asking questions
- Sessions requiring players to be extremely active.
- Selecting activities that do not place undue stress on the muscles, bones and energy systems of the body.
- Repeating activities regularly – constant change and insufficient reinforcement negatively affects learning
- Camouflaging and concealing technical information by using names, characters and stories.
- Encouraging trial and error, keeping instruction to a minimum
- Using equipment and props to increase complexity but continue to make the sessions fun – hurdles, hoops, ladders, bean bags etc
- Including competitive games, but emphasize success other than just winning (i.e. effort)
- Providing considerable encouragement.
- Including 'games and matches' in every session
- Introduction to small sided games – 2v2 to 4v4   play at the end of a practice session – don't sacrifice practice sessions for games at this stage.
- All players to receive fundamental goal keeping skills – catching, throwing and diving (players love to dive!).
- Introduce basic rules of the game – including restarts when ball leaves the field.
- Passing skills can be introduced.

## PLUS 2 COACHING FOR DEVELOPMENT

- Avoiding temptations to place players in specialist positions (i.e. full back, forward or goal keeper)

### **Player Competencies and Assessment**

The SoccerPlus Player Development Curriculum offers parents and coaches' comfort by knowing there is a plan to guide a child's soccer playing experience from the time they enter the program to the end of their youth playing experience. Part of this planning process is identifying the performance expectations/competencies for each stage of development. In addition, regular player assessment will enable coaches to know a player's ability and take the necessary steps to provide appropriate instruction. Assessment also allows coaches to feedback to parents a child's progress and identifies how they can help in the player's development.

With this in mind, the following table provides players, parents, coaches and administrators with a comprehensive list of soccer competencies (skills, techniques, knowledge, tactics) for Plus 2. The matrix represents the recommended time for introducing a competency (✚) and the time when the player should become competent (✓). Note players are not expected to become competent in many competencies by the end of Plus 2.

# SOCCER COACHING ACTIVITIES, SESSION PLANS AND ASSESSMENT

Plus 2 Competencies Matrix

| Stage/Chronological Age (yrs) | 6 yrs | 7 yrs | 8yrs |
|---|---|---|---|
| **Physical Literacy Skills** | | | |
| Run with stops and starts | ✓ | | |
| Run and change directions | ✓ | | |
| Gallop | ✓ | | |
| Skip | ✓ | | |
| Lateral movements - side-step | ✓ | | |
| Rolling, bending low, arching | ✓ | | |
| Balance - on a line | ✓ | | |
| Balance - on one foot | ✓ | | |
| Throw - strong hand | | ✓ | |
| Throw - weak hand | | ✓ | |
| Jump - stride and bound patterns | | Consolidate | |
| Jump – hurdles | | Consolidate | |
| Quick feet and crossovers | | ✓ | |
| Speed - Coordination of arms and legs | + | | |
| Running technique | | Consolidate | |
| Sprinting technique | + | | |

# PLUS 2 COACHING FOR DEVELOPMENT

| Stage/Chronological Age (yrs) | 6 yrs | 7 yrs | 8 yrs |
|---|---|---|---|
| **Dribbling Skills** | | | |
| Turns – basic | | ✓ | |
| Dribbling basics | | ✓ | |
| Ball manipulation | | Consolidate | |
| Feints and dribble | | Consolidate | |
| Control – Foot | | Consolidate | |
| Attacking an opponent 1v1 | | | ✓ |
| Shooting at an open goal | | ✓ | |
| Turns – advanced | ✚ | | |
| Running with the ball | ✚ | | |
| Beating an opponent | ✚ | | |
| Escaping an opponent | | ✚ | |
| **Receiving** | | | |
| Control – Foot | | Consolidate | |
| Control – Thigh | | ✚ | |
| Control – Chest | | | ✚ |
| Control – Head | | | ✚ |
| **Passing** | | | |
| Ground - Inside of foot - 5 yards | ✚ | | |
| Ground - Inside of foot - 10 yards | ✚ | | |
| Ground - Inside of foot - 20 yards | | ✚ | |

SOCCER COACHING ACTIVITIES, SESSION PLANS AND ASSESSMENT

| Stage/Chronological Age (yrs) | 6 yrs | 7 yrs | 8 yrs |
|---|---|---|---|
| Ground – Instep | | ✚ | |
| Long pass | | | ✚ |
| Chip/Lofted pass | | | ✚ |
| Swerve pass - inside of foot | | | ✚ |
| Swerve pass - outside of foot | | | ✚ |
| **Shooting** | | | |
| Instep | | ✚ | |
| Half volley | | | ✚ |
| Volley | | | ✚ |
| One on one with Goal Keeper | | | ✚ |
| **Heading** | | | |
| Basic technique | ✚ | | |
| **Physical Conditioning** | | | |
| Own body weight strength exercises | | | ✚ |
| Core body strength | | | ✚ |
| Dynamic warm-up | | Consolidate | |
| Speed training (Anaerobic) | | ✚ | |

## PLUS 2 COACHING FOR DEVELOPMENT

| Stage/Chronological Age (yrs) | 6 yrs | 7 yrs | 8 yrs |
|---|---|---|---|
| **Mental/Cognitive conditioning** | | | |
| Confidence | | Consolidate | |
| Commitment | | | + |
| Concentration | | Consolidate | |
| Composure | | | + |
| **Goalkeeping** | | | |
| Basic catching techniques | | + | |
| Positioning | | + | |
| Set Plays | | | |
| Throw in | | | + |
| Penalties | | | + |
| **Laws of the Game** | | | |
| Individual and team behavior | + | | |
| Field and equipment | | | + |
| Fair and foul play | + | | |
| Basic rules | + | | |

# SOCCER COACHING ACTIVITIES, SESSION PLANS AND ASSESSMENT

Key:

(✚) Introduction of the skill, techniques, knowledge & tactics

(✓) Expected time when the average player should become competent

Consolidation = period between ✚ & ✓

Note: Understanding the SoccerPlus Long Term Player Development Model™ and in particular the integration between content, methodology and dedicated coaching time, provides the rationale for this timeline. Also, these expectations are based on a 'typical' development pattern for a player introduced to the SoccerPlus Curriculum at Stage One. Expectations and coaching practices should be modified for players above or below the curve.

PLUS 2 COACHING FOR DEVELOPMENT

# Coaching Tips - Do's and Don'ts

## Do's

1. <u>Plan</u> – Begin the session with the end in mind. Develop expectations of what you want your players to be able to perform/know at the end of the session.
2. <u>Follow the curriculum activities</u> - The guess work has been eliminated. Activities are developmentally appropriate and linked to end of stage competencies.
3. <u>Understand development</u> - Become a student of your students! Understanding the abilities of your players cognitively, physically and emotionally is essential to coaching performance.
4. <u>Repeat and Reinforce</u> - Have a theme for your sessions and find every opportunity to focus on 1-2 key points. Build on progress each session and ensure you dedicate time to the basics.
5. <u>Assess players</u> - Watch players perform in practice and in games and focus on their ability to execute the basics: dribbling, turning, shooting and beating an opponent.
6. <u>Demonstrate</u> - Young players need a visual example – very few do well with lengthy explanations. Stop the players and demonstrate the skill – and/or get one of the players to demonstrate.
7. <u>Know your coaching points</u> – 1-2 coaching points per session are just enough – don't try to cram in too many.
8. <u>Finish with a game based on the theme</u> - Reinforce what you have been teaching by emphasizing the focus in the game. Add conditions and scoring mechanisms that encourage creativity and application of the skill.
9. <u>Coach Individuals off the ball</u> - Avoid shouting instructions to players in possession. Instead, allow the activity to flow and speak to the individual. Or, stop the game and make the point to the whole group.
10. <u>Have a "sleever"</u> - Have a favorite activity or two up your sleeve if your session falters.
11. <u>Teach the rules</u> - Young players need to know the basic rules – such as restarts.
12. <u>Teach Fundamental Movement Skills</u> (FMS) - ensure players can run, jump, change pace and have good balance and agility. The foundation for all sports consists of fundamental movement skills – don't leave the development of FMS to someone else!
13. <u>Be enthusiastic</u> - The hardest part of coaching is getting the attention and respect of the players – winning the players over is achieved with a combination of enthusiasm, empathy and preparation.

# SOCCER COACHING ACTIVITIES, SESSION PLANS AND ASSESSMENT

## **Don'ts**

1. <u>Treat everyone as equal</u> - From the perspective of development the players in your group are not equal. They need individual attention and to this end the coaching needs to be differentiated.
2. <u>Over Coach</u> - The younger the player the less talking is needed and more action. Once the activity is established try to stick with 10-15 second points and then play!
3. <u>Overcrowd the space</u> - A common issue is getting in the way – being in the center of the activity. Young children find spatial awareness an issue without having a 6ft coach blocking their view.
4. <u>Commentate</u> - Unlike many sports in the USA, soccer requires players to make the decisions during play. Coaches must avoid telling the players what to do during play.
5. <u>Have more than one voice at a time</u> - Where there are two or more coaches to a group, separate the responsibilities – there needs to be one leader for each activity – not 2 or 3.
6. <u>Set up line drills</u> - There should never be more than 2-3 players in a line.
7. <u>Have players watching</u> - Avoid having substitutes - particularly in the Plus 1 and 2 stages of development. There is no development value in players standing on the sideline – create activities/games that keep them learning.
8. <u>Assume that serious soccer starts at 9-10 years</u> - The most important time in the development of a soccer player is 4-8 years old.
9. <u>Underestimate your impact</u> - Experiences children have in youth sport shape their adherence to sport and exercise in later life. Make the sessions fun and educational and the players will develop and commit long term.
10. <u>Waste valuable coaching time</u> - Time picking up cones and re-establishing the area during practice is time wasted. Set up the equipment before players arrive and let the players pick up the equipment for you.
11. <u>Let team focus dominate individual development</u> - A fundamental flaw in many sessions is lack of individual player development.
12. <u>Set the agenda on the most talented player</u> - Coaches who establish content on the most talented players are setting 90% of players up for failure.

PLUS 2 COACHING FOR DEVELOPMENT

# Coaching Formula

The dynamic interplay between coaching variables differs at each stage of development. Collectively, these variables create the right learning environment for players and provide the greatest opportunity for success. Largely, the environment is determined by the development characteristics of the players and modifications to this starting point can be made based upon the level of player engagement and performance.

From this point forth in the manual, several assumptions are made with regard to the training, coaching and development of the players at the Plus 1 stage. There are four assumptions:

## 1. Player Performance and acquisition of prerequisite skills

Players entering Plus 2 stage of development have acquired the pre-requisite skills. As a benchmark, players should be able to competently perform the five 'Tier 1' skills from the Plus 1 Skills Challenge Pyramid™ (see pg. 48 Plus 1 Skills Challenge Pyramid). Players should also be able to make a reasonable attempt at performing the four Tier 2 activities from the Plus 1 Pyramid. In addition, players should be at or above expectation when assessing the players using the 8 Plus 1 assessment activities[2].

## 2. Accumulative effect of practice and good coaching

Players should have preferably completed at least one year/two seasons of instruction. Accumulation of quality practice time and repetition are important variables for player development (see pg. 31 Repetition and Reinforcement). Ideally players entering Plus 2 stage of development have accumulated approximately 80 hours of experience over two years with a coach and also accrued a similar number of self directed hours playing in the yard with friends and relatives.

## 3. Physical, cognitive and emotional readiness

Physical, cognitive and emotional development has progressed sufficiently for the players to cope with increased demand and difficulty (see pg. 34, Development characteristics helpful to know about 6, 7 & 8 year olds)

## 4. Appropriate content and methodology

Prior to entering into Plus 2, the vast majority of coaching time has been dedicated to dribbling, ball mastery, basic 1v1 attacking and shooting.

---

[2] The 8 activities are: 1) Dribbling and ball mastery, 2) Dribbling and turning, 3) Dribbling and shooting, 4) Ball Mastery, 5) Movement – Balance, 6) Movement – Jumping, 7) Locomotor run and hop and 8) Gallop and skip – see <u>Soccer Coaching Activities, Session Plans and Assessment for Plus 1 Players (4 & 5 Years Old)</u>, pg 103-110.

# SOCCER COACHING ACTIVITIES, SESSION PLANS AND ASSESSMENT

## Plus 1 – Coaching Formula

It is helpful for a coach of Plus 2 players to know the coaching formula for Plus 1 and compare and contrast the differences between the two stages.

| | |
|---|---|
| **Coaching theme:** | Dribbling, ball mastery, basic 1v1 attacking and shooting |
| **Session frequency:** | 1 or 2 training sessions per week (At least 48 hours rest between sessions) |
| **Games frequency:** | Small sided games to occur in training schedule – too early in development to dedicate a day for games |
| **Activities per session:** | 4-5 activities per hour |
| **Session duration:** | 45 minutes to 60 minutes (max) |
| **Activity duration:** | No more than 15 minutes each activity |
| **# of unique activities per session:** | Max of 1 (After the initial session) |
| **Progressions:** | Every 5-6 sessions increase complexity |
| **Individual : team ratio:** | Individual 75% (min) : Team 25% (max) |
| **Player : ball ratio:** | 1:1 |
| **Coach : player ratio:** | 2:12 |
| **# Coaching points:** | 1 or 2 |
| **Small sided game format:** | 1v1 to 3v3 (max) |
| **Player Assessment:** | 1 assessment for every 8-10 training sessions (but at least twice per season) |

Note: SoccerPlus adopts and supports US Soccer Federation's recommendations for game format.

# PLUS 2 COACHING FOR DEVELOPMENT

## Plus 2 – Coaching Formula

| | |
|---|---|
| **Coaching theme:** | Consolidate – dribbling, turns & fundamental movement skills.<br>Running with the ball, escape and take-on moves, passing and receiving, shooting, goalkeeping and laws of the game.<br>See Competency Matrix pg. 38 for a full list. |
| **Session frequency:** | 2 training sessions per week (At least 48 hours rest between sessions) |
| **Games frequency:** | Session 1: dedicate approximately 25% of practice session to small sided games within the group/team.<br>Session 2: dedicate approximately 50% of practice session to small sided games. Include games against other groups.<br>Note: it is too early in the development of players to dedicate an entire session to games. |
| **Activities per session:** | 4-5 activities per hour |
| **Session duration:** | 60 minutes to 75 minutes (max) |
| **Activity duration:** | No more than 15 minutes each activity |
| **# of unique activities per session:** | Max of 2 (After the initial session) |
| **Progressions:** | Every 5-6 sessions increase complexity |
| **Individual : team ratio:** | Individual 75% (min) : Team 25% (max) |
| **Player : ball ratio:** | 1:1 |
| **Coach : player ratio:** | 2:12 |
| **# Coaching points:** | 2 or 3 |
| **Small sided game format:** | 3v3 to 5v5 (max) |
| **Player Assessment:** | 1 assessment for every 8-10 training sessions (but at least twice per season) |

Note: SoccerPlus adopts and supports US Soccer Federation's recommendations for game format.

SOCCER COACHING ACTIVITIES, SESSION PLANS AND ASSESSMENT

## Skills Challenge Pyramid™

The Skills Challenge Pyramid was created by SoccerPlus for the following purposes:

1. Identify a series of progressively challenging skills for the players to attempt.
2. Provide coaches with a simple model to encourage players to develop fundamental soccer skills.
3. Provide some direction for parents and players when practicing outside of the regularly scheduled team/group practices.
4. Provide an easy to implement assessment model for coaches of varying experience.
5. To engage players and coaches in a fun and challenging activity.

**About the Skills Challenge Pyramid™**

The features of the Skills Challenge Pyramid™ include:

- There are 5 Pyramids (Plus 1 – 5).
- Each pyramid has a series of 10 skills.
- A Pyramid consists of 4 'Tiers'
    - Tier 4 – Fundamentals
    - Tier 3 – Intermediate
    - Tier 2 – Advanced
    - Tier 1 - Master
- Activities are numbered 1-10. Activity number 1 is regarded as the easiest skill to learn in the Pyramid and number 10 is regarded as the most difficult.
- The top three activities of the Plus 1 Pyramid (Tiers 1 & 2) form the first three activities of the Plus 2 Pyramid (Tier 4). This relationship continues for the Plus 2-5 Pyramids.
- A simple evaluation system is incorporated for each activity:
    - <u>Below expectation</u> – movements are awkward and uneven, there is little consistency between two or more attempts and the skill is performed below game speed.
    - <u>At expectation</u> – At least 50% or more of the attempts are completed in one smooth movement, are at game speed and appear to be natural (second nature and free flowing).
    - <u>Above expectation</u> – At least 90% or more of the attempts are completed in one smooth movement, are at game speed and appear to be natural (second nature and free flowing).

# PLUS 2 COACHING FOR DEVELOPMENT

## Plus 1 Skills Challenge Pyramid™

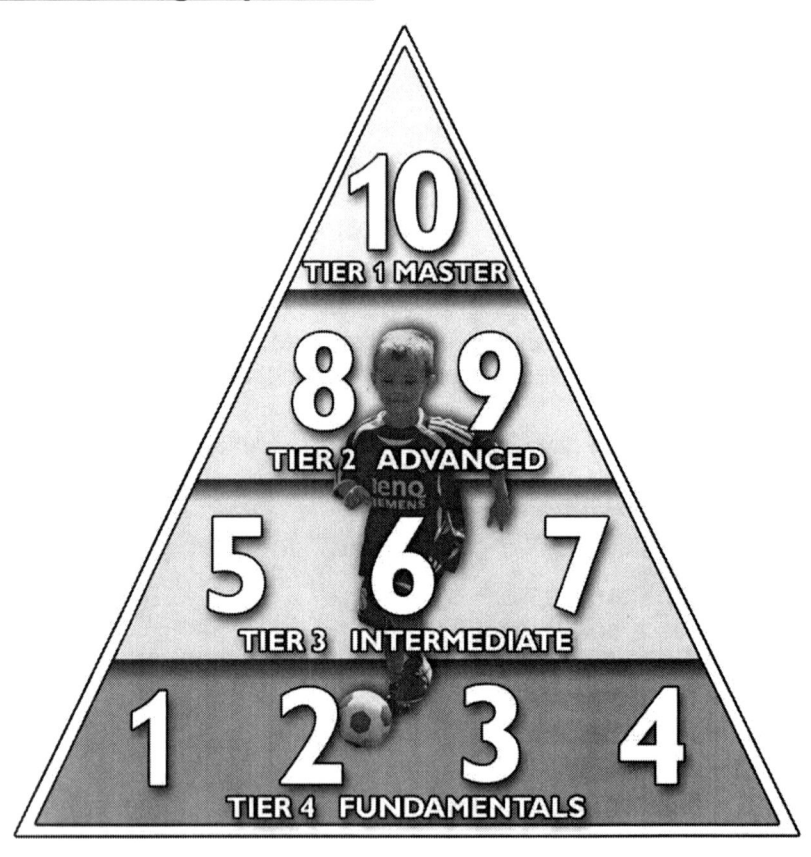

**Tier 4**

1. <u>Laces Dribble</u> – With the toes pointing down towards the ground push the ball forward with the laces, knee bent over ball on contact. After each touch step through with the opposite foot.
2. <u>Toe Taps</u> – using the inside of both feet push the ball from one foot to the other. On the spot initially then moving forward and back when comfortable
3. <u>Sole Taps Forward</u> – Using the toe end of the sole, tap the top of the ball - alternating left and right feet. On the spot initially, with a slow rhythm and then hopping. Once competent in a stationary position, move forwards.
4. <u>Sole Taps Backward</u> – Using the toe end of the sole, tap the top of the ball - alternating left and right feet. On the spot initially, with a slow

# SOCCER COACHING ACTIVITIES, SESSION PLANS AND ASSESSMENT

rhythm and then hopping. Once competent in a stationary position, move backwards.

## Tier 3

5. <u>Step-On Turn</u> – Dribble forward, place the sole of one foot on the ball to stop momentum, step beyond the ball with both feet leaving the ball, turn to face the ball and dribble back. Repeat several times using both feet.
6. <u>Drag Back Turn</u> – Dribble forward, stop forward momentum of the ball by reaching forward with one foot and placing the sole of the foot on top of the ball, drag (roll) the ball back down the side of the body away from the defender and accelerate into a dribble.
7. <u>Back Heel</u> – Dribble forward, step beyond the ball, make contact with the heel of one foot sending the ball backwards, turn and accelerate into a dribble.

## Tier 2

8. <u>Inside Cut</u> – Dribble forward, stop forward momentum of the ball by reaching forward with inside of one foot and 'cutting' the ball back down the inside of the body (away from the defender) in one movement and accelerate into a dribble.
9. <u>Ball Rolls</u> – Using the inside, outside and sole of one foot, roll the ball side to side, backwards and forwards and keeping contact with the ball at all times. Both feet.

## Tier 1

10. <u>Outside Cut</u> – Dribble forward, stop forward momentum of the ball by reaching forward with outside of one foot and 'cutting' the ball back down the outside of the body (away from the defender) in one movement and accelerate into a dribble.

# PLUS 2 COACHING FOR DEVELOPMENT

## Plus 2 Skills Challenge Pyramid™

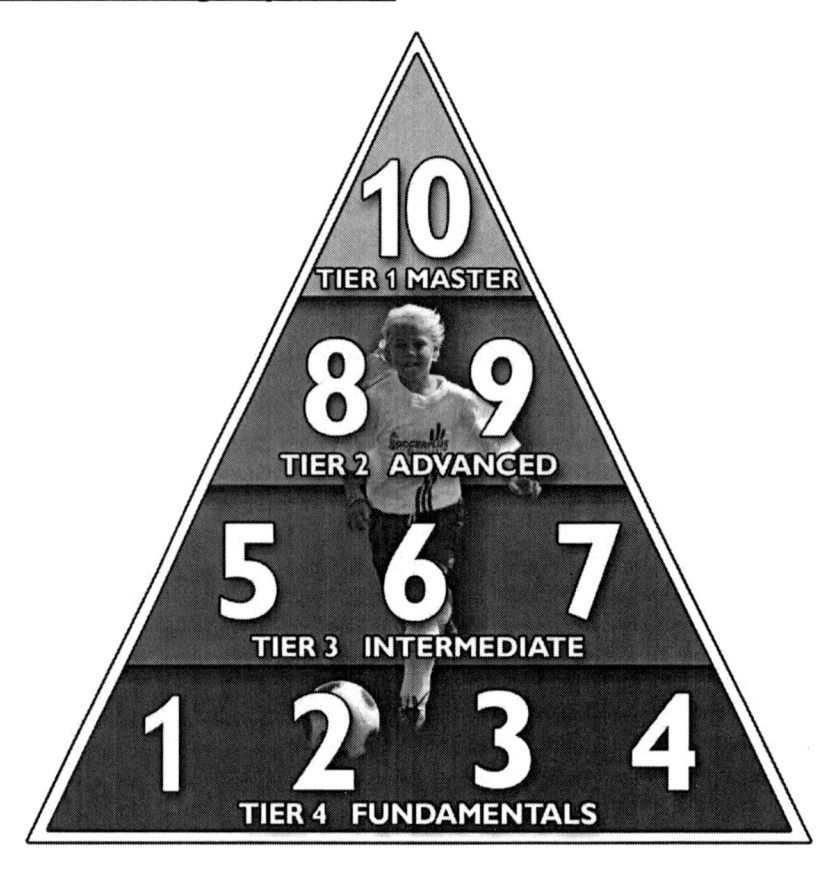

**Tier 4**

1. <u>Inside Cut</u> – Dribble forward, stop forward momentum of the ball by reaching forward with inside of one foot and 'cutting' the ball back down the inside of the body (away from the defender) in one movement and accelerate into a dribble.
2. <u>Ball Rolls</u> – Using the inside, outside and sole of one foot, roll the ball side to side, backwards and forwards and keeping contact with the ball at all times. Use both feet.
3. <u>Outside Cut</u> – Dribble forward, stop forward momentum of the ball by reaching forward with outside of one foot and 'cutting' the ball back down the outside of the body (away from the defender) in one movement and accelerate into a dribble.

# SOCCER COACHING ACTIVITIES, SESSION PLANS AND ASSESSMENT

4.  <u>Take on dribble (outside of foot)</u> – Dribble forward and after a few touches play the ball with the outside of one foot (right) towards the side of the body (moving the ball to the outside of the defender). Accelerate away from the defender.

## Tier 3

5. <u>Single cut dribble</u> – Dribble forward and after a few touches play the ball with the inside of one foot (right) across the body (transferring the ball from one foot to another in front of the defender). The next touch is played with the inside of the other foot (left) to push the ball forward and continue the dribble (past the defender).
6. <u>Forward Drag Rolls</u> – Move forward with the ball in a straight line (walking at first) and dragging the ball with the sole of the foot - pulling the ball across your body. Perform for 10 yards and them repeat – increase speed.
7. <u>Step-pivot turn</u> – Dribble forward, place foot on top of the ball and keeping contact with the ball step beyond the ball with the other foot. Turn and push the ball into a dribble.

## Tier 2

8. <u>Flick turn</u> – Dribble forward, reach out with one foot and place the toe end of the shoe on the ball. Maintain contact with the ball, open up your body shape and flick the ball back and across the body. Quickly transfer feet and accelerate away.
9. <u>Double tap and dribble</u> – Tap the ball back and forth quickly between the left and right feet (toe taps). On the second touch, play the ball at an angle and accelerate into a dribble.

## Tier 1

10. <u>Double cut dribble</u> – Using either foot, push the ball diagonally forward twice with the outside of the foot. Take a step and use the inside of the same foot to cut the ball diagonally forward twice. Take a step between each touch, repeat for 10 touches then change feet.

# Chapter 4
# The Coaching Plan for 8, 10 & 12 Week Seasons

SOCCER COACHING ACTIVITIES, SESSION PLANS AND ASSESSMENT

## The Coaching Plan for 8, 10 & 12 Week Seasons

The following diagrams provide a schedule for 8, 10 and 12 week seasons, based on 1 or 2 training sessions per week. As previously mentioned, it is important for coaches to evaluate needs and progress of players individually. To that end, the Coaching Plans indicate when a coach should evaluate the players.

At Plus 2 it is important to strike a fine balance between reinforcing previously learned skills and introducing new topics. An average child will take approximately 3 years to attain end of stage performance competencies. The duration can certainly increase or decrease based on a number of variables including child development (physical, cognitive, psychological and emotional), training time, frequency of training, skill of the coach and player dedication. An average child attending 40 coaching sessions per year and dedicating a similar amount of time to self improvement will reach the level to progress to Plus 3.

It is likely players in mixed ability groups will emerge at different points on the development continuum. In these circumstances, coaches should be conscious of progressing too quickly and leaving players behind. It is better to select sessions the majority of players can perform and add conditions for advanced performance to increase difficulty.

An optimal model for player development at this stage is 2 sessions per week. Depending on your location, the season length and time of year will differ. See pg. 47, Plus 2 Coaching Formula - for establishing the optimal coaching environment.

PLUS 2 COACHING FOR DEVELOPMENT

# Coaching plan for 8 weeks – 1 session per week

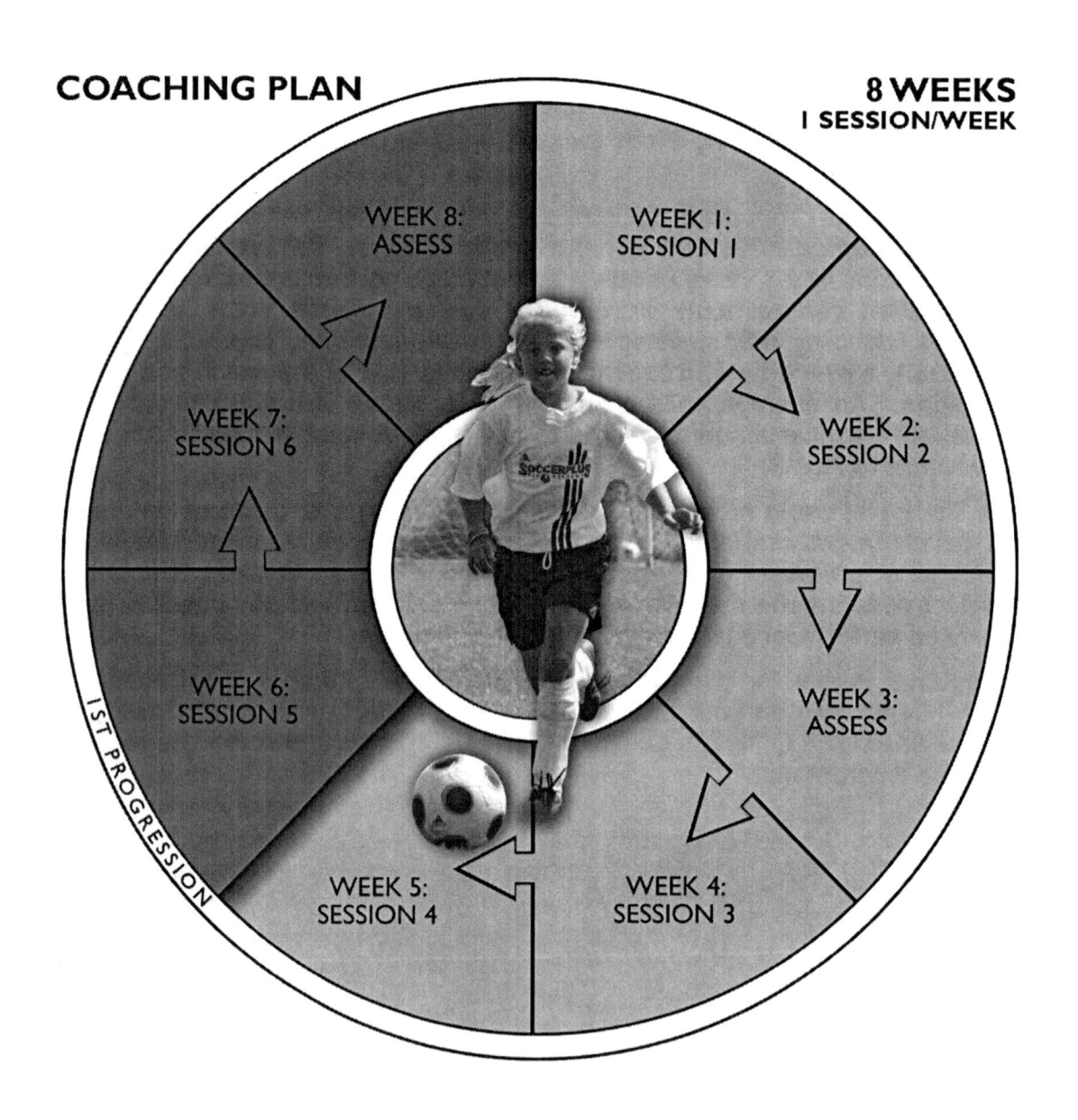

**COACHING PLAN**

**8 WEEKS**
1 SESSION/WEEK

- WEEK 1: SESSION 1
- WEEK 2: SESSION 2
- WEEK 3: ASSESS
- WEEK 4: SESSION 3
- WEEK 5: SESSION 4
- WEEK 6: SESSION 5
- WEEK 7: SESSION 6
- WEEK 8: ASSESS

1ST PROGRESSION

SOCCER COACHING ACTIVITIES, SESSION PLANS AND ASSESSMENT

## Coaching plan for 8 weeks – 2 sessions per week

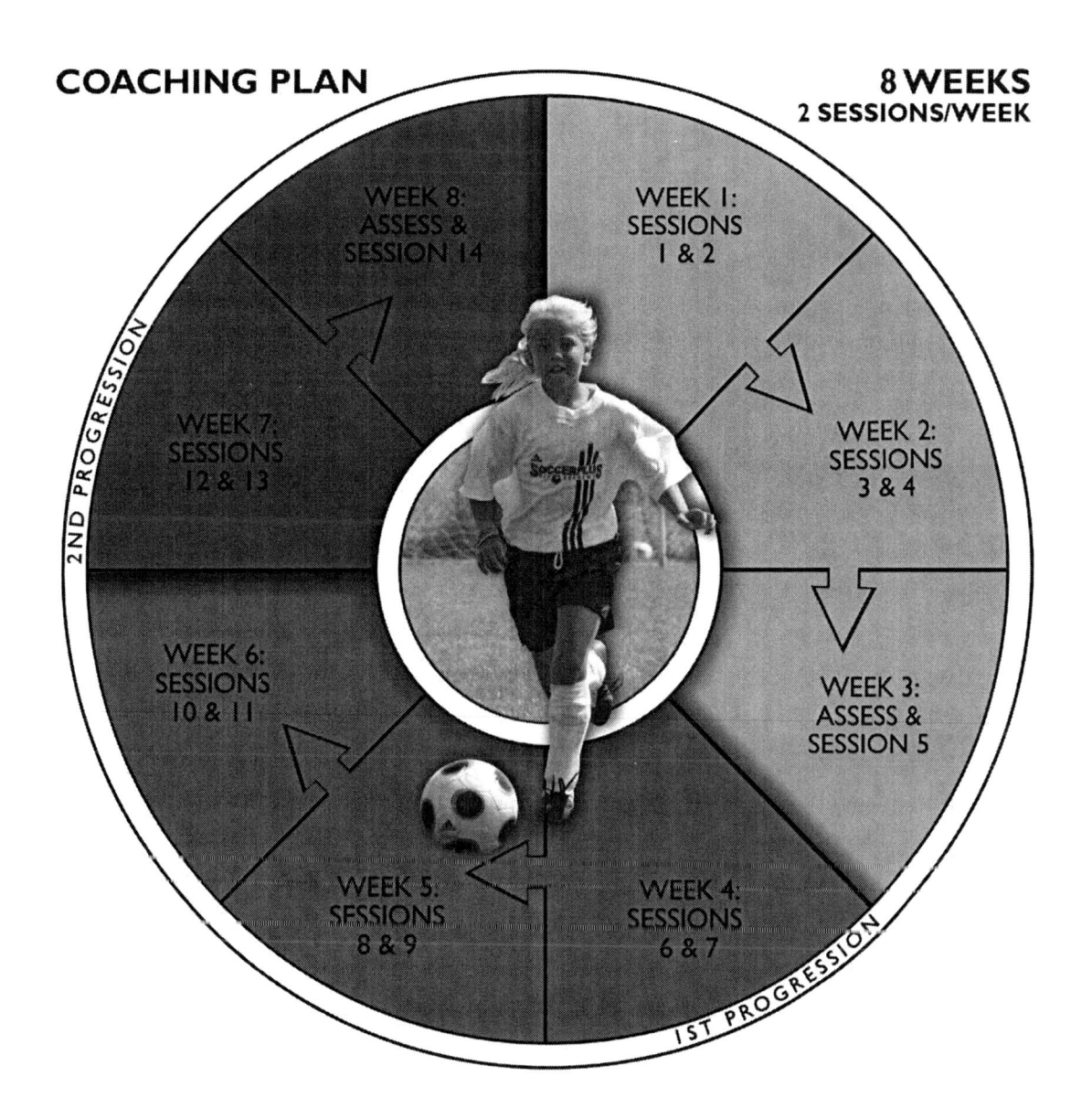

**COACHING PLAN**     **8 WEEKS**
**2 SESSIONS/WEEK**

- WEEK 1: SESSIONS 1 & 2
- WEEK 2: SESSIONS 3 & 4
- WEEK 3: ASSESS & SESSION 5
- WEEK 4: SESSIONS 6 & 7
- WEEK 5: SESSIONS 8 & 9
- WEEK 6: SESSIONS 10 & 11
- WEEK 7: SESSIONS 12 & 13
- WEEK 8: ASSESS & SESSION 14

1ST PROGRESSION

2ND PROGRESSION

PLUS 2 COACHING FOR DEVELOPMENT

# Coaching plan for 10 weeks – 1 session per week

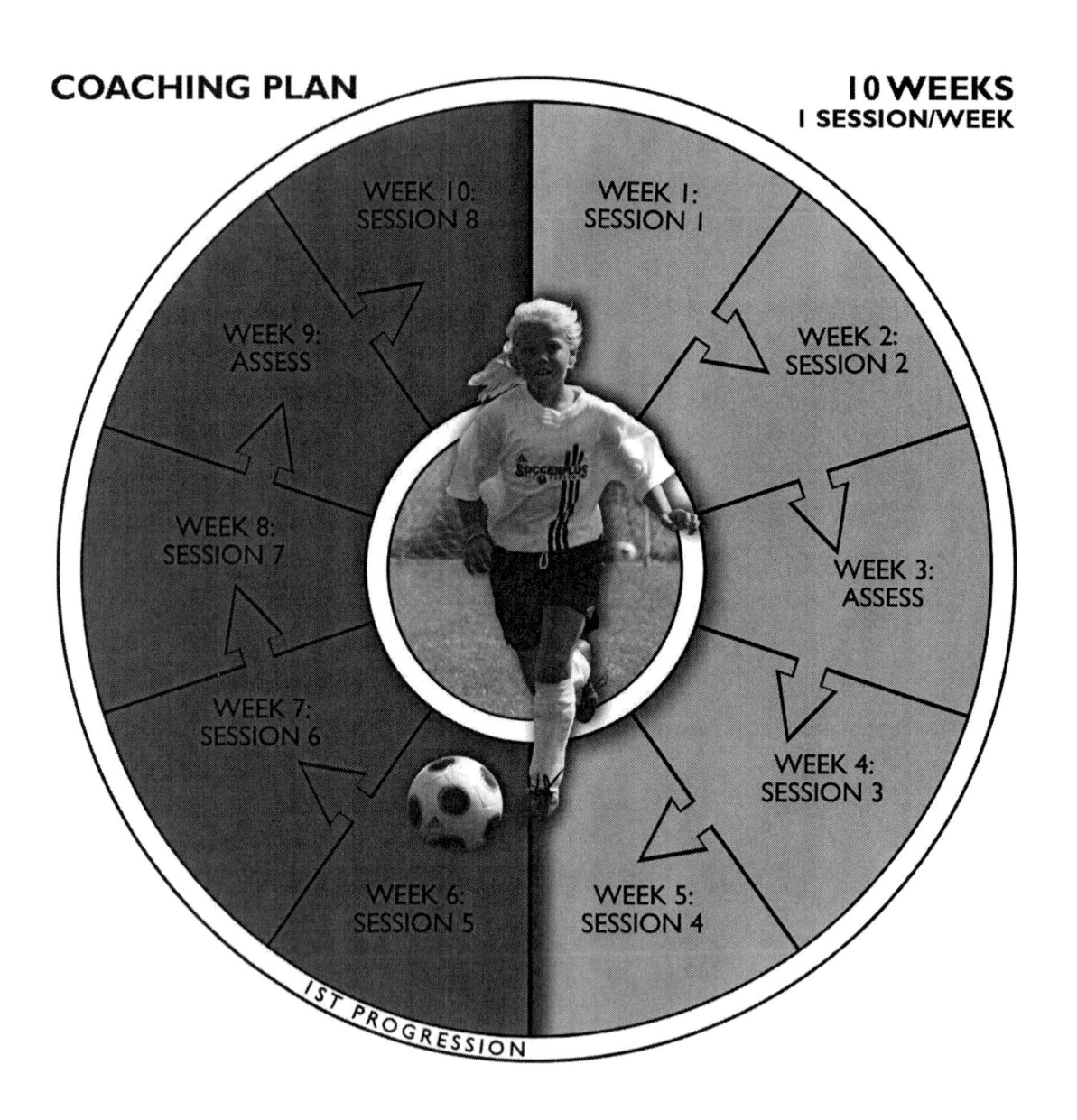

**COACHING PLAN**

**10 WEEKS**
**1 SESSION/WEEK**

- WEEK 1: SESSION 1
- WEEK 2: SESSION 2
- WEEK 3: ASSESS
- WEEK 4: SESSION 3
- WEEK 5: SESSION 4
- WEEK 6: SESSION 5
- WEEK 7: SESSION 6
- WEEK 8: SESSION 7
- WEEK 9: ASSESS
- WEEK 10: SESSION 8

1ST PROGRESSION

57
© SOCCERPLUS ALL RIGHTS RESERVED

SOCCER COACHING ACTIVITIES, SESSION PLANS AND ASSESSMENT

## Coaching plan for 10 weeks – 2 sessions per week

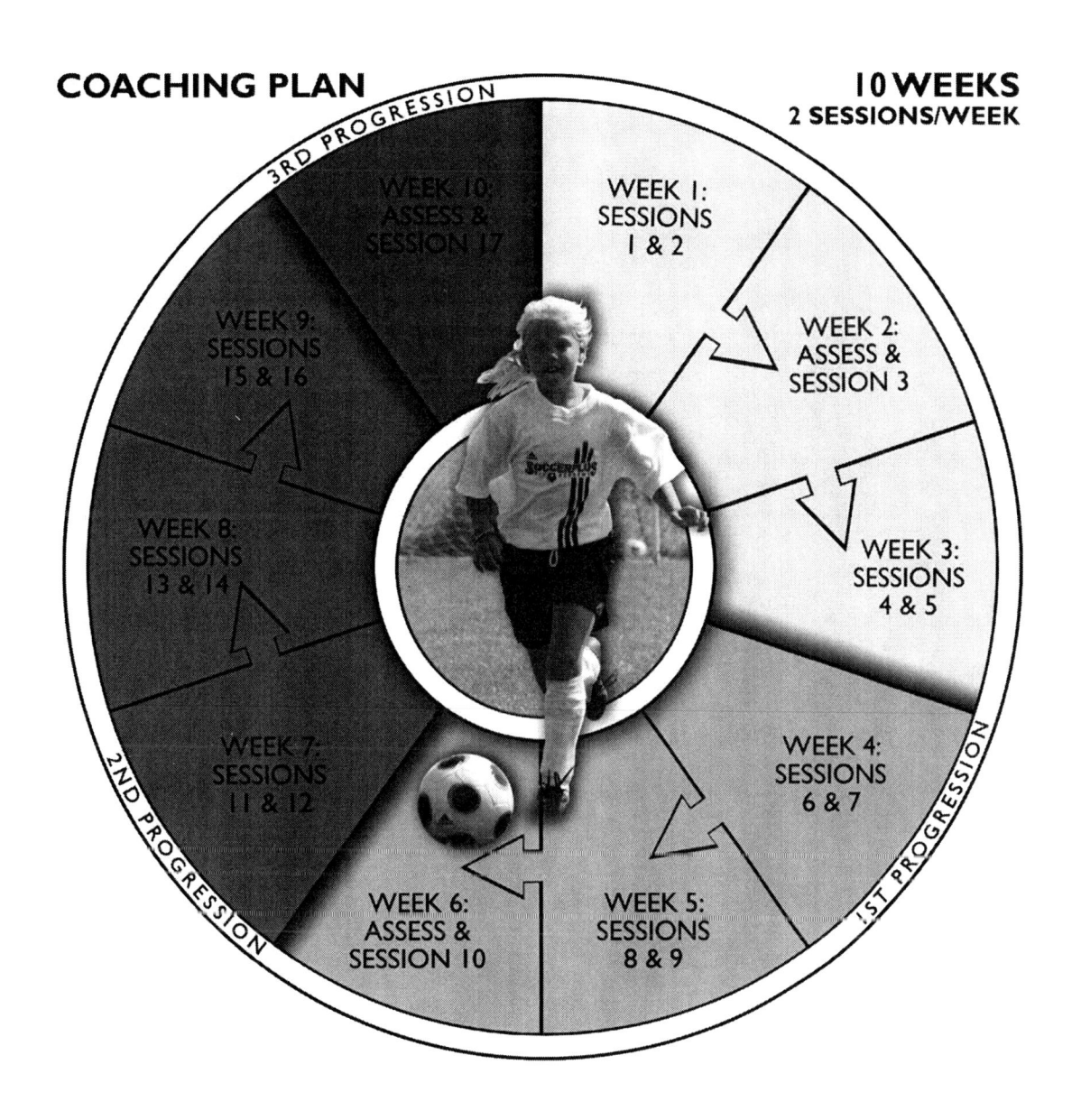

**COACHING PLAN** — **10 WEEKS / 2 SESSIONS/WEEK**

- 3RD PROGRESSION
- 2ND PROGRESSION
- 1ST PROGRESSION

- WEEK 1: SESSIONS 1 & 2
- WEEK 2: ASSESS & SESSION 3
- WEEK 3: SESSIONS 4 & 5
- WEEK 4: SESSIONS 6 & 7
- WEEK 5: SESSIONS 8 & 9
- WEEK 6: ASSESS & SESSION 10
- WEEK 7: SESSIONS 11 & 12
- WEEK 8: SESSIONS 13 & 14
- WEEK 9: SESSIONS 15 & 16
- WEEK 10: ASSESS & SESSION 17

PLUS 2 COACHING FOR DEVELOPMENT

# Coaching plan for 12 weeks – 1 session per week

**COACHING PLAN**

**12 WEEKS**
1 SESSION/WEEK

- WEEK 1: SESSION 1
- WEEK 2: ASSESS
- WEEK 3: SESSION 2
- WEEK 4: SESSION 3
- WEEK 5: SESSION 4
- WEEK 6: SESSION 5
- WEEK 7: SESSION 6
- WEEK 8: SESSION 7
- WEEK 9: SESSION 8
- WEEK 10: SESSION 9
- WEEK 11: ASSESS
- WEEK 12: SESSION 10

1ST PROGRESSION

2ND PROGRESSION

SOCCER COACHING ACTIVITIES, SESSION PLANS AND ASSESSMENT

# Coaching plan for 12 weeks – 2 sessions per week

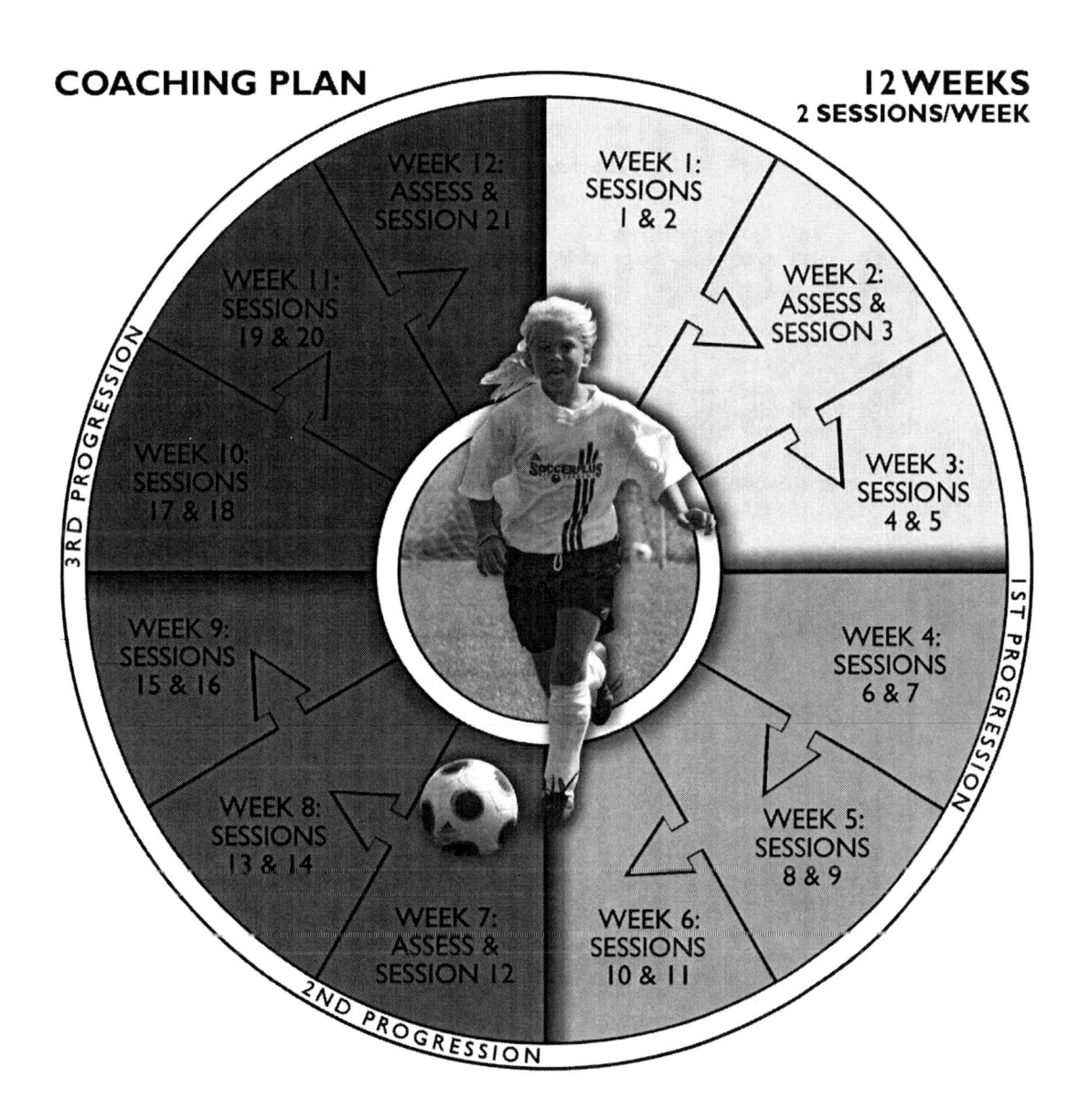

**COACHING PLAN**  **12 WEEKS**
2 SESSIONS/WEEK

- WEEK 1: SESSIONS 1 & 2
- WEEK 2: ASSESS & SESSION 3
- WEEK 3: SESSIONS 4 & 5
- WEEK 4: SESSIONS 6 & 7
- WEEK 5: SESSIONS 8 & 9
- WEEK 6: SESSIONS 10 & 11
- WEEK 7: ASSESS & SESSION 12
- WEEK 8: SESSIONS 13 & 14
- WEEK 9: SESSIONS 15 & 16
- WEEK 10: SESSIONS 17 & 18
- WEEK 11: SESSIONS 19 & 20
- WEEK 12: ASSESS & SESSION 21

1ST PROGRESSION
2ND PROGRESSION
3RD PROGRESSION

PLUS 2 COACHING FOR DEVELOPMENT

# Chapter 5 Coaching Activities and Session Plans

SOCCER COACHING ACTIVITIES, SESSION PLANS AND ASSESSMENT

# Coaching Activities & Session Plans

This section of the manual includes activities and session plans organized into two transitional phases for Plus 2; *Early to Mid Phase* and *Mid to Late Phase*.

## Early to Mid Phase

To ensure a seamless transition for Plus 1 to Plus 2 stages of development, we have provided 64 unique activities and 18 session plans organized by a coaching theme. These activities are suitable for players at or above performance expectation for Plus 1. Integrating activities from the Plus 1 handbook is important to ensure players are capable of meeting the higher demands of Plus 2 (Please refer to the Plus 1 handbook for such content).

## Mid to Late Phase

There are numerous new skills and topics introduced for the first time during the 'Early to Mid Phase' of Plus 2. To this end, it is anticipated players will be ready for the 'Mid to Late Phase' of Plus 2 after 3-5 sessions of regular exposure to 'Early to Mid Phase' content. Moving to small group activities (2v2 etc) begins a transition from almost exclusive dedication, focus and time on individual development to team play. As this is a major step in the process it is incredibly important for coaches to make certain players have achieved a clear understanding and proficiency of skills such as dribbling, passing, receiving, attacking and defending as an individual, heading and shooting. We have provided 44 unique activities and 11 session plans for the 'Mid to Late Phase'.

## Design your own session plans

It is, of course, difficult to anticipate in a handbook the exact needs of the players and coach. To that end, the sessions in this manual present content based on themes – i.e. passing. The coach will most likely want to combine activities from a couple of themes in one session – the variations are endless. For example, a session devoted completely to heading is not appropriate, so a coach may wish to select a dribbling warm-up, choose a couple of heading activities as the main theme and finish with a small sided game that rewards heading in the points system.

Also, coaches should refer back to the coaching formulas for Plus 1 and Plus 2 and specifically the '# of unique activities per session'. With this in mind, finding the right balance of previously learned and unique activities will factor significantly in the success of the session and the learning experience.

# PLUS 2 COACHING FOR DEVELOPMENT

Activities and session plans cover the following topics:

**Dribbling Skills**

- Turns, ball manipulation, feints and dribble, running with the ball.

**Passing & Receiving**

- Passing along the ground – 5-20 yards, instep, driven, chip/lofted, swerve.
- Receiving – Foot, Thigh, Chest, Head.

**Attacking and Defending**

- Attacking - attacking an opponent 1v1, beating an opponent – take-on moves and escaping an opponent.
- Defending – techniques for tackling, body positioning, applying pressure, defending as an individual and in pairs.

**Shooting**

- Instep, half volley, volley, one on one with the Goalkeeper

**Heading**

- Basic technique, heading to clear and heading for goal.

Note: Introducing basic goalkeeping to all players is important at the Plus 2 stage of development. Due to the specialism of this position and coaching goalkeeping, we have devoted an entire manual to this position.

The activities in this handbook and over 600 more are available online at www.soccerinteractive.com. Over 50% of all activities are supported by video or animation so coaches are able to watch the activities coached by a professional before taking to the field. In addition, there are over 200 session plans organized into the 5 stages of development.

Visit www.SoccerInteractive.com and sign up for a free trial.

# SOCCER COACHING ACTIVITIES, SESSION PLANS AND ASSESSMENT

## Plus 2 - Early to Mid Stage Activities

| Activities | Theme | Page |
|---|---|---|
| 1 v 1 - 2 goals | Attacking, Defending | pg. 66 |
| 1 v 1 - 4 Gates | Defending, Attacking | pg. 67 |
| 1 v 1 Challenge | Defending, Attacking | pg. 68 |
| 1 v 1 to Goal | Attacking, Defending | pg. 69 |
| 1 v 1 to Goal #2 | Attacking, Defending | pg. 70 |
| 10 Continuous Attacks | Attacking, Defending | pg. 71 |
| 1st Team to 4 | Attacking, Defending | pg. 72 |
| 4 by 4 Squares | Passing, Receiving | pg. 73 |
| 4 Group Passing | Passing, Receiving | pg. 74 |
| 4 v 4 Defending | Defending | pg. 75 |
| Agility Race | Movement | pg. 76 |
| All Up and All Back | Attacking, Defending | pg. 77 |
| Antz Nests | Dribbling | pg. 78 |
| Attacking Moves - 1 v 1 | Attacking, Defending | pg. 79 |
| Balancing in Pairs | Movement | pg. 80 |
| Block Tackle | Defending | pg. 81 |
| British Bull Dog | Dribbling | pg. 82 |
| Can You? Plus 2 | Ball Mastery | pg. 83 |
| Coconut Shy | Passing, Receiving | pg. 84 |
| Cooperation Games 1 | Movement, Team work | pg. 85 |
| Cooperation Games 2 | Movement, Team work | pg. 86 |
| Cooperation Games 3 | Movement, Team work | pg. 87 |
| Cooperation Games 4 | Movement, Team Work | pg. 88 |
| Count Down | Dribbling, Passing | pg. 89 |
| Creating Space 1 v 1 | Shooting, Attacking, Defending | pg. 90 |
| Defending 1 v 1 A | Defending | pg. 91 |
| Defending 1 v 1 B | Defending | pg. 92 |
| Defending 1 v 1 Recover | Defending, Attacking | pg. 93 |
| Defending 3 Goals | Defending | pg. 94 |
| Dribble, Turn, Pass | Dribbling, Ball Mastery | pg. 95 |
| Dribbling Basics | Dribbling, Creating Space | pg. 96 |
| Dribbling Tag | Dribbling, Creating Space | pg. 97 |
| Driven Pass/Shot | Shooting, Passing | pg. 98 |
| End Zone | Passing, Receiving | pg. 99 |
| Escape & Possession | Dribbling | pg. 100 |
| Escape Move - Drag Back | Dribbling, Creating Space | pg. 101 |
| Escape Move - Step Over | Dribbling, Creating Space | pg. 102 |

## PLUS 2 COACHING FOR DEVELOPMENT

| | | |
|---|---|---|
| Fetch | Dribbling, Ball Mastery | pg. 103 |
| Flip 'em | Dribbling, Ball Mastery | pg. 104 |
| Four Rings | Movement, Defending, Attacking | pg. 105 |
| Heading 1 v 1 | Heading | pg. 106 |
| Heading 1 v 1 v 1 v 1 | Heading | pg. 107 |
| Heading Basics | Heading | pg. 108 |
| Hot Shot 1 | Shooting, Attacking | pg. 109 |
| Hot Shot 2 | Shooting, Attacking | pg. 110 |
| Individual Ball Warm Up 1 | Dribbling | pg. 111 |
| Individual Ball Warm Up 2 | Dribbling | pg. 112 |
| Individual Receiving | Passing, Receiving | pg. 113 |
| Looters | Dribbling, Attacking, Defending | pg. 114 |
| Match 2 v 2 | Game | pg. 115 |
| Mirrors 1 v 1 | Dribbling | pg. 116 |
| Numbers Game | Dribbling, Attacking, Shooting, Defending | pg. 117 |
| Numbers Hot Shot | Shooting, Attacking, Defending | pg. 118 |
| Numbers Turn | Shooting, Attacking | pg. 119 |
| One Goal 1 v 1 | Attacking, Defending | pg. 120 |
| Pairs Passing & Moving | Passing, Receiving | pg. 121 |
| Passing Through The Arch | Passing, Receiving | pg. 122 |
| Passing Through The Gate | Passing, Receiving | pg. 123 |
| Patterns | Dribbling | pg. 124 |
| Possession 1 v 1 | Passing, Receiving | pg. 125 |
| Shapes and Colors | Movement | pg. 126 |
| Short Passing Basics | Passing, Receiving | pg. 127 |
| Short Passing for Points | Passing, Receiving | pg. 128 |
| Soccer Rugby | Game | pg. 129 |
| Squares | Passing, Receiving | pg. 130 |
| Striker Breakaway | Dribbling, Shooting | pg. 131 |
| Take On - Inside Outside | Dribbling, Creating Space | pg. 132 |
| Treasure Chest | Dribbling, Attacking, Defending | pg. 133 |
| Tree House | Dribbling | pg. 134 |
| Winner Stays On | Attacking, Shooting, Defending | pg. 135 |
| World Cup | Shooting, Attacking | pg. 136 |

# 1 v 1 - 2 goals

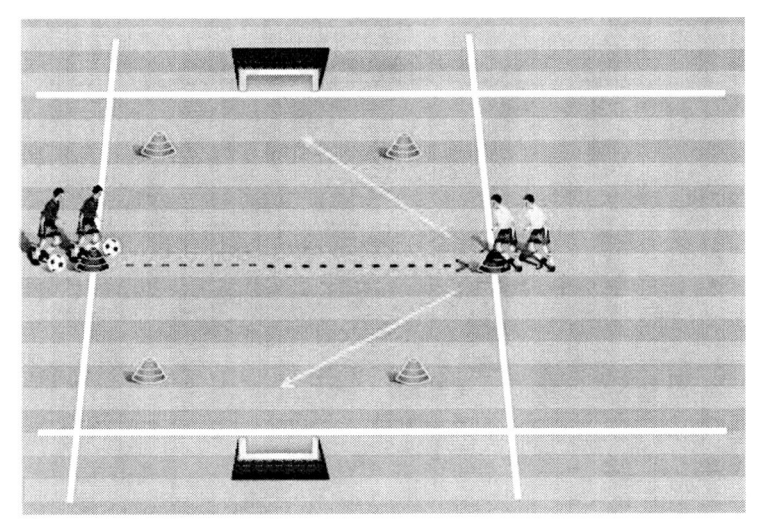

**Materials Needed**

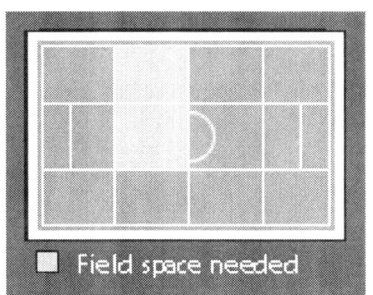

Area 20 x 20 yds
- Balls
- Cones
- Training Vests

## 1 v 1 - 2 goals (Two goals)

### Description:
Players in small groups of no more than 4. 1st player passes ball across to the opposite line and immediately defends against the attacker. The attacking player tries to score in either goal set to either side. To score a goal the player has to be beyond the coned shooting line that is about 2-3 yards from goal. If the defender wins the ball they can score a goal. Players change lines each time to ensure everybody defends and attacks.

### Coaching Points
- Players to use take-on moves to beat the defender
- Be aware of the open goal to score in
- Defenders to transition quickly to attackers

### Progressions:
1. Team competition so players return to their own line after each attack and each team gets 3 minutes to score as many goals as possible before changing.
2. Progress to 2v2 so introducing the option of passing.

# 1 v 1 - 4 Gates

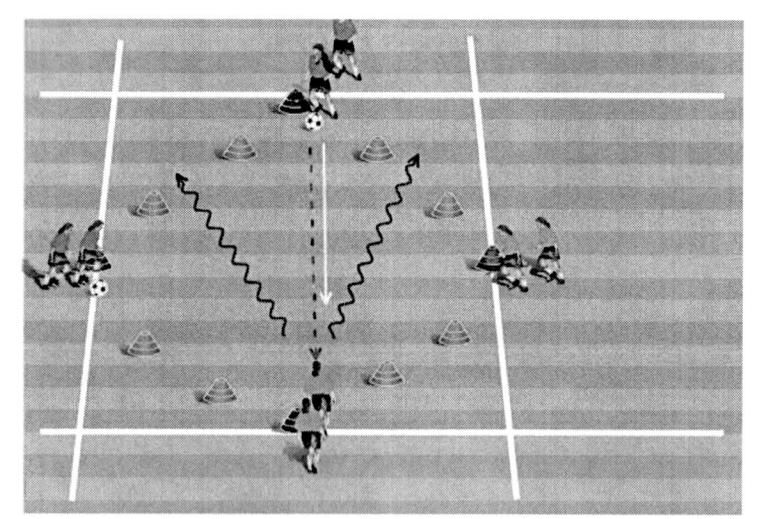

**Materials Needed**

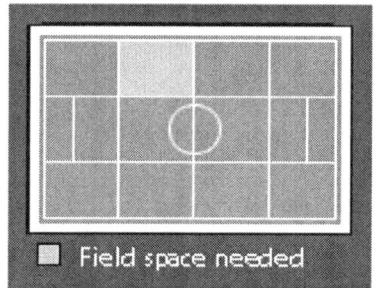

Area 20 x 20 yds
- Balls
- Cones
- Training Vests

## 1 v 1 - 4 Gates (Defending, Attacking)

### Description:
Four pairs positioned on each side of the area. Start by alternating - Play games one after another (two teams opposite each other compete). The server sends a ball across the area to the attacker. The attacker attempts to score by dribbling the ball through either of the two gates either side of the server (defender). If the defender wins the ball they can score through the opposite two gates.

### Coaching Points
- Defense - close down space quickly
- Defense - force attacker to their weaker side
- Defense - win possession when the attacker makes an error
- Attack - You have to beat a player to score
- Attack - Realism in the moves
- Attack - Speed to move away from the defender

### Progressions:
Play two games concurrently (two teams opposite each other compete).

# 1 v 1 Challenge

## Materials Needed

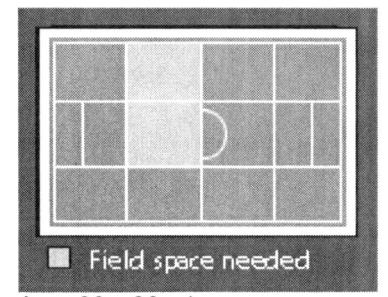

Area 30 x 30 yds
- Balls
- Cones
- Training vests

## 1 v 1 Challenge (Defending, Attacking)

### Description:
Players work in pairs. One player is the attacker with the ball and one player is the defender. The attacker's objective is to try and dribble through as many of the gates (two cones 2 yds apart) as possible. The defender must try to stop the attacker from scoring. After 45 seconds change roles.

### Coaching Points
- Defense - try to slow the attacking player
- Defense - don't be overly concerned with winning the ball
- Defense - use body strength to force play to one direction
- Attack - awareness of the open space
- Attack - keep the ball moving but have control
- Attack - encourage take on or escape moves

### Progressions:
Change the emphasis of defending to win possession - the first defender to win the ball gets a point - first defender to 3 points wins.

# 1 v 1 to Goal

## Materials Needed

Area 25 x 25 yds
- Balls
- Cones
- Training Vests

## 1 v 1 to Goal (Attacking)

### Description:
Two players start side by side 25 yards from goal. The server (standing to one side of the goal) plays a ball into the area and shouts "GO". Players must turn and compete for the ball and attempt a shot at goal.

### Coaching Points
- Speed of reaction
- First touch towards goal but away from defender
- Awareness of keepers and defenders positions

### Progressions:
Add a time limit on the attack.

# 1 v 1 to Goal #2

**Materials Needed**

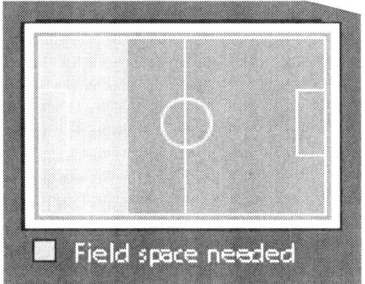

Area 25 x 25 yds
- Balls
- Cones

## 1 v 1 to Goal #2 (Attacking, Defending)

### Description:
Split the team into two groups - defenders and attackers. The first defender plays a ball to the first attacker and then must run around the cone and chase down the attacker. Attacker must control the pass and quickly dribble at goal to finish.

### Coaching Points
- Technique of first touch
- Dribble at speed
- Dribble to cut off path of defender
- Shooting technique (side foot, laces)

### Progressions:
1) Switch sides where service originates.
2) Add two attackers/defenders.
3) Defenders play a flighted ball.

# 10 Continuous Attacks

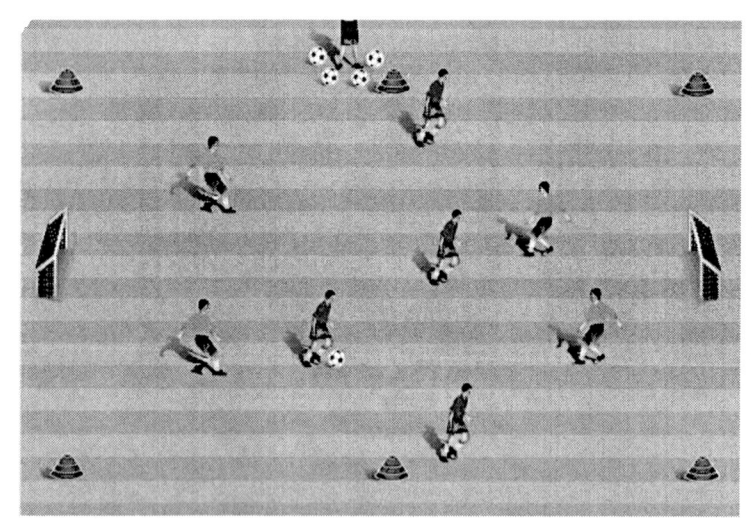

**Materials Needed**

Area 40 x 30 yds
- Balls
- Cones
- Goals
- Training Vests

## 10 Continuous Attacks (Attacking, Defending)

### Description:
4v4. 4 attacking players start the game on the centre line and the 4 players on the defending team are separated into two pairs - each defending one half of the field. The defending teams cannot enter into the opposing half of the field. The coach starts each attack by feeding the ball into the attackers. The 4 attackers attack one end of the field creating a 4 v 2 situation. If the defenders win the ball they must clear the ball off the field. The attackers have 10 continuous attacks to score as many goals as possible. Attacks must alternate from one end to the other (i.e. 5 attacks at each end).

### Coaching Points
- Positive attitude towards attacking by all attackers
- Look to go past a defender at every opportunity
- Shoot when the opportunity presents itself

### Progressions:
1) Introduce a goalkeeper into each goal to increase the difficulty for the attackers.
2) Every attacking player to be in the attacking half for a goal to count.

# 1st Team to 4

## Materials Needed

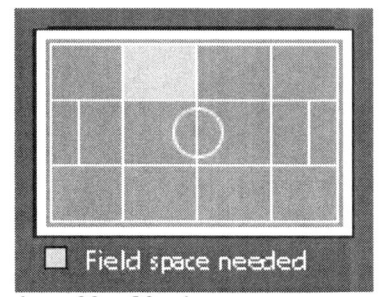

Area 20 x 20 yds
- Balls
- Cones
- Training Vests

## 1st Team to 4 (Attacking, Defending)

### Description:
Two teams play 4v4 into four small goals with no goalkeepers. The first team to score in all four goals is the winner. This will encourage attackers to move away from defenders as they look for an open goal to score into. Depending on number of players in the session this can be 3v3 or 5v5.

### Coaching Points
- A positive attitude to scoring by all players
- Use turns to move away from players to look for an open goal
- Accuracy of finishing

### Progressions:
1) Each player can only score in one goal so everybody becomes a goal scorer.
2) Put a time limit on the game to increase the desire from the players to score goals quickly.
3) Give the goals a number 1-4 and players have to score in that sequence.

# 4 by 4 Squares

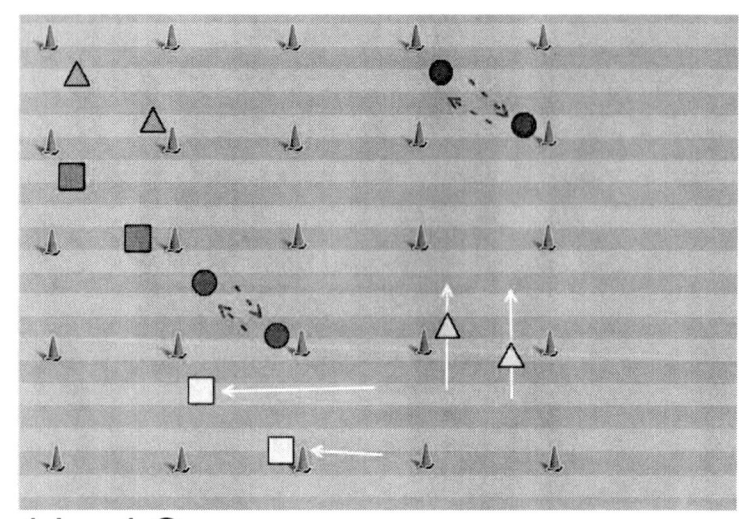

**Materials Needed**

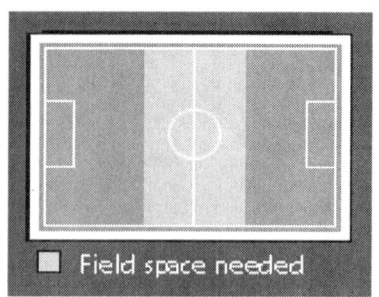

Area 40 x 40 yds
- Balls
- Cones

## 4 by 4 Squares (Passing, Receiving)

### Description:
Set out 16 squares measuring 10 x 10 yds - 4 squares long and 4 squares wide. Each pair starts in one square – passing the ball back and forth to reach 10 passes. On completion of 10 passes, the pair move to an unoccupied square and repeat another 10 passes.

### Coaching Points
- Look up for space
- Accelerate into the space
- Correct execution of the skill

### Progressions:

1) 10 one touch passes.
2) Move to a square not adjacent.
3) Heading – 5 high - 5 low.
4) Side volleys – 5 left and 5 right.

# 4 Group Passing

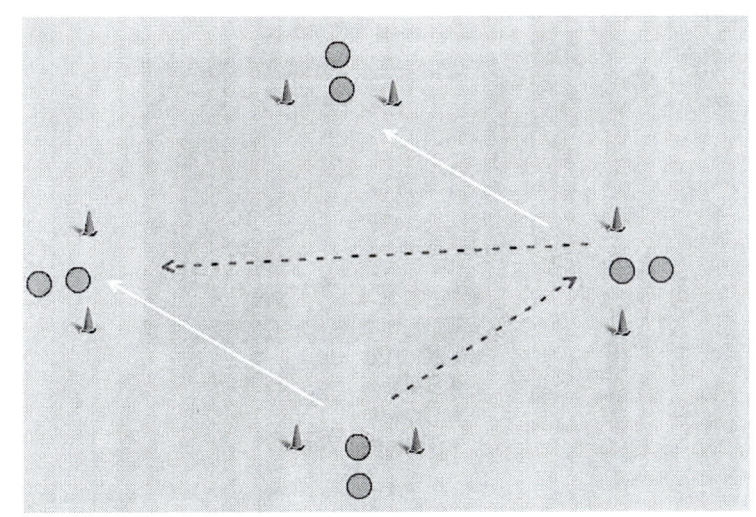

**Materials Needed**

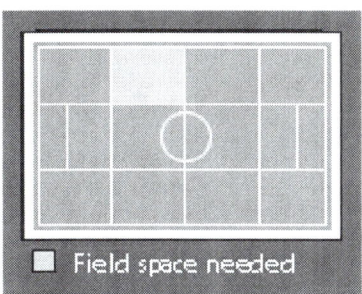

Area: 20 x 20
- Balls
- Cones

## 4 Group Passing (Passing)

### Description:
Players are split into 4 groups with 2 players being in each group. One ball is used. The exercise starts with the player with the ball playing a pass to one group and moving to another. Whoever plays the pass must move to a different group. You can't play a pass to a group which has 1 player.

### Coaching Points
- Movement away from the ball
- Quality of pass
- Speed of movement

### Progressions:
Play 1 touch passes

# 4 v 4 Defending

**Materials Needed**

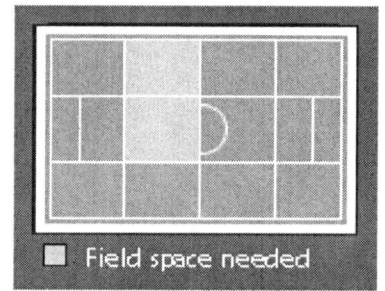

Area 20 x 20 yds
- Balls
- Cones
- Training Vests

## 4 v 4 Defending (Defending)

**Description:**
The defenders have to protect the center of the area (5 x 5 yd). The attackers have a ball each and have to try and beat the defender and dribble into the center. If the defender wins the ball he/she should dribble to the outside of the area to score a point. Switch roles every 1 minute.

**Coaching Points**
- Apply pressure
- Get into the staggered position
- Be patient

**Progressions:**
Have 3 balls on each cone. When an attack has finished, the attacker goes back to the cone and collects the next ball. The 4 attackers combine their score and then the defenders switch positions with the attackers and attempt to beat the score.

# Agility Race

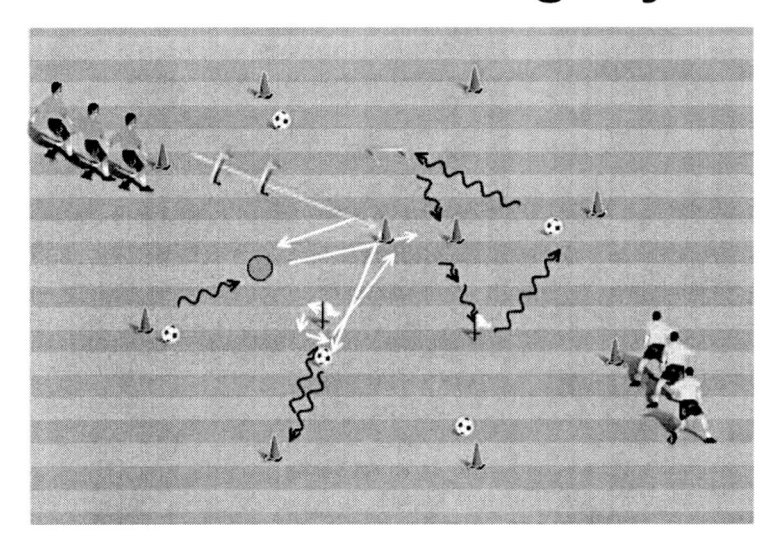

## Materials Needed

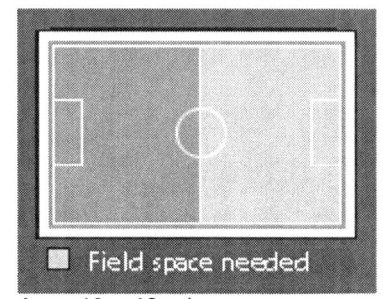

Area 40 x 40 yds
- Balls
- Cones
- Training Vests
- Ladders, hurdles
- Rings, band & pillows

## Agility Race (Movement)

### Description:
5 mins & 6-36 players. Teams of 3 players. Each team has a home cone (starting point). Sticks, hurdles, ladders, speed bands, cones, rings and wobble pillows placed in area. Coach shouts the order of each activity (ie. hurdle, cone, ring - 1st player sprints out to perform the activity and then returns 'home' for 2nd player to go. Combinations of dribbling the ball and performing without.

### Coaching Points
- Perform activity with good form
- Explosive moves
- Maximum intensity whilst working

### Progressions:
Activities: 1. Dribble to the stick, leave the ball and circle the stick (facing to middle of area), sprint to the center, return to the ball and hand over to partner. 2, 3, 4 - same as 1 but players must perform an exercise through the ladders, rings and hurdles before returning. 5. Coach shouts equipment items (i.e. hurdle, stick, cone) and players have to dribble the ball to those items in that order - progress to performing an activity at each equipment item - such as 5 lateral jumps over hurdles and under over the sticks etc. 6. Balance - dribble to the wobble pillow and hold balance (variety - one or two feet) for 5 seconds before moving to the next. Rings can replace wobble pillows for the youngest players.

# All Up and All Back

## Materials Needed

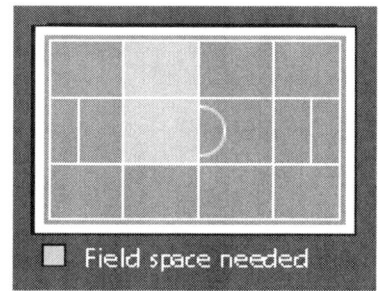

Area 40 x 20 yds
- Ball per player
- Cones
- Training Vests
- Goals

## All Up and All Back (Attacking, Defending)

### Description:
A line of cones mark the center line of the field. Players play a regular game of soccer (3v3 to 5v5), but a goal does not count for the attacking side unless all players are in the attacking half of the field. Also, a goal counts as double if all defenders are not in the defensive half when the ball enters the goal.

### Coaching Points
- Attack – provide angles for support
- Defense – get behind the ball
- Think quickly and concentrate on the rules

### Progressions:
Add conditions such as one touch finish and two touches everywhere else.

# Antz Nests

## Materials Needed

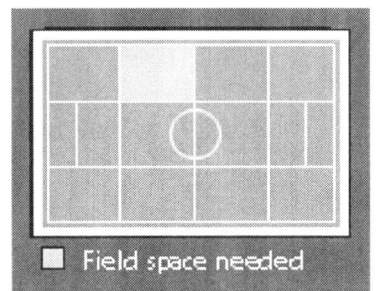

Area 20 x 20 yds
- Ball per Player
- Cones
- Training Vests

## Antz Nests (Dribbling, Turns)

### Description:
Four equal teams of Antz must work quickly to build their ants nest. In the four corners of the square the coach sets 3x3 yd squares. The objective is to fill the nest with supplies first – three balls.

### Coaching Points
- Quick turns and dribble
- Look around to see which groups are closest to winning
- Stay upright when competing for a ball

### Progressions:
Each Ant has a name (characters from the movie) – Z, Weaver, Princess Bala and Barbatus. When the coach shouts a name, the ants of the same name from each team collect supplies (balls) from the center of the square – one at a time only. The objective is to fill the nest with supplies first – three balls.

Story: 'Z, Weaver, Princess Bala and Barbatus need to collect supplies for the Antz nest before the supplies run out – three rival colonies are also sharing so the team must move fast?'

### Progression/variations:

Eliminate balls each round so there are not enough for each team to have three balls. Allow the players to steal one ball at a time from an opposing group until they have three.

# Attacking Moves - 1 v 1

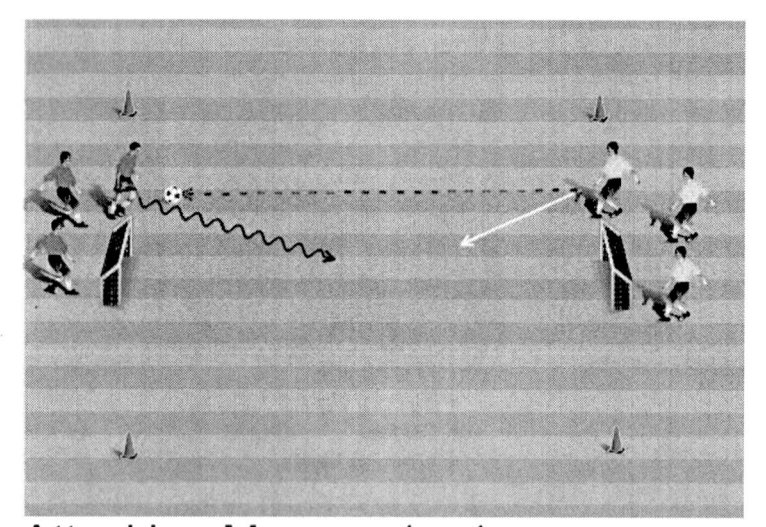

**Materials Needed**

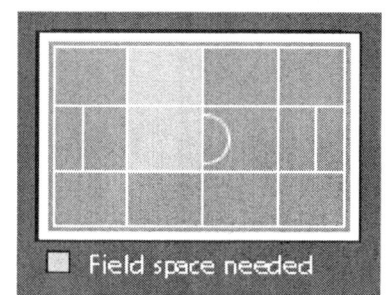

Field space needed

Area 30 x 20 yds
- Several balls
- Cones
- Training vests
- Small Goals

## Attacking Moves - 1 v 1 (Attacking, Possession)

### Description:
3-4 players at each end of the field. First player in each line play 1v1 - defender plays ball to the attacker and attacker performs a take-on move. If backed up, attacker creates space with an escape-move.

### Coaching Points
- Approach defender at comfortable speed
- Sell the defender with take on move
- Create space using escape move

### Progressions:
This activity is a progression from take on and escape moves. Like all practices, the skills need to be performed realistically - fakes have to be good to fool the defender and then accelerate away. Coach player to be clinical - once the attacker has beaten the defender go to goal and score - don't allow defender to recover. Progress to the 'game with gates' or small sided game.

# Balancing in Pairs

**Materials Needed**

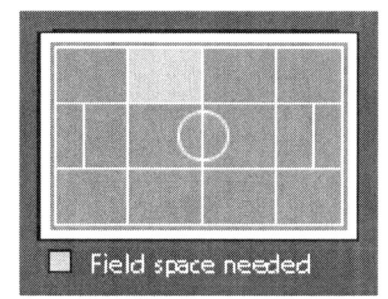

Area 20 x 15 yds
- 1 Ball per pair
- 4 Cones

## Balancing in Pairs (Movement)

**Description:**
Players in pairs, completing various patterns of movement.
1) Throw and catch with two hands. 2) Catch, stretch high, bring into chest and then throw to partner, 3) Catch, stretch high, brush the ground with the ball, bring back to chest and throw to partner, 4) Catch, stretch high, brush the ground with the ball, circle twice around the body, bring into the chest and throw to partner.

**Coaching Points**
- Maintain balance for all movements
- Two feet on the ground & two hands on the ball
- Throw chest height

**Progressions:**
Balance on one foot while completing the movement pattern.

# Block Tackle

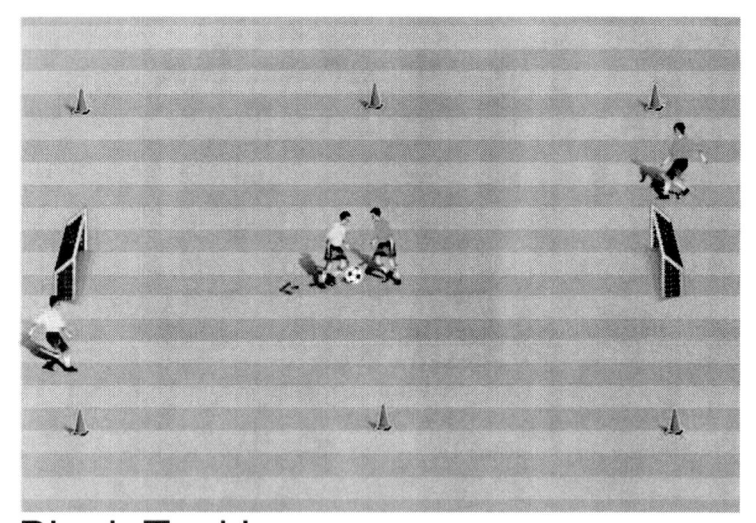

## Materials Needed

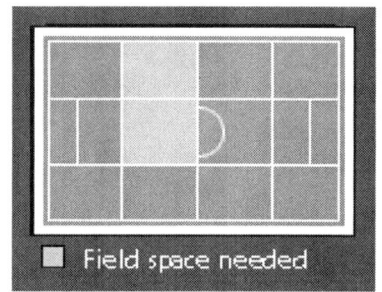

Field space needed

Area 20 x 10 yds
- Ball per player
- Cones
- Training Vests
- Goals

## Block Tackle (Defending)

### Description:
Play 1v1 - One goal at each end of the area. Firstly teach the block tackle technique: Players stand face to face with hands on their partners shoulder. One ball between each pair. One player counts to 3 and then the players perform a block tackle - both players tackling at the same time. When the ball is won, the players attempt to score. 4 players to an area, next 2 on when goal is scored.

### Coaching Points
- Non-kicking foot by the side of the ball
- Block tackle with inside of foot
- Lean into challenge with body weight forward
- Do not kick at the ball

### Progressions:

The correct technique (lower the body by bending knees, place non-tackling foot beside the ball, contact the ball with inside of foot, cushion on impact, force the ball away from opponent. Progress to taking a step back and perform again – players need to get the 'feel' – no kicking through the ball!

# British Bull Dog

## Materials Needed

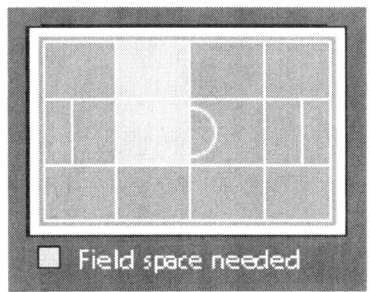

Area 30 x 15 yds
- Ball per player
- Cones
- Training Vests

## British Bull Dog (Dribbling & Movement)

### Description:
One player is selected to be the 'Bull Dog' and starts at the end line. The other players 'Cats' line up at the other end of the rectangle facing the person in the middle. The first time through without soccer balls – then all players other than Bull Dog has balls to dribble. Cats who were tagged join the Bull Dog.

### Coaching Points
- Encourage players to use body movements to elude the bull dog
- When dribbling, keep soccer balls close to allow quick changes in direction
- Lift head to avoid collision and see routes for escape

### Progressions:

One player is selected to be the 'Bull Dog' and starts at the end line. The other players 'Cats' line up at the other end of the rectangle facing the person in the middle. The first time through without soccer balls – then all players other than Bull Dog has balls to dribble. The Cats start the game by chanting in unison "British Bull Dog 1, 2, 3", the Bull Dog then responds by giving the command "BRITISH BULL DOG" – the Cats then try to make their way to the opposite end of the rectangle without being tagged by Bull Dog. Any Cat who is tagged or dribbles outside the rectangle must step out of the area. Once the remaining Cats have made it to the other end line, the Cats who were tagged join the Bull Dog. The game continues until there is only one player left to be tagged. That player then gets to be Bull Dog for the next round. Change the way players move from one end to the other - gallop, skip, walk, or slide. Bull Dog and Cats become crabs – must remain in crab position to move. Instead of tagging the players, Bull Dog must pull the training vests hanging in the back of the Cats shorts (the tail).

# Can You? Plus 2

**Materials Needed**

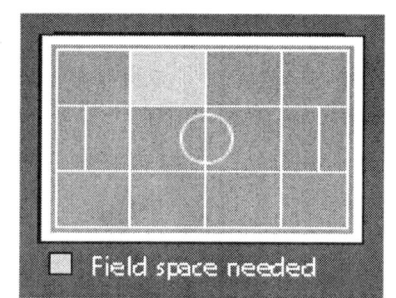

Area 20 x 20 yds
- Ball per Player
- Cones

## Can You? Plus 2 (Ball Mastery)

**Description:**
Coach to lead patterns of movement asking can you ....? Basic and more advanced movements.

**Coaching Points**
- Concentrate on great execution
- Build up pace to game speed
- Get in a good body position to protect the ball

**Progressions:**
Use this activity to teach players skills from the Plus 2 Skills Pyramid:
**Tier 4**
1. Inside cut, 2. Ball rolls, 3. Outside cut, 4. Take on dribble (outside of foot)
**Tier 3**
5. Single cut dribble, 6. Forward drag rolls, 7. Step-pivot turn,
**Tier 2**
8. Flick turn, 9. Double tap and dribble
**Tier 1**
10. Double cut dribble

# Coconut Shy

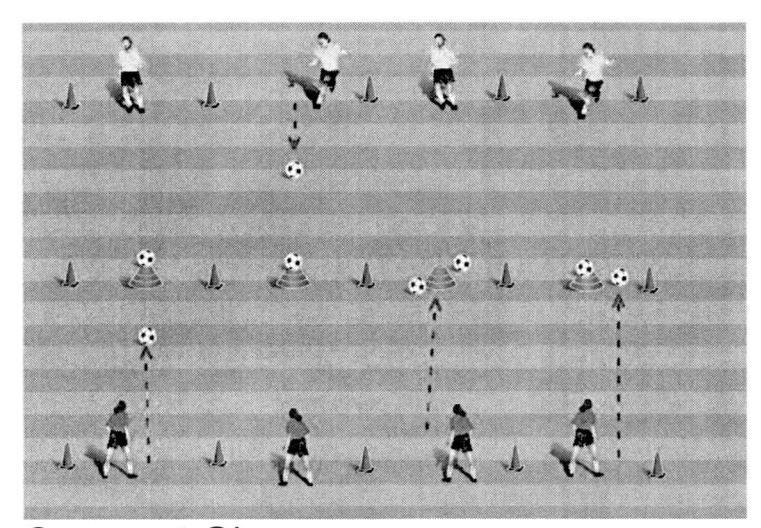

**Materials Needed**

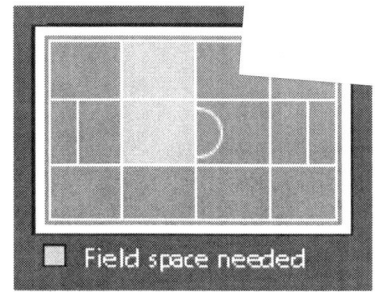

Area 30 x 20 yds
- Ball per player
- Cones

## Coconut Shy (Passing and Receiving)

**Description:**
A line of cones 5 yds apart are placed along the center (10 yds) of the rectangle. A ball is placed on top of each cone. 2 Players stand opposite each other 20 yds apart. The objective is to pass the ball from behind the line and hit the ball off the cone. The first pair to reach 5 hits wins.

**Coaching Points**
- For accuracy, pass ball with the inside of the foot
- Run onto the ball straight
- Kick through the ball for power

**Progressions:**

Players compete against each other to score 5 points

# Cooperation Games 1

## Materials Needed

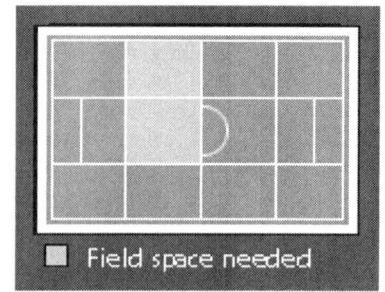

Area 20 x 20 yds
- Ball per player
- Cones
- Training Vests

## Cooperation Games 1 (Movement and team work)

### Description:
Caterpillar Sit – split the group in two – 4-8 players in each - players are seated on the floor with their legs stretched flat out in front of them. One player behind the other, in a line similar to a train or caterpillar. Players have to move in close enough to each other so that each player can place their feet just below the hips/quadriceps of the player in front. The group has to work together to reach a target (end line). No hands are permitted to touch the floor, except the hands of the last person in the group. Add obstacles (cones) to increase difficulty. Once the players have had a chance to practice the activity, you can organize relays between the groups.

### Coaching Points
- Encourage good technique for sprinting, catching and hopping etc
- Add pressure by applying times and competition
- Intersperse between skill activities

### Progressions:
**Soccer Ball Pyramid** – At any point in the session the coach shouts "PYRAMID". The time starts on the command and players rush to collect the balls and carefully stack them on each other so they form a pyramid. **Catching relay** – 2,3 or 4 teams compete. The team stands in a staggered formation - two yards apart. On the command of "GO", the team have to throw and catch objects from one person to the next in a zigzag pattern. If the object is dropped, start again with the first person. A good activity to determine who gets to play a game first – first two teams to finish play first! **Circle relay** – players stand in a circle – 5-7 yards from the center. The coach stands in the middle and throws/passes a ball to a player. The player to the right of the person receiving the ball must set off around the circle (running, side step, skipping, hopping etc) and the ball is passed in the opposite direction (either by hands or feet) – can the player beat the ball back? Add multiple balls and change the passing rules – i.e. pass to every other person.

# Cooperation Games 2

**Materials Needed**

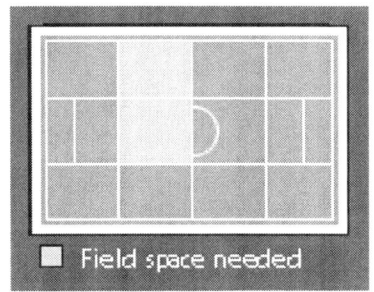

Area 20 x 20 yds
- Ball per player
- Cones
- Training Vests

## Cooperation Games 2 (Movement and team work)

**Description:**
Follow the leader juggling in pairs – 'A' starts performing one juggle – B follows. B then leads with two juggles – A follows.
No hands – see how many ways players can get the ball into the air – no hands allowed.
Around the body – juggle the ball from the right foot to right thigh to right shoulder to head to left shoulder to left thigh to left foot - all with one touch on each surface.

**Coaching Points**
- Add pressure by applying times and competition
- Intersperse between skill activities

**Progressions:**
**Follow the leader juggling** – In pairs, each player with a ball. Player A starts with performing one juggle – Player B follows. Player B then leads for two juggles – player A follows. Use feet, thigh, shoulder, head etc. **'No hands'** – Players are set the task of seeing how many ways they can get the ball into the air – no hands allowed. **Around the body** – objective is to juggle the ball from right foot-right thigh-right shoulder-head-left shoulder-left thigh-left foot. – all with one touch. **Group juggles** - 3-5 players in a group attempt to keep the ball up for as many touches. **Get into groups** – coach calls a number and players must form groups of that number. **Chain gang** – players must form a chain by linking arms and complete certain tasks set by the coach – such as run around the goal and back.

# Cooperation Games 3

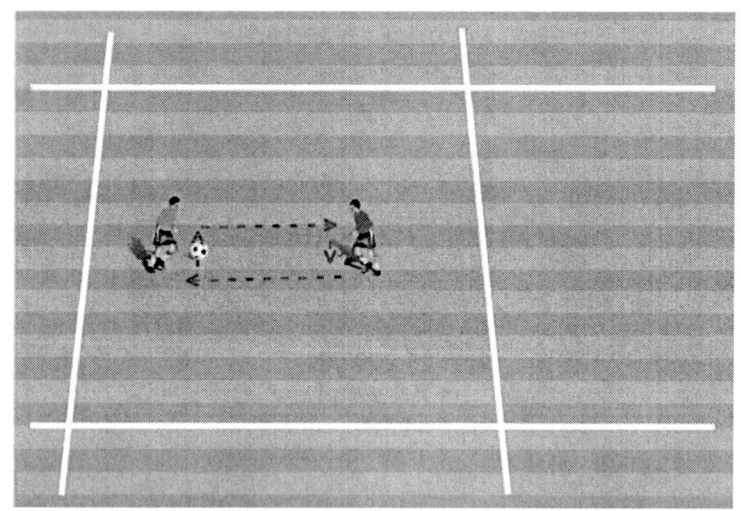

**Materials Needed**

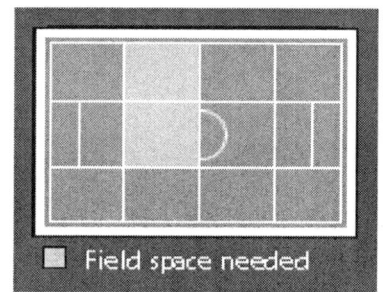

Area 20 x 20 yds
- Ball per player
- Cones
- Training Vests

## Cooperation Games 3 (Movement and team work)

### Description:
Straight line passing – In pairs 5 yards apart – one ball. 'A' passes the ball from the right hand – 'B' catches with two hands and passes to A with the right hand. Change direction.
Straight line passing with feet. In pairs 5 yards apart – one ball. A passes the ball along ground using the right foot – B controls the ball and passes to A with right foot. Change direction.

### Coaching Points
- Communicate with each other to coordinate release
- Start slow and increase pace and intensity
- Get a rhythm going

### Progressions:
**Straight line passing –** In pairs 5 yards apart – one ball (soccer/medicine). A passes the ball at chest height from the right hand – B catches with two hands and passes to A with right hand. Change direction. **Straight line passing with feet –** In pairs 5 yards apart – one ball. A passes the ball along the ground using the right foot – B controls the ball and passes to A with right foot. Change direction. **Circle passing –** A passes with the right hand and B catches with left hand – pass across the body and throw back with right hand. Change direction. **Circle passing with feet–** A passes with the right foot and B receives with the left foot – pass across the body using one touch and then play back to A with the right foot. Change direction. **Two Balls Circle passing –** Perform the same exercise, but this time both players throw balls simultaneously. Change direction. **Two Balls Circle passing with feet–** Perform the same exercise, but this time both players pass balls simultaneously. Change direction.

# Cooperation Games 4

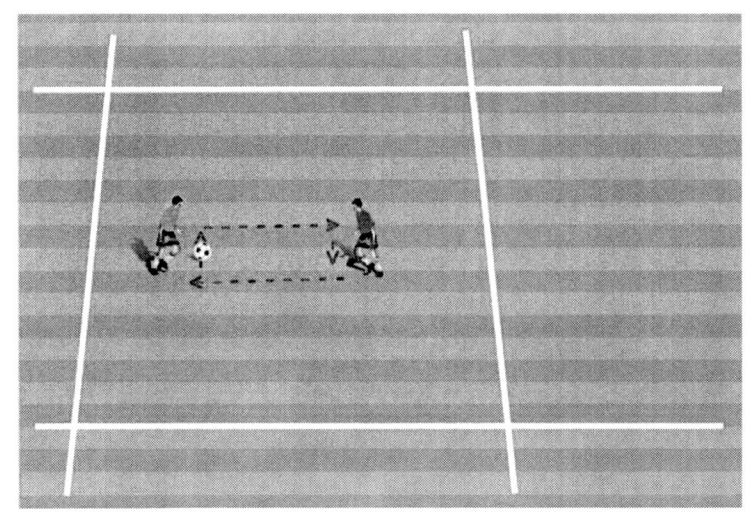

## Materials Needed

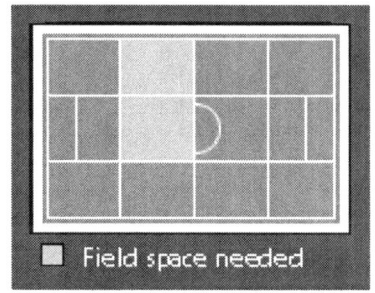

Area 20 x 20 yds
- Ball per player
- Cones
- Training Vests

## Cooperation Games 4 (Movement, Team Work)

### Description:
2 ball rebound throw– players attempt to coordinate the throw so the balls rebound off each other in mid air – how many in a row? 2 ball rebound pass with feet – players attempt to coordinate the pass so the balls rebound off each other along the ground. Start 3 yards apart and increase distance. 2 ball over under throw – one player throws the ball over and the other ball is a chest pass. 2 ball over under with feet – one player chips a ball that is played along the ground.

### Coaching Points
- Communicate with each other to coordinate release
- Start slow and increase pace and intensity
- Get a rhythm going

### Progressions:

# Count Down

## Materials Needed

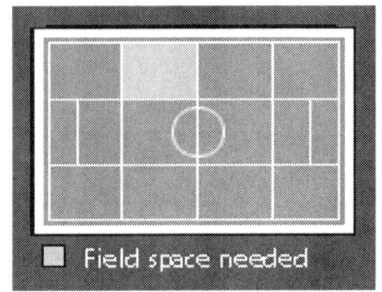

Area 30 x 20 yds
- Several balls
- Cones
- Training Vests

## Count Down (Dribbling, Passing, Possession)

### Description:
Two teams six play 5v5 in an area 30 yards long and 20 yards wide. At each end of the rectangle is an end zone stretching the width of the area and 5 yards deep – a target player stands in this area. The coach feeds balls into the area – teams compete to win possession and then send balls to their team mate (target player) in their end zone. If the target player successfully controls the ball within the area, the player passing the ball joins the target player. The 'count down' continues as teammates join the target players until all players are in the end zone.

### Coaching Points
- Attack – be creative to beat your opponent
- Attack – after passing the ball support the play
- Attack – target player must remain on the move
- Defense – protect the target
- Defense – communicate with your partner
- Defense – be patient to win possession

### Progressions:

1) Final pass must be one touch.
2) Target player must control the ball with two touches.

# Creating Space 1 v 1

**Materials Needed**

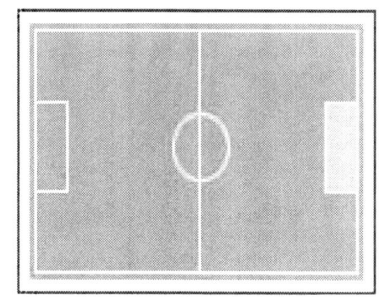

Area 20 x 20 yds
- 8 balls
- Cones
- Training Vests

## Creating Space 1 v 1 (Shooting, Attacking, Defending)

**Description:**
Place 8 balls 15-20 yards from goal. Start with 2 Defenders and Attackers on the goal line. On the command of "GO" the attackers sprint to collect any ball. The defender is partnered with one attacker and must prevent the attacker from scoring. The attacker must attempt to create space to create a scoring opportunity. Start without a goal keeper and then add one in. When all the balls have been used, change the attackers and defenders.

**Coaching Points**
- Attack - move quickly to the ball
- Attack - use escape and take on moves to beat the defender
- Attack - shoot at every opportunity
- Defend - restrict attackers space
- Defend - don't dive into a tackle
- Defend - prevent attacker facing the goal

**Progressions:**
Progess to 2v2.

# Defending 1 v 1 A

**Materials Needed**

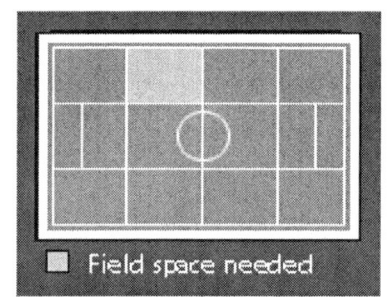

Area 10 x 10 yds
- Ball per pair
- Cones
- Training Vests

## Defending 1 v 1 A (Defending)

### Description:
In pairs 10 yds apart. One player (defender) passes the ball to the attacker. The defender follows the pass and closes the space. Coach the players to get into a good staggered position. Walk through to begin with the defenders passive (no tackles). Then allow the players to compete for the ball and attack the other end. The defender then becomes the attacker.

### Coaching Points
- Close space quickly
- Staggered stance and low center of gravity
- Stop opponent scoring – then win possession (patience)
- Get tight to attacker if their back is to goal – no turns
- Focus on the ball and not on body feints
- Stay balanced and on balls of feet

### Progressions:

Progress to pairs facing each other 3 yds apart. Defender plays ball through the attacker's legs and the attacker turns to collect the ball. The defender closes spaces and attempts to stop the attacker from turning.
Progress to two pairs facing each other 20 yds apart. One pair starts with the ball and passes to the other pair. On the third pass, the person receiving the ball attempts to attack the opposing end line. The other pair are defenders - one applies pressure and the other covers. Discuss the role of the second defender in covering the first and how two players can 'double team' an opponent in trouble.

# Defending 1 v 1 B

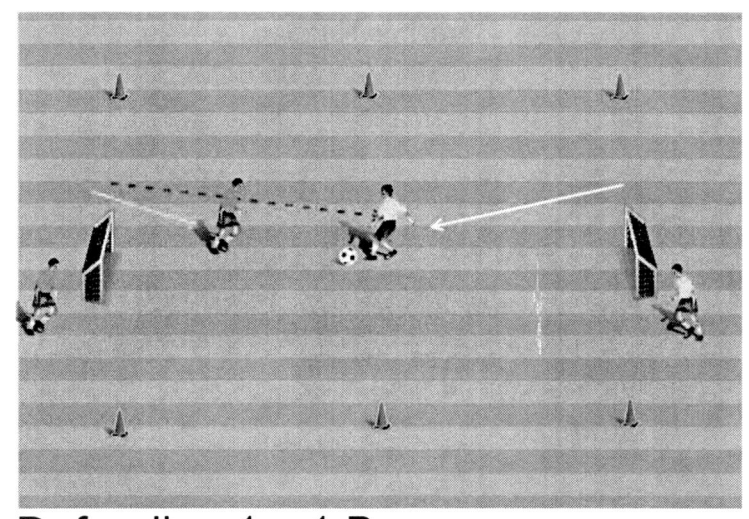

**Materials Needed**

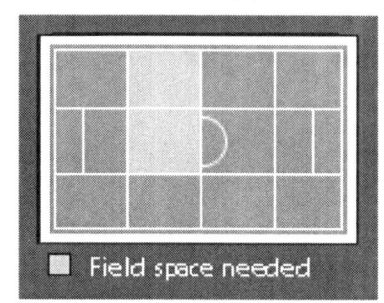

Area 20 x 10 yds
- Ball per player
- Cones
- Training Vests
- Goals

## Defending 1 v 1 B (Defending)

### Description:
Play 1v1 - One goal at each end of the area. From the defensive end of the field, the defender passes the ball firmly along the ground to the attacker. On receipt, the attacker attacks the defender and attempts to score a goal. If the defender wins the ball, he/she can also score in the attacker's goal. 4 players to an area – next defender and attacker start when ball leaves the area or a goal is scored. Gradually introduce coaching points.

### Coaching Points
- Close space quickly to keep attacker away from goal
- Staggered stance and low center of gravity
- Stop opponent scoring - win possession (patience)
- Get tight to attacker – no turns
- Focus on the ball and not on body feints
- Stay balanced and on balls of the feet

### Progressions:
1) Change starting position of defender to the side – curved run to cover the goal.
2) Attacker and defender start from either side of the goal – defender passes the ball in the area and attacker and defender chase forward – attacker must turn and score.

# Defending 1 v 1 Recover

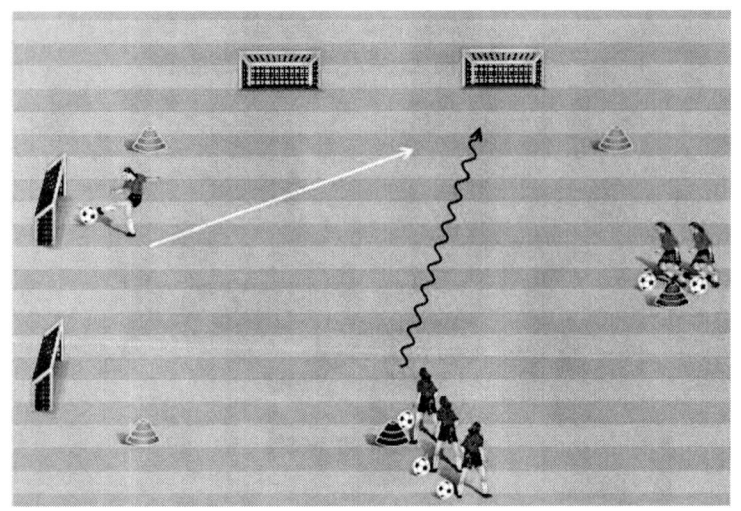

**Materials Needed**

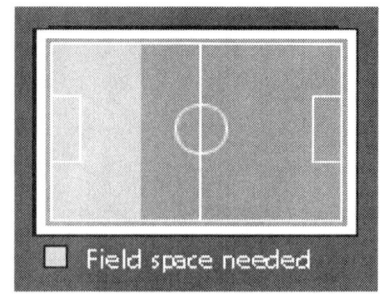

Area 30 x 30 yds
- Balls
- Cones
- Training Vests

## Defending 1 v 1 Recover (Defending, Attacking)

### Description:
Two groups of 3 players. One team starts with the ball and has an unopposed dribble and shot at one of two goals opposite the starting position. The attacker must be in the shooting zone (cones placed 10 yds from the goals to shoot. Immediately after the shot (score or miss) the attacker recovers to become a defender against the first attacker from the opposite line. The other team cannot go until the ball is shot.

### Coaching Points
- Defender must quickly recover to defend after attacking
- Attacker to go at pace at the defender - minimal time to recover

### Progressions:
1. A timed team competition to see who scores the most goals
2. Adjust the pitch dimensions and starting distances from goal to ensure attacker has to beat defender.

# Defending 3 Goals

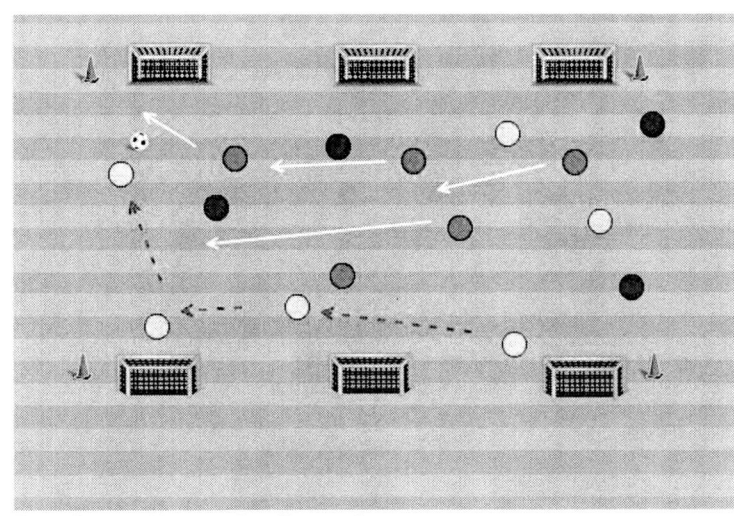

**Materials Needed**

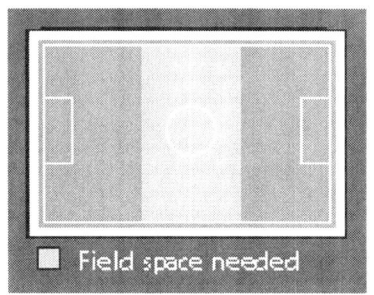

Area 60 x 20 yds
- Balls
- Cones
- Training Vests
- 6 small goals or flags

## Defending 3 Goals (Defending)

### Description:
Two teams defend and attack 3 goals each. 3v3 to 5v5. Plus 2 stage of development focus on the individual defender 1v1. For Plus 3-5 introduce the principles of pressure and cover in small teams.

### Coaching Points
- #1 priority is to protect the goals
- Position body to stop the shot
- Shift defense as attack moves across field

### Progressions:
This activity is a progression for many defensive practices.

# Dribble, Turn, Pass

**Materials Needed**

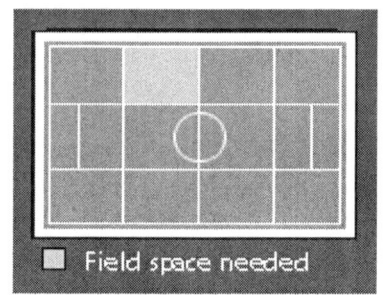

Area 20 x 20 yds
- Ball per player
- Cones
- Training Vests

## Dribble, Turn, Pass (Dribbling, Ball Mastery)

### Description:
3 cones form a triangle in the area. 3 players dribble at the same time to the next cone in the same direction. When arriving at the cone, the player performs a turn specified by the coach and dribbles back to the starting cone. Repeat.

Progress to instructing the player to pass the ball when they reach the cone to the player in front (i.e. all players pass the ball at the same time)

### Coaching Points
- Minimal touches to turn
- Accurate pass back and good 1st touch to receive the pass
- Timing so that everybody works at the same time

### Progressions:
1. Dribble the opposite way around the triangle and vary the turns.
2. Players dribble half way, make the turn, pass ball back and sprint to the next cone to receive the incoming pass.

# Dribbling Basics

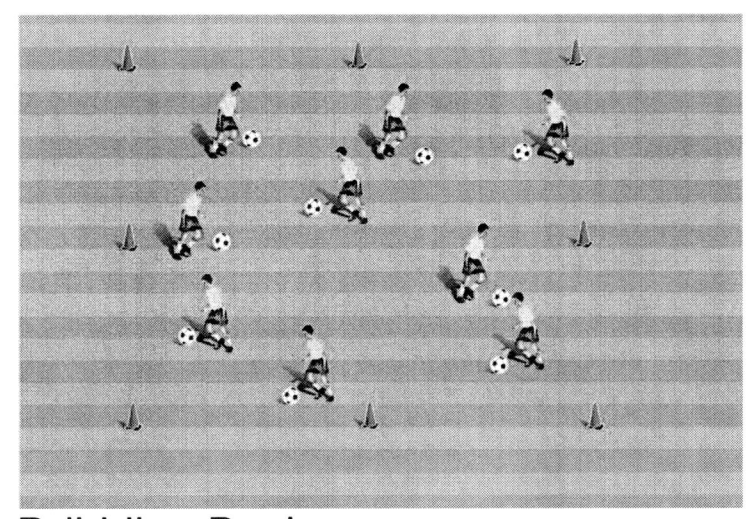

**Materials Needed**

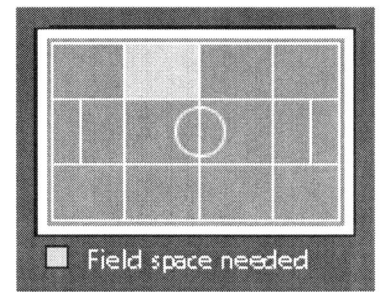

Area 20 x 20 yds
- Ball per player
- Cones

## Dribbling Basics (Dribbling, creating space)

**Description:**
Players dribble the ball randomly in the area. On command of "FREEZE", players demonstrate control by placing the foot on the ball. Balance by bending the knees and determine if there is adequate space by extending the arms in all directions. Red light – Green light can be used (Red = Stop, Green = Go and Yellow = Turn). Progress to turns, fakes, and exchanging balls.

**Coaching Points**
- "Feel the ball - see the field"
- Keep the ball moving
- Dribble with the laces

**Progressions:**
Dribbling activities form a large part of training for young players. The aim is to get touches on the ball. To this end, this activity has several progressions and the coach must decide the competency levels of the players. Importantly, the players should be encouraged to dribble in a normal running style – with the laces and toes forward. Dribbling with the inside of the foot slows down play, restricts quick changes of direction and telegraphs play to a defender.

Progression/variations
The possibilities are endless: Use activitites from the Skills Challenge Pyramid, and add escape and take on moves.

# Dribbling Tag

**Materials Needed**

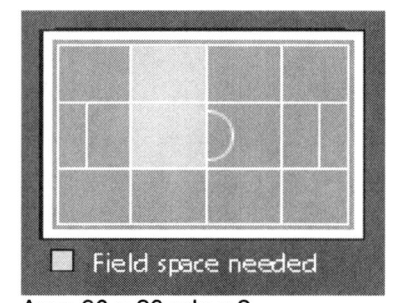

Area 30 x 20 yds x 2
- Ball per player
- Cones
- Training Vests

## Dribbling Tag (Dribbling, Creating Space)

**Description:**
Two 30 x 20 yds areas with 5 yds of space between. Two teams of 4 players create a 3v1 scenario in each area. Every player has a ball (including the defensive player). The defender attempts to tag as many players as he/she can in 30 seconds. At the end of 30 seconds, rotate the players. Add the total score for the teams. If a player dribbles outside of the area - count one point for the defender.

**Coaching Points**
- Use the laces
- Find space – head up
- Change pace to escape the defender

**Progressions:**
Award additional points if the attacking player performs a skill/move practiced during the session.
1) Increase/decrease the amount of time to encourage success and learning.
2) Adjust the area according to the number of players in each grid.

# Driven Pass/Shot

## Materials Needed

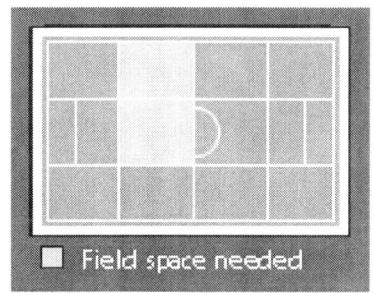

☐ Field space needed

Area: 10 x 20 yds
- Ball per person
- Cones
- Goal

## Driven Pass/Shot (Shooting, Passing)

**Description:**
In pairs, 20 yards apart, drive the ball back and forth with the instep (laces). Keep balls on the ground and strike through the middle of the ball – minimizing rotation of the ball.

Open the area to 20 yards and drive the ball to each other.

**Coaching Points**
- Strike the ball with the laces
- Approach the ball from the front
- Drive through the ball for power

**Progressions:**

Close the gap to 10 yards and then play directly out of the hands – a volley. Progress to a half volley
Add a goal and goal keeper. Starting close to the goal, the attacker plays a wall pass (one - two) with a server and shoots at goal. Play volleys and half volleys out of the hands to begin and then progress to a ball served by the coach. To avoid long lines, separate the team in two and perform in two goals or have the other group perform a different activity – such as squares.

# End Zone

**Materials Needed**

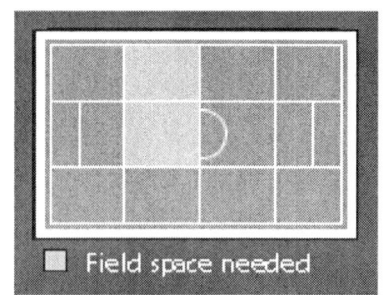

Area 40 x 20 yds
- Ball per player
- Cones
- Training Vests

## End Zone (Passing, Receiving)

**Description:**
Two teams - 5v5 - nominate one person (target player) to stand in the end zone at the opponents end of the field. Each team must attempt to pass the ball to the target person. If the target player successfully controls the ball in the end zone, the person passing the ball also becomes a target player. Try to get all players in the end zone.

**Coaching Points**
- Weight of pass needs to be firm to reach target
- Target player must offer supporting angles
- First touch needs to cushion the ball

**Progressions:**
1) The pass into the end zone must be lofted and received on the full (volley).
2) Set a minimum number of touches before ball is served into the area (reduces aimless passes and encourages teamwork).
3) Coach elects the receiving surface for the target player (i.e. foot, thigh, chest etc).

# Escape & Possession

**Materials Needed**

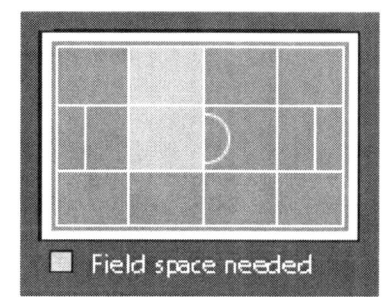

Area 20 x 20 yds
- Balls
- Cones

## Escape & Possession (Dribbling)

**Description:**
Players must dribble around keeping their ball under close control and perform an escape move when they reach a cone (drag back, outside hook, step over, 'L' etc). Transition into possession - In pairs, one attacker and one defender – the attacker must keep the ball from the defender. 1 minute, keep points.

**Coaching Points**
- Awareness of defenders and space
- Close control of the ball
- Quick change of direction and speed.

**Progressions:**
1) Focus on possession encouraging attacker to use the body to protect the ball.
2) Allow defenders to go for any ball.
3) Remove a cone and see if players can protect ball with touches and keeping it close (1 minute, keep points).

# Escape Move - Drag Back

**Materials Needed**

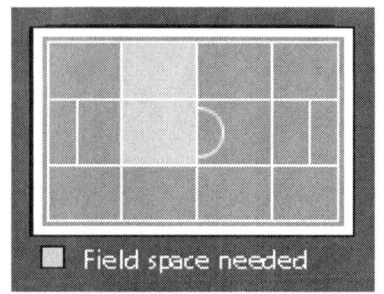

Area 30 x 20 yds
- Ball per player
- Cones

## Escape Move - Drag Back (Dribbling, Creating Space)

### Description:
One ball per player in an open grid to begin. Isolate the skill by performing on-the-spot. Dribbling forward, stop the ball with the sole of the foot and roll the ball back down the side of the body then dribble back. Progress to: 1) Performing the skill on the move, 2) 1v1 passive defending, 3) 1v1 active defending 4) Game with gates, 5) Small sided game.

### Coaching Points
- Several touches on the ball with the sole
- Sell the move to the defender
- Accelerate away after the move

### Progressions:
The freedom to experiment and practice 'escape' skills against an opponent is critical to their development. The more proficient a player becomes at dribbling and creating space as a young player, the more confident they will become in a game situation and the more likely they are to perform the skill. Repetition is very important, but ensuring the technique is correct - the player must be able to 'sell' the opponent and escape. This activity is a good warm-up with the ball. The starting point will depend on the players proficiency - the skill can be progressed from performing on-the-spot to a small sided game. To emphasize the skill in a small sided game award points/goals to a player who escapes a defender.

# Escape Move - Step Over

**Materials Needed**

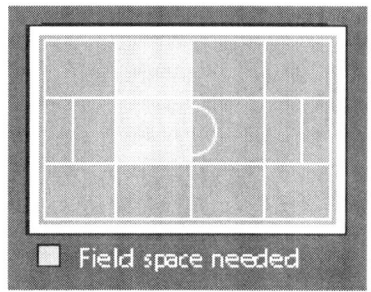

Area 30 x 20 yds
- Ball per player
- Cones

## Escape Move - Step Over (Dribbling, Creating Space)

**Description:**
One ball per player in an open grid to begin. Isolate the skill by performing on-the-spot. Dribbling forward, the attacker steps over the top of the ball with the foot furthest from the defender and quickly pivots 180 degrees (away from the defender). The attacker quickly turns and accelerates away.
Progress to: 1) Performing the skill on the move, 2) 1v1 passive defending, 3) 1v1 active defending 4) Game with gates, 5) Small sided game.

**Coaching Points**
- Start in stationary position - not a dribble
- Repeat and repeat again
- Accelerate away leaving defender behind

**Progressions:**
The freedom to experiment and practice 'escape' skills against an opponent is critical to their development. The more proficient a player becomes in dribbling and creating space as a young player, the more confident they will become in a game situation and the more likely they are to perform the skill. Repetition is very important and ensuring the technique is correct is essential (the players are able to 'sell' the opponent and escape). This activity is a good warm-up with the ball. The starting point will depend on the players' proficiency - the skill can be progressed from performing on one spot, to a small sided game. To emphasize the skill in a small sided game award points/goals to a player who escapes a defender.

**SOCCERPLUS**
THE DICICCO METHOD

soccer interactive.com

# Fetch

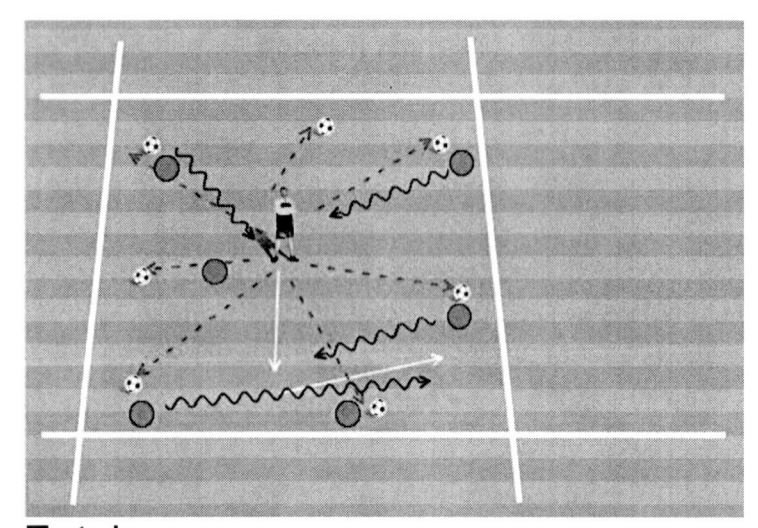

## Materials Needed

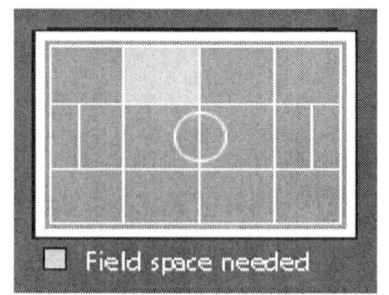

Area 20 x 20 yds
- Ball each player
- Cones

## Fetch (Dribbling, Ball Mastery)

### Description:
No more than 5 minutes - 4-8 players. Ball each. Coach kneels on the ground. Players surround the coach so they are close enough for the coach to reach their ball when the player puts their foot on top. Coach rolls the balls randomly in the area and the players sprint to collect and dribble back, stopping the ball within touching distance for the coach.

### Coaching Points
- Move quickly to the ball
- Dribble with laces
- Use different surfaces to change direction

### Progressions:
1) Coach becomes mobile and the players dribble the ball and change direction as the coach moves. The coach pauses for 2 seconds and picks up balls within touching distance.
2) On receiving the ball, the players must perform a task before dribbling back - i.e. toe taps, turn, dribble around a cone etc.
3) Select 2-3 players and they perform the coach's role - players must dribble to a different server each time.

# Flip 'em

**Materials Needed**

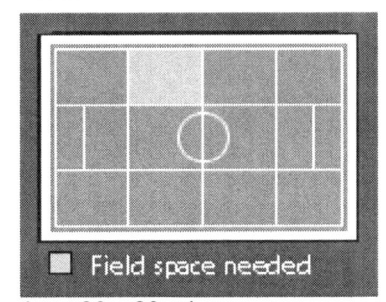

Area 20 x 20 yds
- Balls
- Cones
- Training Vests

## Flip 'em (Dribbling, Ball Mastery)

**Description:**
Players start in the area with a ball each at their feet. There are cones spread randomly around the area with some the correct way up and some upside down. Players dribble around the area performing a specified ball mastery exercise and every time they reach a cone they have to flip it over the opposite way. 1) Toe taps, 2) Sole taps, 3) Laces dribble, 4) Lateral rolls.

**Coaching Points**
- Soft light touches on the ball
- Start slowly then build up the speed
- Control the ball next to each cone

**Progressions:**
Players must make at least 10 touches of the ball between each cone and the winner is the player who turns over the most cones in one minute. After a few minutes split the group into two teams with each team having one minute to turn all the cones over a certain way – one team the correct way up and the other team upside down. Again all players have to perform ball mastery exercise between cones with a minimum of 10 touches before turning the next cone.

# Four Rings

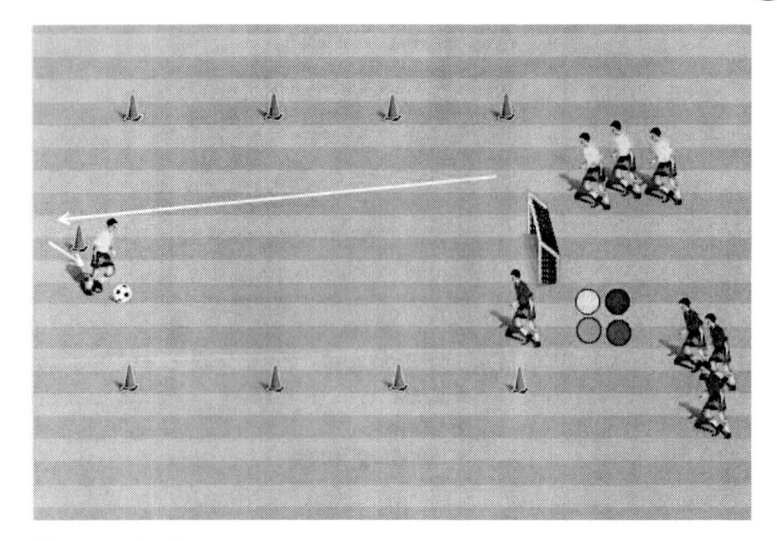

## Materials Needed

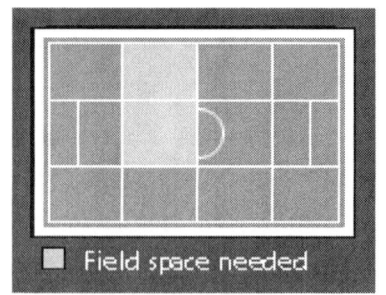

Field space needed

Area 20 x 10 yds
- Ball per player
- Cones
- Training Vests
- Speed rings
- Small goal

## Four Rings (Movement, Defending, Attacking)

### Description:
In an area 20 x 10 yds the coach places a goal at one end. At the same end as the goal and behind the end line four rings are placed 1 foot apart to form a square. On the command of "GO", one attacking player sprints to the far end to collect a ball and the defender performs an activity in the speed rings.

### Coaching Points
- Attack - change pace of attack
- Attack - front foot of defender
- Attack - use body feints and ball movements to beat defender
- Defense - close down the space between attacker and goal
- Defense – force attacker to weaker foot
- Defense – be patient to win possession

### Progressions:
Speed ring activities: 1) Two footed, leap from ring 1 to 2, 2 to 3 and 3 to 4. 2) One foot hop (same leg). 3) Knee high. 4) Butt kicks. 5) Scissor kicks. 6) Two leg hops. 7) Add others. Keep in mind that all movements should be quick, there should be minimal contact with the ground, the player should be balanced and on the balls of their feet.

### Variances:
1) 2 attackers vs 1 defender. 2) 2v2 with recovering defender (start the recovering defender 15 yards from the end line) – 20 x 20 yds. 3) add two goals to switch point of attack.

# Heading 1 v 1

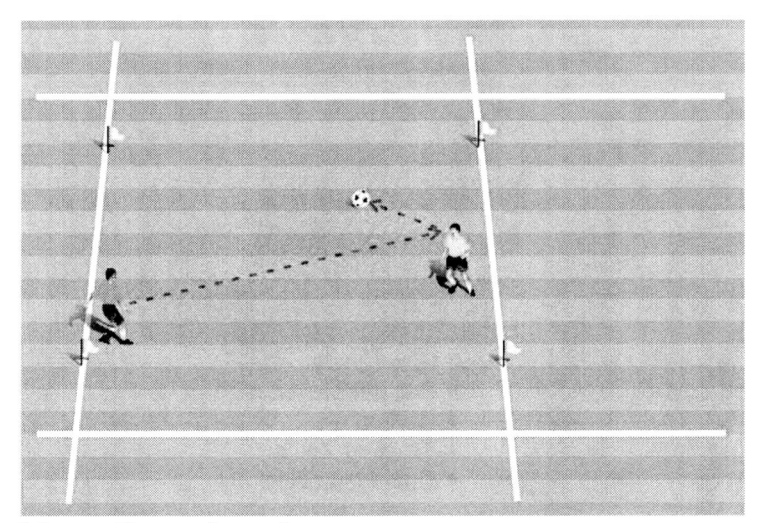

## Materials Needed

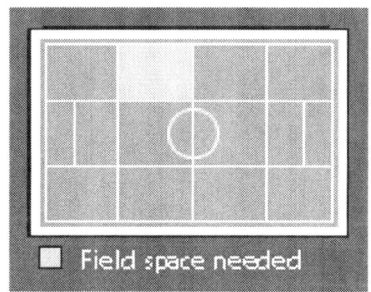

Area 10 x 10 yds
- Ball per player
- Cones
- Training Vests
- Coaching sticks

## Heading 1 v 1 (Heading)

### Description:
In pairs, players stand 10 yards apart in an 8 yds wide goal, marked with coaching sticks. Player A throws a two handed underarm throw to Player B at head height. Player B attempts to head the ball at the goal defended by Player A. A goal counts as one point. Alternate the serve. First to 3 or 5 points wins the game.

### Coaching Points
- Reiterate basic technique
- Set up header using a cushion header
- Attacking header should be headed down and in the corners

### Progressions:
Progress to alternating the service height - low for a diving header and high to jump and power header downwards. Next step is to move to Heading 1v1v1v1.

# Heading 1 v 1 v 1 v 1

## Heading 1 v 1 v 1 v 1 (Heading)

**Materials Needed**

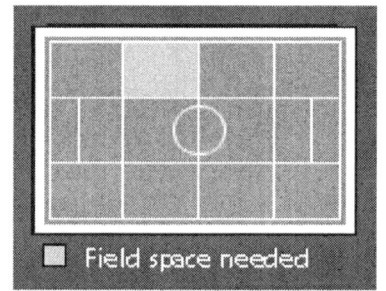

Area 10 x 10 yds
- Ball per player
- Cones
- Training Vests
- Coaching sticks

### Description:
Four players play against each other to score 5 headed goals. Place 4 coaching sticks in the corner to form a 10 x 10 yds square with 4 goals. One of the four players start with the ball (A). Player A serves to the person directly opposite (B). Player B can head for any of the 3 goals defended by players A, C and D. The play is dead if a goal is scored, the ball is saved or the ball hits the post. The next server is the player to the right of the first server (rotate around). First player to score 3 goals wins.

### Coaching Points
- Reiterate basic technique
- Set up header is a cushion header
- Attacking header should be headed down and in the corners

### Progressions:
Players can play as pairs - aiming for only two goals.

# Heading Basics

## Materials Needed

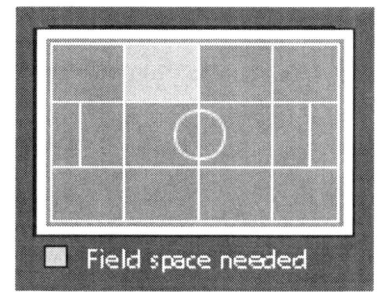

Field space needed

Area 10 x 10 yds
- 1 Ball between 2

## Heading Basics (Heading)

**Description:**
In pairs, one player performs the heading (A) and the other serves the ball (B). 1) Player A lies on his/her stomach and rests on the elbows. Kneeling and 2 yds apart from Player A, Player B feeds the ball with two hands. Using the back and abdominal muscles, Player A heads the ball back to B. 2) A gets into a 'crab' position and this time uses the neck muscles to generate power to head the ball back.

**Coaching Points**
- Contact with the forehead
- Keep eyes open and watch the ball
- Use knees, back and neck to generate power

**Progressions:**

1) 'A' kneels in front of 'B' and as the ball is served, 'A' attacks the ball with the head, breaking the fall with the hands. 2) Standing heading. 3) Jumping and heading downwards. 4) Jumping and heading for distance. 5) Jumping over a passive defender. 6) Challenging a defender for the ball. Progress to Heading 1v1, Heading 1v1v1v1.

# Hot Shot 1

**Materials Needed**

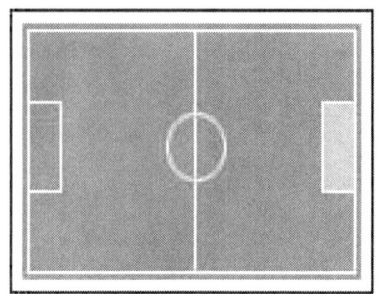

Area 20 x 20 yds
- Ball per player
- Flat markers (or cones)
- Training Vests
- Goal

## Hot Shot 1 (Shooting)

**Description:**
Split into two teams. One team is shooting against the clock and the other is collecting the balls. Team A shoots first. The starting position for all players is next to the left post. On the call of "GO", the first player sprints to a cone on the 18 yard line, then back to a small 2 x 2 yds shooting box where the ball is laid off for the shot. Player 1 shoots at goal first time and player 2 follows the path of player 1 – player 3 passes to 2 etc.

**Coaching Points**
- Strike with laces
- Place ball low in the corners
- Don't stand admiring pass or shot

**Progressions:**

Change the shooting positions:
1) Ball from the side.
2) Ball from behind.
3) Bouncing ball.
4) Full volley.
5) Header etc.

# Hot Shot 2

## Materials Needed

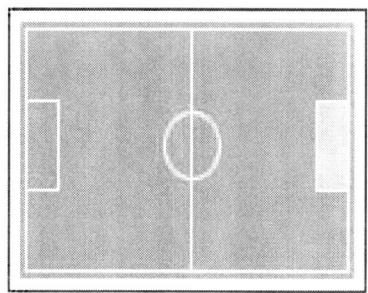

Area 30 x 10 yds
- Balls - 2 for every player
- Cones
- Training Vests
- Goals

## Hot Shot 2 (Shooting)

**Description:**
The team is separated into two – team A lines up 5 yards outside the penalty area to the left and right 25 yds from goal. A server kneels facing away from goal with all the balls. The other team provides two players for each post and the remaining players collect the balls missing the goal. A cone is placed 5 yards along the goal line outside of each post and the two post players stand next to the cone. On the command of "GO" the server feeds a ball to the left for the first attacker to run onto – they must strike the ball before a line 5 yds inside the penalty box. Every 2-3 sec the server feeds another ball – alternating between sides. The goalkeeper has to react very quickly to save the rapid fire shots. A post player on each side assists the GK – each time a goal is scored, a new post player enters (they must start on the cone). After a minute the teams change over.

**Coaching Points**
- Get onto the ball quickly
- Adjust feet to shoot in a balanced position
- Lift head prior to the shot to pick a spot to aim for

**Progressions:**

Create different shooting positions and different serves.

# Individual Ball Warm Up 1

**Materials Needed**

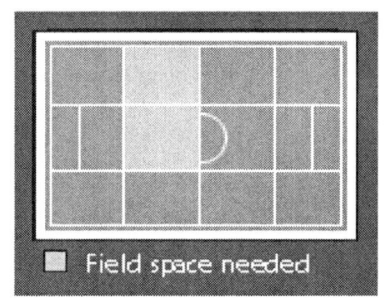

Area 20 x 20 yds
- Ball per player
- Cones

## Individual Ball Warm Up 1 (Dribbling)

**Description:**
Players have a ball each. Set the players tasks - don't let the ball stop moving! Don't let the ball go outside the area. Progress to having the players react to the coach's commands. Toe taps, boxes, stop and go, change balls, etc.

**Coaching Points**
- Keep the ball moving at all times
- Soft touches and keep head up
- Move into the open space

**Progressions:**
Each time you play add a different movement, turn and mastery skill. For example: Movement sequence: 1) **Dribble with laces** - slow down and push the ball lightly with the laces (left, right and both) 2) **Boxes** – push the ball from side-to-side, right to the left foot and back again, 3) **Toe taps** – hopping from one foot to the other touching the top of the ball with the opposite foot each time. Ball stays does not move. 4) **Sole drag back** – hopping between feet, move backwards dragging the ball back alternating between the sole of the shoes, 5) **Sole push** – push the ball forward with the sole of the shoes, 6) **Laterals** – move to the left by dragging the right foot over the top of the ball (rolling the foot over the top of the ball). Move right with the left foot. Turns: It is anticipated players at the end of this stage of development will be able to perform the following turns 1) **Inside of the foot**, 2) **Outside of the foot**, 3) **Drag back**, 4) **Step over**, 5) **Back heel**. Add others! This is also an excellent opportunity to bring in fundamental movements such as running, skipping, galloping, balancing, dodging etc. As this is your warm up ensure you inject the enthusiasm and excitement with the players.

**SOCCERPLUS**
**THE DICICCO METHOD**

**soccer interactive.com**

# Individual Ball Warm Up 2

**Materials Needed**

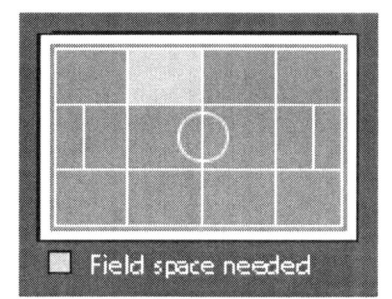

Field space needed

Area 20 x 20 yds
- Ball per player
- Cones

## Individual Ball Warm Up 2 (Dribbling)

**Description:**
Each player has a ball and dribbles around the inside of the square. The coach challenges the players to complete a variety of tasks within 30 seconds. For example 1) Travel to all 4 sides of the box in any order, 2) How many touches on the ball can you get with your right foot or left foot?, 3) How many people can you tag?, 4) How many soccer balls dribbled by other players can you tag?

**Coaching Points**
- Keep the ball moving at all times
- Keep your head up
- Move into the open space

**Progressions:**
As this is the warm up the coach must inject enthusiasm and energy into the players at this stage of the practice. Coaches can be creative with these small 30 second games.
Introduce skills from the appropriate Skills Challenge Pyramid

# Individual Receiving

**Materials Needed**

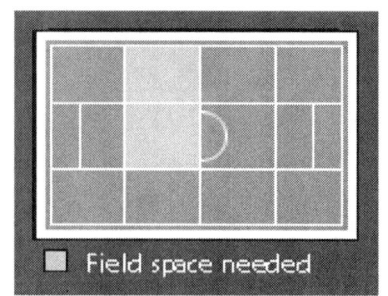

Area 20 x 20 yds
- Ball per player
- Cones

## Individual Receiving (Receiving)

### Description:
Players have a ball each and dribble around the area. The players must react to the coach's command. When the coach calls "FOOT" - players throw ball into the air to receive with their laces, "THIGH" - players receive with the thigh, "CHEST" receive with the chest, "HEAD" cushion header into players path.

### Coaching Points
- Keep eyes on the ball
- Present surface to the ball
- Cushion ball

### Progressions:
The coach can be creative with the commands.

# Looters

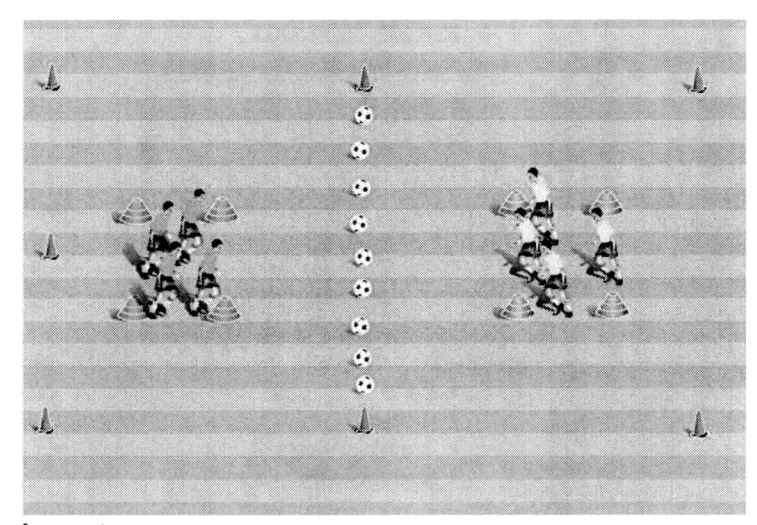

**Materials Needed**

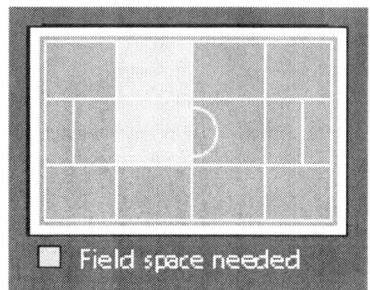

Area 40 x 20 yds
- Ball per player
- Cones
- Training Vests

## Looters (Dribbling, attacking, and defending)

### Description:
Two or more teams. To play the activity with two teams, two 5 x 5 yds square are marked 5 yards from each end line. Players from both teams stand inside their team square and all the balls are lined up on center line of the area. On the command of "GO" players leave their square and attempt to dribble a ball back to their square. An opponent cannot steal the ball. Play until all balls are in either of the two squares.

### Coaching Points
- Get to the ball quickly
- Move into space
- Dribble with laces for speed

### Progressions:

1) All players can enter either square to steal (Loot) the balls (90 second time limit), 2) Split each team into attackers and defenders – each cannot enter the other half of the field and must pass to get the ball back to the square, 3) Create equal numbers of small 'home' squares around the area – once the ball enters this area, the ball cannot be removed.

# Match 2 v 2

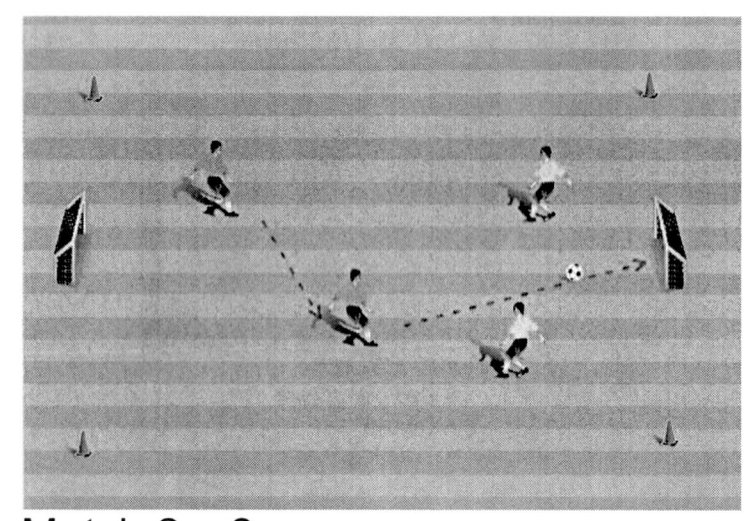

**Materials Needed**

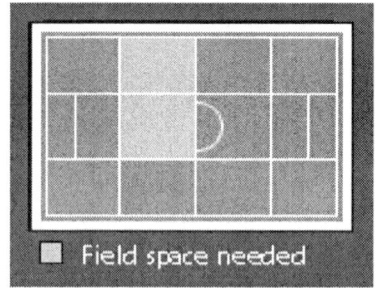

Area 20 x 10 yds
- Balls
- Cones
- Training Vests
- Small Goals

## Match 2 v 2 (Game)

**Description:**
A small sided game 2v2 or 3v3 is a good way to finish a practice session.

Other than emphasizing the main theme of the session, let the players play with little or no coaching - 10-15 minutes at the end of the session.

**Coaching Points**
- Little or no coaching
- Encourage players to try skills practiced during the session

**Progressions:**
Dribbling is the a main emphasis for developing players at Plus 1-3, so don't discourage dribbling by over emphasizing passing. When the ball leaves the field take the nearest ball - dribble in. No goal keepers with 2v2 - progress to 3v3 (one player is nominated as a 'rush goalie' - plays in and out of goal). Change players regularly.

# Mirrors 1 v 1

**Materials Needed**

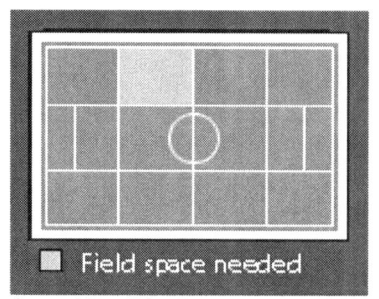

Area 15 x 15 yds
- Ball between 2
- Cones

## Mirrors 1 v 1 (Dribbling)

**Description:**
One player with a ball must dribble to either cone before the player without the ball can get to the same cone. The player getting to the cone first wins a point. Players then return to the middle to repeat. Switch roles every time. First to 10 points wins.

**Coaching Points**
- Demonstrate the 'lunge' move to unbalance the defender
- Try to shift the weight of the defender
- Accelerate to the cone

**Progressions:**
Introduce a third cone placed 10 yards behind the defender (without the ball). The attacker can elect to attempt 2 pts by dribbling to the third cone before the defender can turn and get there first before the attacker.

# Numbers Game

## Materials Needed

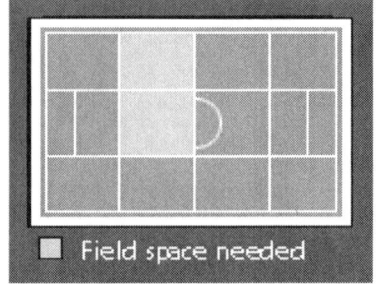

Field space needed

Area 30 x 20 yds
- Ball per player
- Cones
- Training Vests
- Goals x 2
- Hurdles, ladders, rings etc

## Numbers Game (Dribbling, attacking, shooting, defending)

### Description:
A coach's favorite – players play individually and as a small group to score a goal!

### Coaching Points
- Get to the ball quickly
- Look for the goal not protected
- Move quickly to the goal

### Progressions:
Two, three of four teams situated on each side of the field. One or two goals at end - coach rolls a ball out and calls a number. The player in each team corresponding to the number/s runs out and attempts to score a goal.

1) Players run around a cone before coming onto the field, 2) Run through the ladder, 3) Under and over the hurdle etc, 4) Player must play the ball to their team on the sideline and receive it back before scoring, 5) Two or more numbers are called and each player must touch the ball before scoring.

# Numbers Hot Shot

**Materials Needed**

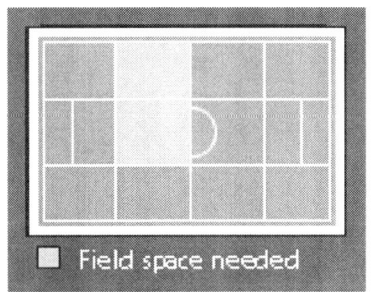

Area 30 x 20 yds
- Ball per player
- Cones
- Training Vests
- Goal

## Numbers Hot Shot (Shooting, Attacking, Defending)

### Description:
Players separated into 4 teams and each team stands between two cones, equal distance from goal on each corner of the area. At one end this is a goal and at the other end are 4 cones with 4 balls balanced on them. When a number is called, the player runs to compete for the ball. A goal = 1pt, dislodge their teams ball off the cone = 2pts, knock off another team's ball = 2pts to other team.

### Coaching Points
- Quick sprint to the ball
- Use a turn to change direction
- Dribble and shoot with laces

### Progressions:
1) Multiple numbers called at once.
2) Add a goal keeper.

# Numbers Turn

## Materials Needed

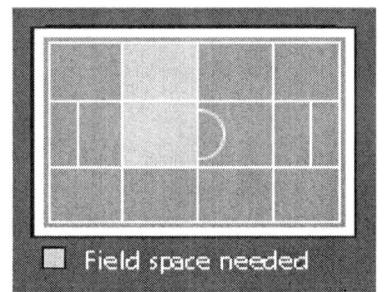

**Field space needed**

Area 30 x 20 yds
- Ball per player
- Cones
- Training Vests
- Goal

## Numbers Turn (Shooting, Attacking)

### Description:
Players are separated into 2, 3 or 4 teams and each team stands between two cones. A square, 5 x 5 yds is created between the players and the goal. Place a cone for each team 10 yards behind the teams. When a number is called the players run out to the center square, collect one of the balls and dribble around the cone behind their team. Once around the cone, the players go for goal and attempt to be the first team to score. 1pt for each goal - first team to 5 points wins the game.

### Coaching Points
- Quick sprint to the ball
- Use a turn to change direction
- Dribble and shoot with laces

### Progressions:
1) Multiple numbers called at once.
2) One ball – players compete to score.

# One Goal 1 v 1

**Materials Needed**

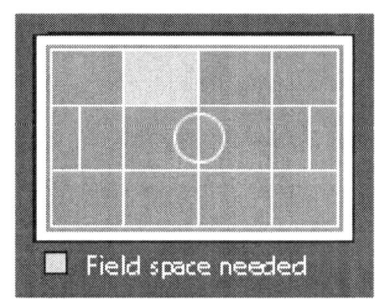

Field space needed

Area 10 x 10 yds
- Ball per player
- Cones

## One Goal 1 v 1 (Attacking, Defending)

### Description:
Players are in pairs with a ball. Within a 10 x 10 square players place a goal (cone with ball on top) in the center. Players play for one minute. If a goal is scored, player retains possession, if ball goes out of the square the ball goes to the opponent. Between each game (or every other game), bring player together and make coaching points.

### Coaching Points
- Attack - change pace of attack
- Attack - attack the front foot of the defender
- Attack - use body feints and ball movements to beat defender
- Defense – force play to weaker foot
- Defense – keep attacker from goal
- Defense – be patient to win possession

### Progressions:
Each game is played against a different opponent – score based on coaching focus: i.e. – Defending 1 pt win and extra 2pts for no goals conceded.

# Pairs Passing & Moving

**Materials Needed**

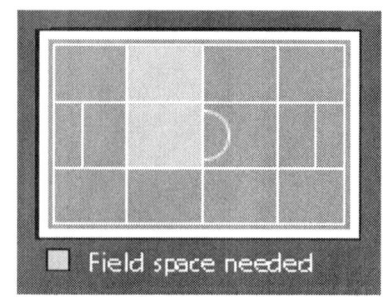

Area 30 x 30 yds
- Balls
- Cones

## Pairs Passing & Moving (Passing, Receiving)

### Description:
Players are in pairs. Gates are created with cones and situated randomly in the area. Pairs must pass through a gate then move onto another unoccupied gate. Emphasize firm accurate passing and moving quickly between gates. Start with no time limit, then challenge players to get as many gates as possible in 30 seconds. Change partners & repeat.

### Coaching Points
- Proper passing technique
- Pass then move - don't watch
- Communicate with your partner

### Progressions:
1) Increase/decrease time. 2) Create a competition amongst pairs. 3) Players must perform a move before passing through the gate.

# Passing Through The Arch

**Materials Needed**

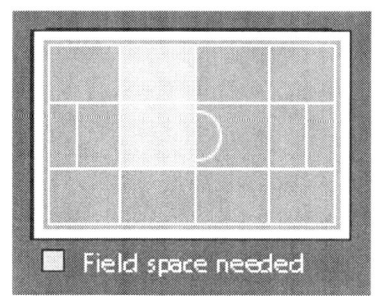

Area 10 x 10 yds
- Ball per player
- Cones

## Passing Through The Arch (Passing, Receiving)

**Description:**
Start with pairs – 5 yards apart - each person standing between cones 2 yards apart. Pass back and forth taking one controlling touch and a touch to pass.
Set a goal (training arches or cones) in the center of the area 2-3 yards apart. Players win a point for each successful pass – 30 seconds and then pairs change.

**Coaching Points**
- Lock (firm) ankle
- Inside of foot
- Supporting foot next to ball
- Strike through the center of the ball
- On your toes
- Arms out for balance

**Progressions:**

Rapid fire – one touch in pairs 3 yards apart .

# Passing Through The Gate

**Materials Needed**

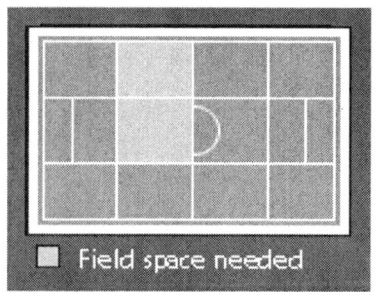

Area 10 x 10 yds
- Ball per player
- Cones

## Passing Through The Gate (Passing, Receiving)

### Description:
Ideal as a warm-up and for players getting touches on the ball. Start with pairs – 5 yards apart - each person standing between cones 2 yards apart. Pass back and forth taking one controlling touch and a touch to pass. Enforce proper technique (plant foot next to ball, pass with inside of foot, follow through, etc.) Move to the main activity:
3 players – 'A' passes through 'B's' legs to 'C'. 'A' then follows pass and presents the bridge to 'C'. 'C' then passes through 'A's' legs to 'B' etc.

### Coaching Points
- Lock (firm) ankle
- Inside of foot
- Supporting foot next to ball
- Strike through the center of the ball
- On your toes
- Arms out for balance

### Progressions:
This activity or parts of this activity can be incorporated into most sessions – ideal as a warm-up and for players getting touches on the ball. Start with pairs, 5 yds apart, with each person standing between cones 2 yds apart. Pass back and forth taking one controlling touch and a touch to pass.

Progression/variations
1) Two cones 10 yards apart – In pairs, A passes to B who turns - dribbles around the cone and passes to A who turns - dribbles around the cone, etc, 2) A goal (training arches or cones) in the center of the area 2-3 yards apart – point for each successful pass – 30 seconds and then pairs change (all players on one side of the area move down, 3) Rapid fire – one touch in pairs 3 yards apart.

# Patterns

**Materials Needed**

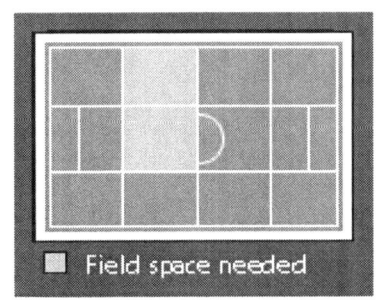

Area 20 x 20 yds
- Ball per player
- Cones

## Patterns (Dribbling)

**Description:**
Players dribble around the area and react to the pattern of play the coach calls out.
Start with basic commands such as dribbling with the laces, turn etc. Then increase complexity by adding patterns such as: Inside/inside/inside/miss, Inside/inside/inside and drag back. Inside/outside/inside/outside. Outside/inside/outside/inside. Inside/Outside sole. Sole/sole/step over.

**Coaching Points**
- Keep ball close and under control
- Keep ball moving at all times
- Keep head up and move the ball into the open space.

**Progressions:**
Patterns are designed to challenge the players. Instruct the players shout the pattern out loud as they perform. Once proficient players can perform this activity as a good pre-game warm-up.

# Possession 1 v 1

**Materials Needed**

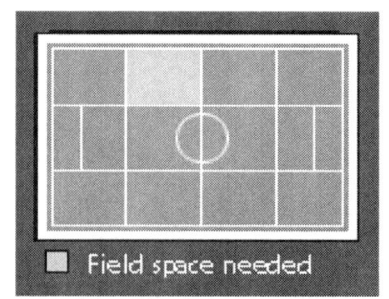

Area 20 x 20 yds
- 1 Ball per pair
- 4 Cones

## Possession 1 v 1 (Possession)

**Description:**
In pairs - one attacker and one defender. On the command of "GO", the attacker attempts to maintain possession for 20 seconds - preventing the defender from stealing the ball.

**Coaching Points**
- Use body as a barrier to the ball
- Control and move the ball away from pressure
- Use body to hold off and push opponent away from the ball

**Progressions:**
The defender attempts to touch the ball as many times as he/she can in 30 seconds.

# Shapes and Colors

**Materials Needed**

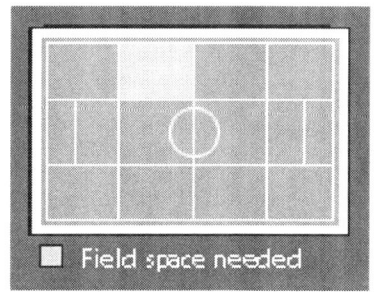

Area 20 x 20 yds
- Flat Markers
- Colored Cones

## Shapes and Colors (Movement)

**Description:**
Players perform different balances and moves in response to the coach's instructions. In the area, place colored markers (or colored objects) on the ground. Instruct the players to follow the coach's commands. For example, "GO A YELLOW MARKER" or "SQUARE". Once the player gets to that object, ask them to perform an exercise – for example - balance alternately on one, two, three, four, and then five body parts. Have them hold each balance for three to five seconds (The players should strive for control when balanced).

**Coaching Points**
- Ask players who perform a skill well to demonstrate
- Reward creativity – create a points system

**Progressions:**

Other instructions include: 1) Skip, run, side step, gallop, hop, jump etc to the blue. 2) Multiple colors – red, green blue. 3) Include a ball – bounce the ball on your head, foot thigh etc without bouncing 4) Balance ball on your foot for 5 seconds.

# Short Passing Basics

**Materials Needed**

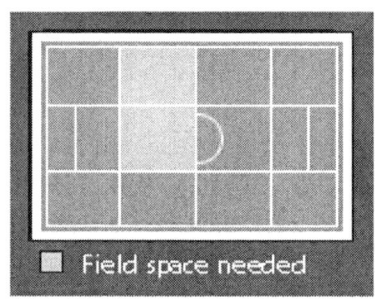

Area 10 x 10 yds
- Ball per player
- Cones

## Short Passing Basics (Passing, receiving)

### Description:
Players passing back and forth (2 or more touches) - Progress to moving side to side along the line.

### Coaching Points
- Lock (firm) ankle
- Inside of foot
- Supporting foot next to ball
- Strike through the center of the ball
- On your toes
- Arms out for balance

### Progressions:
This activity, or parts of this activity can be incorporated into most sessions – ideal as a warm-up and for players getting touches on the ball. Start with pairs – 5 yards apart - each person standing between cones (2 yards apart). Pass back and forth taking one controlling touch and a touch to pass.

# Short Passing for Points

**Materials Needed**

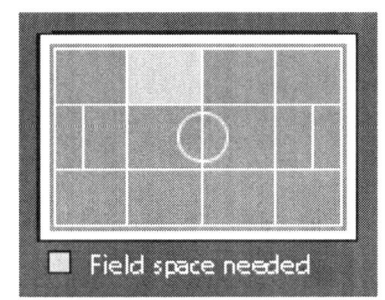

Area 20 x 20 yds
- Balls
- Cones
- Training Vests

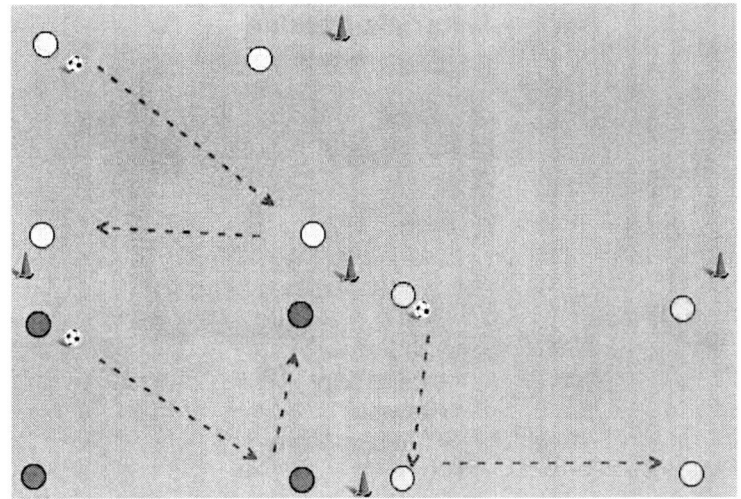

## Short Passing for Points (Passing, Receiving)

**Description:**
If you have 12 players split them into 3 teams of 4 players. Each team has their own 10 x 10 yds area. One soccer ball per team. The team must pass their ball around their area. Each team has 5 points, every time the balls goes out of bounds or a player stops moving they lose a point.

**Coaching Points**
- Use inside of foot to play short pass
- Ensure non-kicking foot is next to the ball
- Follow through towards target
- Soft receiving touch

**Progressions:**
Teams can move between squares.

# Soccer Rugby

**Materials Needed**

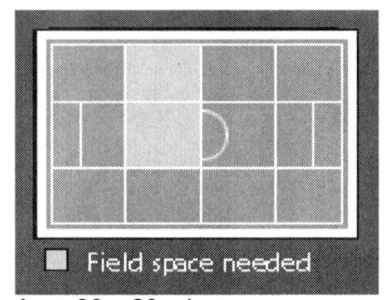

Area 30 x 20 yds
- Balls 6-10
- Cones
- Training Vests

## Soccer Rugby (Game)

**Description:**
To encourage players to dribble the ball forward and beat an opponent, introduce the 'backward pass' rule of Rugby. Play 3v3. On receiving the ball a player should attempt to dribble forward - a pass can be made, but it must be made behind the player with the ball. This encourages players to be positive on the ball and attacking while in possession. Set a cone 5 yards from each goal - once the players cross this line they can pass/shoot forward.

**Coaching Points**
- Be positive on the ball
- Attacking the open space
- Keep the ball close and under control

**Progressions:**
Allow a player to shoot before the cone if an escape or take on move is made.

# Squares

**Materials Needed**

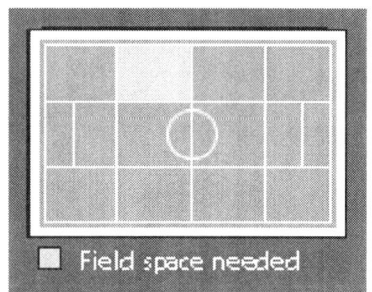

Area 15 x 15 yds
- Ball per player
- Cones

## Squares (Passing, Receiving)

**Description:**
All players stand inside a square marked with cones. One ball only required per game. Trying to keep the ball on the ground and using the inside or outside of the foot only, the players attempt to eliminate each other until one player remains. The ball is passed around one touch as the coach introduces rules: 1) One touch or you are out. 2) If you kick the ball out of the square (last touch) – out! 3) If you could have stopped the ball from leaving the square – out! 4) If you are 'nutmegged' through the legs – out! 5) If you play the ball in the air and it is caught – out! 6) If you attempt to catch the ball but drop it – out!

**Coaching Points**
- Ball on the ground
- Quick play
- No arguments – one adjudicator

**Progressions:**
Eliminated players can form another square – when eliminated from one square join the others – play for 5 minutes (person who changes squares the least wins the game).

# Striker Breakaway

**Materials Needed**

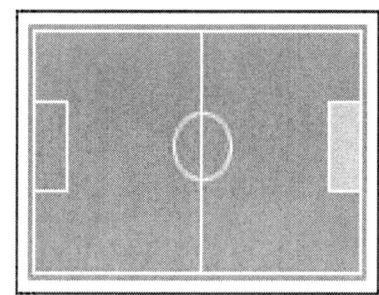

Area 10 x 30 yds
- 10-12 balls
- Cones
- Training Vest

## Striker Breakaway (Dribbling and shooting)

### Description:
Three pairs compete. Two teams start from either end of the area and the other pair are the goal keepers. The first person from each pair dribbles the ball towards the opposite goal (simultaneously). A time limit of 5 seconds to score. Once the ball is dead (scored a goal, saved by the goal keeper etc), the attacker moves out of the way and joins the opposite line. The next player then goes. Give each team 5 attacks each player and then change the goalkeepers.

### Coaching Points
- Attack at pace - get the ball out of the feet
- Lift your head as you decide what type of shot to take
- Be ready for a rebound and a second opportunity to score

### Progressions:
Add a defender

# Take On - Inside Outside

## Materials Needed

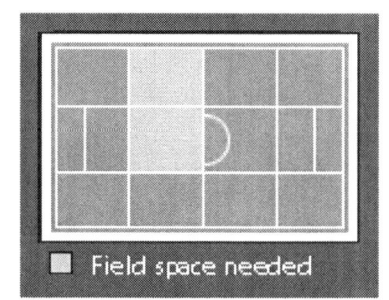

Area 30 x 20 yds
- Ball per player
- Cones

## Take On - Inside Outside (Dribbling, Creating Space)

### Description:
One ball per player in an open grid to begin. Isolate the skill by performing on-the-spot. The attacker dribbles the ball towards the defender. As the defender approaches, the attacker starts to dribble at an angle to one side of the defender using the inside of the foot. As the defender commits to the challenge, the attacker uses the outside of the same foot and pushes the ball to the other side of the defender. The attacker can then accelerate away.

### Coaching Points
- Determine a speed of approach for each individual
- Realistic movement to unbalance the defender
- Accelerate away leaving defender behind

### Progressions:
Progress to 1) Performing the skill on the move, 2) 1v1 passive defending, 3) 1v1 active defending 4) Game with gates. 5) Small sided game. The freedom to experiment and practice 'take on' skills against an opponent is critical to their development. The more proficient a player becomes in dribbling and creating space as a young player, the more confident they will become in a game situation and the more likely they are to perform the skill. Repetition is very important, but ensuring the technique is correct is essential (the players are able to 'sell' the opponent and escape). This activity is a good warm-up with the ball.

# Treasure Chest

## Materials Needed

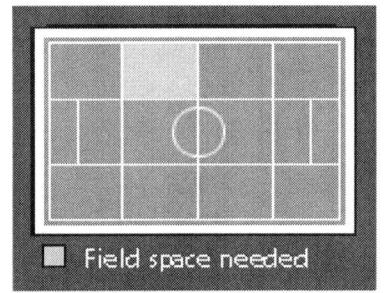

Field space needed

Area 20 x 20 yds
- Balls
- Cones
- Training Vests

## Treasure Chest (Dribbling, Attacking, Defending)

### Description:
Split group into two even teams. Players stand in teams opposite the coach 20 yds away with a pile of balls. Two small goals (Treasure Chest) are placed 10 yds between the players and the coach facing towards the outside of the square. Goals are sufficiently spaced to create a lane for players to run between. On the coach's command, players sprint to a cone placed near the coach. Players round the cone and the coach drops one ball (Treasure). Players compete to score in either goal.

### Coaching Points
- Beat the defender using various moves
- Take a chance on goal
- Be creative

### Progressions:
1) Coach can drop two balls into play; first one to score gets a point.
2) Adjust the distance players have to sprint.
3) Create boundaries around the perimeter to force close control.

# Tree House

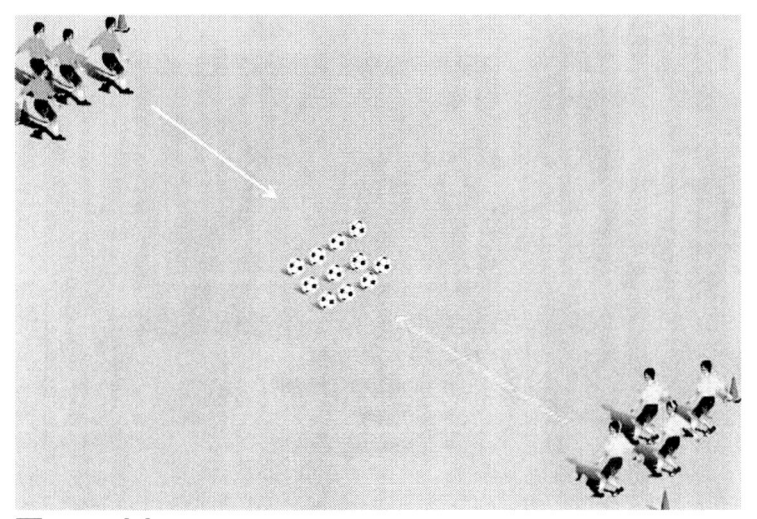

**Materials Needed**

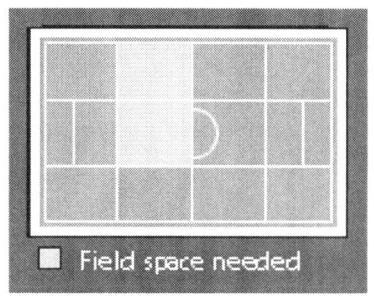

Area 20 x 20 yds
- Balls
- Cones

## Tree House (Dribbling)

**Description:**
At either end of the area you have a tree house. At one end you have the 'Greedy Gorillas' and at the other end you have the 'Cheeky Chimps'. In the middle are all the soccer coconuts. On the call of "GO" the Chimps and Gorillas run to the middle and collect a coconut and return back to their tree house before going to collect another one.

**Coaching Points**
- Keep ball moving
- Keep ball close
- Keep head up

**Progressions:**
Have the Chimps and Gorillas attack each others tree house. After one minute see who has the most coconuts.

# Winner Stays On

**Materials Needed**

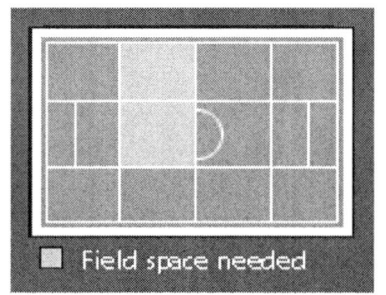

Area 30 x 20 yds
- Ball per player
- Cones
- Training Vests

## Winner Stays On (Attacking, Shooting, Defending)

**Description:**
Three teams. Two teams play 3v3 and one team wait on the sideline. Teams attempt to score in two or all four goals. The team scoring first stay on the field and the losing team moves to the sideline – the team on the sideline come on. The new ball is served back in by the coach.

**Coaching Points**
- Get to the ball quickly
- Look for the goal not protected
- Move quickly to the goal

**Progressions:**
Stipulate the number of passes before shooting.

# World Cup

**Materials Needed**

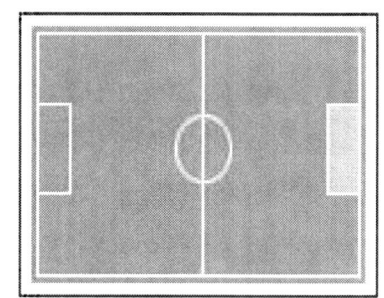

Area 20 x 20 yds
- Ball per player
- Cones
- Training Vests
- Goal

## World Cup (Shooting, Attacking)

### Description:
World Cup singles is each player for himself/herself! World Cup Doubles is played in pairs. Game starts with 1 goalkeeper and all the other players in the area. Create a nogo area 5 yds from goal to protect the goalkeeper (flat markers are perfect). Depending on the numbers, the objective is to play three rounds – eliminating 1-2 or 3 individuals/teams per round. If a player/team scores they are through to the next round. Last touch counts to encourage predatory instincts around goal. Players/Teams eliminated have a drink and collect the balls. The final is between the two individuals/teams and is first to two goals.

### Coaching Points
- Take every opportunity to score
- Be ready for rebounds
- Strike low with laces

### Progressions:
1) Add a defender to help the goal keeper.
2) Create a 'super' goal based on what has been taught in the session - i.e. bent shot, or headed goal. If a super goal is scored the game is over.

# SOCCER COACHING ACTIVITIES, SESSION PLANS AND ASSESSMENT
## Plus 2 - Early to Mid Stage Sessions

| Sessions | Page |
|---|---|
| 1. Dribbling #1 (Plus 1-2) (Dribbling, Ball Mastery) | pg. 138 |
| 2. Dribbling #2 (Plus 1-2) (Dribbling, Ball Mastery) | pg. 139 |
| 3. Dribbling #3 (Plus 1-2) (Dribbling, Ball Mastery) | pg. 140 |
| 4. Dribbling #4 (Plus 1-2) (Dribbling, Ball Mastery) | pg. 141 |
| 5. Dribbling #5 (Plus 1-2) (Dribbling, Ball Mastery) | pg. 142 |
| 6. Dribbling #6 (Plus 1-2) (Dribbling, Ball Mastery) | pg. 143 |
| 7. Passing #1 (Plus 1-2) (Passing, Receiving) | pg. 144 |
| 8. Passing #2 (Plus 1-2) (Passing, Receiving) | pg. 145 |
| 9. Passing #3 (Plus 1-2) (Passing, Receiving) | pg. 146 |
| 10. FMS #1 (Plus 1-2) (Movement Skills) | pg. 147 |
| 11. Attacking #1 (Plus 1-2) (Attacking, Defending) | pg. 148 |
| 12. Attacking #2 (Plus 1-2) (Attacking, Defending) | pg. 149 |
| 13. Defending #1 (Plus 1-2) (Defending, Attacking) | pg. 150 |
| 14. Defending #2 (Plus 1-2) (Defending, Attacking) | pg. 151 |
| 15. Shooting #1 (Plus 1-2) (Shooting, Attacking) | pg. 152 |
| 16. Shooting #2 (Plus 1-2) (Shooting, Attacking) | pg. 153 |
| 17. Heading #1 (Plus 1-2) (Heading) | pg. 154 |
| 18. Cooperation Games (Plus 1-2) (Fun Activities) | pg. 155 |

# Dribbling #1 (Plus 1-2)
# Dribbling, Ball Mastery

## Activity 1: Dribbling Basics
Focus: Dribbling, creating space

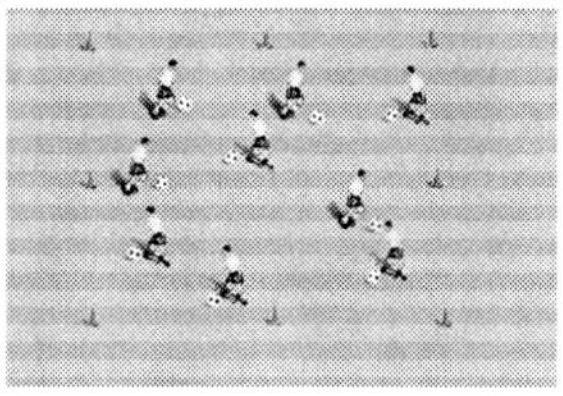

1. Area 20 x 20 yds
2. Ball per player
3. Cones

### Objective
Players dribble the ball randomly in the area. On command of "FREEZE", players demonstrate control by placing the foot on the ball. Balance by bending the knees and determine if there is adequate space by extending the arms in all directions. Red light – Green light can be used (Red = Stop, Green = Go and Yellow = Turn). Progress to turns, fakes, and exchanging balls.

### Coaching Points
1. "Feel the ball - see the field"
2. Keep the ball moving
3. Dribble with the laces

## Activity 2: Tree House
Focus: Dribbling

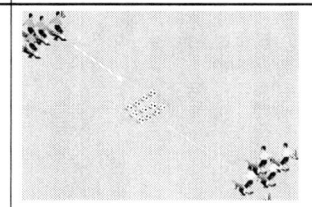

1. Area 20 x 20 yds
2. Balls
3. Cones

### Objective
At either end of the area you have a tree house. At one end you have the 'Greedy Gorillas' and at the other end you have the 'Cheeky Chimps'. In the middle are all the soccer coconuts. On the call of "GO" the Chimps and Gorillas run to the middle and collect a coconut and return back to their tree house before going to collect another one.

### Coaching Points
1. Keep ball moving
2. Keep ball close
3. Keep head up

## Activity 3: Dribbling Tag
Focus: Dribbling, Creating Space

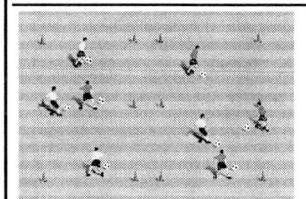

1. Area 30 x 20 yds x 2
2. Ball per player
3. Cones
4. Training Vests

### Objective
Two 30 x 20 yds areas with 5 yds of space between. Two teams of 4 players create a 3v1 scenario in each area. Every player has a ball (including the defensive player). The defender attempts to tag as many players as he/she can in 30 seconds. At the end of 30 seconds, rotate the players. Add the total score for the teams. If a player dribbles outside of the area - count one point for the defender.

### Coaching Points
1. Use the laces
2. Find space – head up
3. Change pace to escape the defender

## Activity 4: Match 2 v 2
Focus: Game

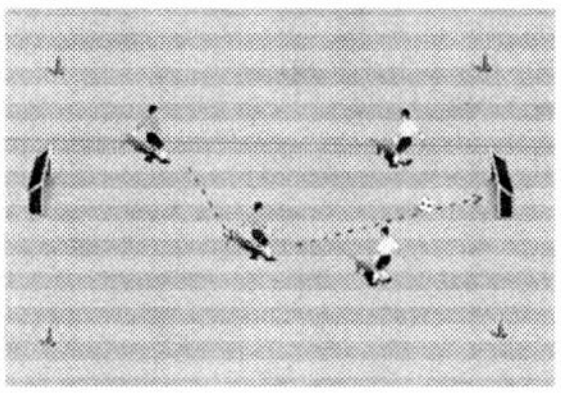

1. Area 20 x 10 yds
2. Balls
3. Cones
4. Training Vests
5. Small Goals

### Objective
A small sided game 2v2 or 3v3 is a good way to finish a practice session.

Other than emphasizing the main theme of the session, let the players play with little or no coaching - 10-15 minutes at the end of the session.

### Coaching Points
1. Little or no coaching
2. Encourage players to try skills practiced during the session

**SOCCERPLUS**
**THE DICICCO METHOD**

soccer interactive.com

# Dribbling #2 (Plus 1-2)
# Dribbling, Ball Mastery

## Activity 1: Individual Ball Warm Up 1
## Focus: Dribbling

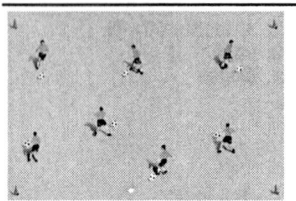

1. Area 20 x 20 yds
2. Ball per player
3. Cones

### Objective
Players have a ball each. Set the players tasks - don't let the ball stop moving! Don't let the ball go outside the area. Progress to having the players react to the coach's commands. Toe taps, boxes, stop and go, change balls, etc.

### Coaching Points
1. Keep the ball moving at all times
2. Soft touches and keep head up
3. Move into the open space

## Activity 2: Escape Move - Drag Back
## Focus: Dribbling, Creating Space

1. Area 30 x 20 yds
2. Ball per player
3. Cones

### Objective
One ball per player in an open grid to begin. Isolate the skill by performing on-the-spot. Dribbling forward, stop the ball with the sole of the foot and roll the ball back down the side of the body then dribble back. Progress to: 1) Performing the skill on the move, 2) 1v1 passive defending, 3) 1v1 active defending 4) Game with gates, 5) Small sided game.

### Coaching Points
1. Several touches on the ball with the sole
2. Sell the move to the defender
3. Accelerate away after the move

## Activity 3: Antz Nests
## Focus: Dribbling, Turns

1. Area 20 x 20 yds
2. Ball per Player
3. Cones
4. Training Vests

### Objective
Four equal teams of Antz must work quickly to build their ants nest. In the four corners of the square the coach sets 3x3 yd squares. The objective is to fill the nest with supplies first – three balls.

### Coaching Points
1. Quick turns and dribble
2. Look around to see which groups are closest to winning
3. Stay upright when competing for a ball

## Activity 4: Numbers Game
## Focus: Dribbling, attacking, shooting, defending

1. Area 30 x 20 yds
2. Ball per player
3. Cones
4. Training Vests
5. Goals x 2
6. Hurdles, ladders, rings etc

### Objective
A coach's favorite – players play individually and as a small group to score a goal!

### Coaching Points
1. Get to the ball quickly
2. Look for the goal not protected
3. Move quickly to the goal

# Dribbling #3 (Plus 1-2)
# Dribbling, Ball Mastery

## Activity 1: Patterns
### Focus: Dribbling

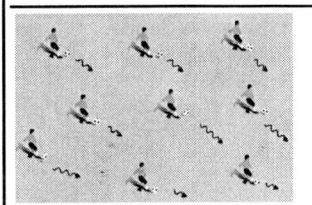

1. Area 20 x 20 yds
2. Ball per player
3. Cones

### Objective
Players dribble around the area and react to the pattern of play the coach calls out.
Start with basic commands such as dribbling with the laces, turn etc. Then increase complexity by adding patterns such as: Inside/inside/inside/miss, Inside/inside/inside and drag back. Inside/outside/inside/outside. Outside/inside/outside/inside. Inside/Outside sole. Sole/sole/step over.

### Coaching Points
1. Keep ball close and under control
2. Keep ball moving at all times
3. Keep head up and move the ball into the open space.

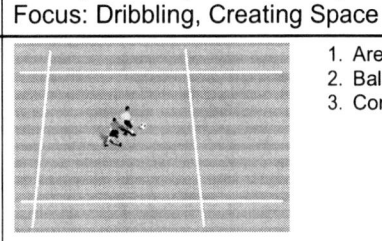

## Activity 2: Escape Move - Step Over
### Focus: Dribbling, Creating Space

1. Area 30 x 20 yds
2. Ball per player
3. Cones

### Objective
One ball per player in an open grid to begin. Isolate the skill by performing on-the-spot. Dribbling forward, the attacker steps over the top of the ball with the foot furthest from the defender and quickly pivots 180 degrees (away from the defender). The attacker quickly turns and accelerates away.
Progress to: 1) Performing the skill on the move, 2) 1v1 passive defending, 3) 1v1 active defending 4) Game with gates, 5) Small sided game.

### Coaching Points
1. Start in stationary position - not a dribble
2. Repeat and repeat again
3. Accelerate away leaving defender behind

## Activity 3: Can You? Plus 2
### Focus: Ball Mastery

1. Area 20 x 20 yds
2. Ball per Player
3. Cones

### Objective
Coach to lead patterns of movement asking can you ....? Basic and more advanced movements.

### Coaching Points
1. Concentrate on great execution
2. Build up pace to game speed
3. Get in a good body position to protect the ball

## Activity 4: Soccer Rugby
### Focus: Game

1. Area 30 x 20 yds
2. Balls 6-10
3. Cones
4. Training Vests

### Objective
To encourage players to dribble the ball forward and beat an opponent, introduce the 'backward pass' rule of Rugby. Play 3v3. On receiving the ball a player should attempt to dribble forward - a pass can be made, but it must be made behind the player with the ball. This encourages players to be positive on the ball and attacking while in possession. Set a cone 5 yards from each goal - once the players cross this line they can pass/shoot forward.

### Coaching Points
1. Be positive on the ball
2. Attacking the open space
3. Keep the ball close and under control

**SOCCERPLUS** — THE DICICCO METHOD

soccer interactive.com

# Dribbling #4 (Plus 1-2)
# Dribbling, Ball Mastery

## Activity 1: Individual Ball Warm Up 2
Focus: Dribbling

1. Area 20 x 20 yds
2. Ball per player
3. Cones

### Objective
Each player has a ball and dribbles around the inside of the square. The coach challenges the players to complete a variety of tasks within 30 seconds. For example 1) Travel to all 4 sides of the box in any order, 2) How many touches on the ball can you get with your right foot or left foot?, 3) How many people can you tag?, 4) How many soccer balls dribbled by other players can you tag?

### Coaching Points
1. Keep the ball moving at all times
2. Keep your head up
3. Move into the open space

## Activity 2: Take On - Inside Outside
Focus: Dribbling, Creating Space

1. Area 30 x 20 yds
2. Ball per player
3. Cones

### Objective
One ball per player in an open grid to begin. Isolate the skill by performing on-the-spot. The attacker dribbles the ball towards the defender. As the defender approaches, the attacker starts to dribble at an angle to one side of the defender using the inside of the foot. As the defender commits to the challenge, the attacker uses the outside of the same foot and pushes the ball to the other side of the defender. The attacker can then accelerate away.

### Coaching Points
1. Determine a speed of approach for each individual
2. Realistic movement to unbalance the defender
3. Accelerate away leaving defender behind

## Activity 3: Dribble, Turn, Pass
Focus: Dribbling, Ball Mastery

1. Area 20 x 20 yds
2. Ball per player
3. Cones
4. Training Vests

### Objective
3 cones form a triangle in the area. 3 players dribble at the same time to the next cone in the same direction. When arriving at the cone, the player performs a turn specified by the coach and dribbles back to the starting cone. Repeat. Progress to instructing the player to pass the ball when they reach the cone to the player in front (i.e. all players pass the ball at the same time)

### Coaching Points
1. Minimal touches to turn
2. Accurate pass back and good 1st touch to receive the pass
3. Timing so that everybody works at the same time

## Activity 4: Looters
Focus: Dribbling, attacking, and defending

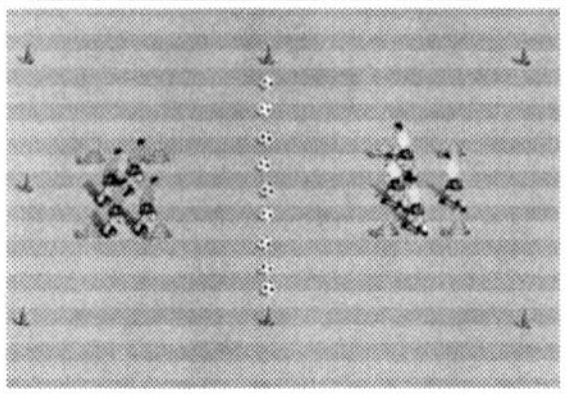

1. Area 40 x 20 yds
2. Ball per player
3. Cones
4. Training Vests

### Objective
Two or more teams. To play the activity with two teams, two 5 x 5 yds square are marked 5 yards from each end line. Players from both teams stand inside their team square and all the balls are lined up on center line of the area. On the command of "GO" players leave their square and attempt to dribble a ball back to their square. An opponent cannot steal the ball. Play until all balls are in either of the two squares.

### Coaching Points
1. Get to the ball quickly
2. Move into space
3. Dribble with laces for speed

# Dribbling #5 (Plus 1-2)
# Dribbling, Ball Mastery

## Activity 1: Fetch
### Focus: Dribbling, Ball Mastery

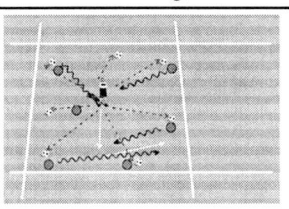

1. Area 20 x 20 yds
2. Ball each player
3. Cones

### Objective
No more than 5 minutes - 4-8 players. Ball each. Coach kneels on the ground. Players surround the coach so they are close enough for the coach to reach their ball when the player puts their foot on top. Coach rolls the balls randomly in the area and the players sprint to collect and dribble back, stopping the ball within touching distance for the coach.

### Coaching Points
1. Move quickly to the ball
2. Dribble with laces
3. Use different surfaces to change direction

## Activity 2: Mirrors 1 v 1
### Focus: Dribbling

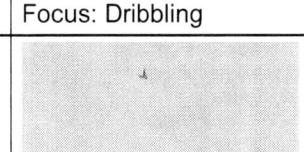

1. Area 15 x 15 yds
2. Ball between 2
3. Cones

### Objective
One player with a ball must dribble to either cone before the player without the ball can get to the same cone. The player getting to the cone first wins a point. Players then return to the middle to repeat. Switch roles every time. First to 10 points wins.

### Coaching Points
1. Demonstrate the 'lunge' move to unbalance the defender
2. Try to shift the weight of the defender
3. Accelerate to the cone

## Activity 3: Flip 'em
### Focus: Dribbling, Ball Mastery

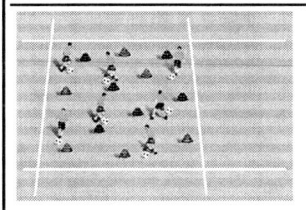

1. Area 20 x 20 yds
2. Balls
3. Cones
4. Training Vests

### Objective
Players start in the area with a ball each at their feet. There are cones spread randomly around the area with some the correct way up and some upside down. Players dribble around the area performing a specified ball mastery exercise and every time they reach a cone they have to flip it over the opposite way. 1) Toe taps, 2) Sole taps, 3) Laces dribble, 4) Lateral rolls.

### Coaching Points
1. Soft light touches on the ball
2. Start slowly then build up the speed
3. Control the ball next to each cone

## Activity 4: Treasure Chest
### Focus: Dribbling, Attacking, Defending

1. Area 20 x 20 yds
2. Balls
3. Cones
4. Training Vests

### Objective
Split group into two even teams. Players stand in teams opposite the coach 20 yds away with a pile of balls. Two small goals (Treasure Chest) are placed 10 yds between the players and the coach facing towards the outside of the square. Goals are sufficiently spaced to create a lane for players to run between. On the coach's command, players sprint to a cone placed near the coach. Players round the cone and the coach drops one ball (Treasure). Players compete to score in either goal.

### Coaching Points
1. Beat the defender using various moves
2. Take a chance on goal
3. Be creative

# Dribbling #6 (Plus 1-2)
# Dribbling, Ball Mastery

## Activity 1: British Bull Dog
## Focus: Dribbling & Movement

1. Area 30 x 15 yds
2. Ball per player
3. Cones
4. Training Vests

### Objective
One player is selected to be the 'Bull Dog' and starts at the end line. The other players 'Cats' line up at the other end of the rectangle facing the person in the middle. The first time through without soccer balls – then all players other than Bull Dog has balls to dribble. Cats who were tagged join the Bull Dog.

### Coaching Points
1. Encourage players to use body movements to elude the bull dog
2. When dribbling, keep soccer balls close to allow quick changes in direction
3. Lift head to avoid collision and see routes for escape

## Activity 2: Dribbling Tag
## Focus: Dribbling, Creating Space

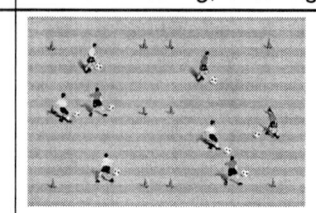

1. Area 30 x 20 yds x 2
2. Ball per player
3. Cones
4. Training Vests

### Objective
Two 30 x 20 yds areas with 5 yds of space between. Two teams of 4 players create a 3v1 scenario in each area. Every player has a ball (including the defensive player). The defender attempts to tag as many players as he/she can in 30 seconds. At the end of 30 seconds, rotate the players. Add the total score for the teams. If a player dribbles outside of the area - count one point for the defender.

### Coaching Points
1. Use the laces
2. Find space – head up
3. Change pace to escape the defender

## Activity 3: Escape & Possession
## Focus: Dribbling

1. Area 20 x 20 yds
2. Balls
3. Cones

### Objective
Players must dribble around keeping their ball under close control and perform an escape move when they reach a cone (drag back, outside hook, step over, 'L' etc). Transition into possession - In pairs, one attacker and one defender – the attacker must keep the ball from the defender. 1 minute, keep points.

### Coaching Points
1. Awareness of defenders and space
2. Close control of the ball
3. Quick change of direction and speed.

## Activity 4: All Up and All Back
## Focus: Attacking, Defending

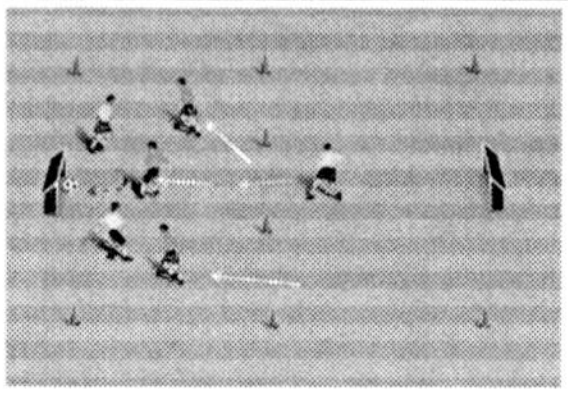

1. Area 40 x 20 yds
2. Ball per player
3. Cones
4. Training Vests
5. Goals

### Objective
A line of cones mark the center line of the field. Players play a regular game of soccer (3v3 to 5v5), but a goal does not count for the attacking side unless all players are in the attacking half of the field. Also, a goal counts as double if all defenders are not in the defensive half when the ball enters the goal.

### Coaching Points
1. Attack – provide angles for support
2. Defense – get behind the ball
3. Think quickly and concentrate on the rules

# Passing #1 (Plus 1-2)
# Passing, Receiving

## Activity 1: 4 by 4 Squares
### Focus: Passing, Receiving

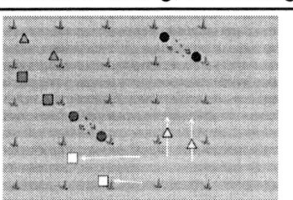

1. Area 40 x 40 yds
2. Balls
3. Cones

### Objective
Set out 16 squares measuring 10 x 10 yds - 4 squares long and 4 squares wide. Each pair starts in one square – passing the ball back and forth to reach 10 passes. On completion of 10 passes, the pair move to an unoccupied square and repeat another 10 passes.

### Coaching Points
1. Look up for space
2. Accelerate into the space
3. Correct execution of the skill

## Activity 2: Short Passing Basics
### Focus: Passing, receiving

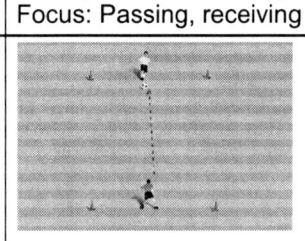

1. Area 10 x 10 yds
2. Ball per player
3. Cones

### Objective
Players passing back and forth (2 or more touches) - Progress to moving side to side along the line.

### Coaching Points
1. Lock (firm) ankle
2. Inside of foot
3. Supporting foot next to ball
4. Strike through the center of the ball
5. On your toes

## Activity 3: Passing Through The Gate
### Focus: Passing, Receiving

1. Area 10 x 10 yds
2. Ball per player
3. Cones

### Objective
Ideal as a warm-up and for players getting touches on the ball. Start with pairs 5 yards apart - each person standing between cones 2 yards apart. Pass back and forth taking one controlling touch and a touch to pass. Enforce proper technique (plant foot next to ball, pass with inside of foot, follow through, etc.) Move to the main activity:
3 players – 'A' passes through 'B's' legs to 'C'. 'A' then follows pass and presents the bridge to 'C'. 'C' then passes through 'A's' legs to 'B' etc.

### Coaching Points
1. Lock (firm) ankle
2. Inside of foot
3. Supporting foot next to ball
4. Strike through the center of the ball
5. On your toes

## Activity 4: End Zone
### Focus: Passing, Receiving

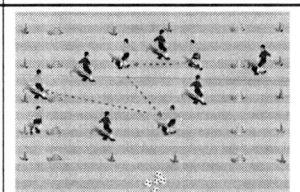

1. Area 40 x 20 yds
2. Ball per player
3. Cones
4. Training Vests

### Objective
Two teams - 5v5 - nominate one person (target player) to stand in the end zone at the opponents end of the field. Each team must attempt to pass the ball to the target person. If the target player successfully controls the ball in the end zone, the person passing the ball also becomes a target player. Try to get all players in the end zone.

### Coaching Points
1. Weight of pass needs to be firm to reach target
2. Target player must offer supporting angles
3. First touch needs to cushion the ball

SOCCERPLUS
THE DICICCO METHOD

soccer interactive.com

# Passing #2 (Plus 1-2)
# Passing, Receiving

## Activity 1: 4 Group Passing
## Focus: Passing

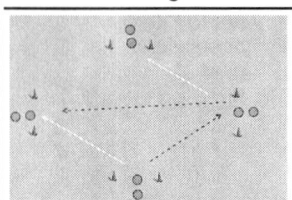

1. Area: 20 x 20
2. Balls
3. Cones

### Objective
Players are split into 4 groups with 2 players being in each group. One ball is used. The exercise starts with the player with the ball playing a pass to one group and moving to another. Whoever plays the pass must move to a different group. You can't play a pass to a group which has 1 player.

### Coaching Points
1. Movement away from the ball
2. Quality of pass
3. Speed of movement

## Activity 2: Passing Through The Arch
## Focus: Passing, Receiving

1. Area 10 x 10 yds
2. Ball per player
3. Cones

### Objective
Start with pairs – 5 yards apart - each person standing between cones 2 yards apart. Pass back and forth taking one controlling touch and a touch to pass. Set a goal (training arches or cones) in the center of the area 2-3 yards apart. Players win a point for each successful pass – 30 seconds and then pairs change.

### Coaching Points
1. Lock (firm) ankle
2. Inside of foot
3. Supporting foot next to ball
4. Strike through the center of the ball
5. On your toes

## Activity 3: Individual Receiving
## Focus: Receiving

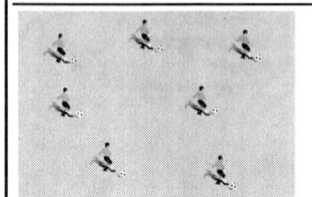

1. Area 20 x 20 yds
2. Ball per player
3. Cones

### Objective
Players have a ball each and dribble around the area. The players must react to the coach's command. When the coach calls "FOOT" - players throw ball into the air to receive with their laces, "THIGH" - players receive with the thigh, "CHEST" receive with the chest, "HEAD" cushion header into players path.

### Coaching Points
1. Keep eyes on the ball
2. Present surface to the ball
3. Cushion ball

## Activity 4: Count Down
## Focus: Dribbling, Passing, Possession

1. Area 30 x 20 yds
2. Several balls
3. Cones
4. Training Vests

### Objective
Two teams six play 5v5 in an area 30 yards long and 20 yards wide. At each end of the rectangle is an end zone stretching the width of the area and 5 yards deep – a target player stands in this area. The coach feeds balls into the area – teams compete to win possession and then send balls to their team mate (target player) in their end zone. If the target player successfully controls the ball within the area, the player passing the ball joins the target player. The 'count down' continues as teammates join the target players until all players are in the end zone.

### Coaching Points
1. Attack – be creative to beat your opponent
2. Attack – after passing the ball support the play
3. Attack – target player must remain on the move
4. Defense – protect the target
5. Defense – communicate with your partner

SOCCERPLUS
THE DICICCO METHOD

soccer interactive.com

# Passing #3 (Plus 1-2)
# Passing, Receiving

## Activity 1: Pairs Passing & Moving
### Focus: Passing, Receiving

1. Area 30 x 30 yds
2. Balls
3. Cones

### Objective
Players are in pairs. Gates are created with cones and situated randomly in the area. Pairs must pass through a gate then move onto another unoccupied gate. Emphasize firm accurate passing and moving quickly between gates. Start with no time limit, then challenge players to get as many gates as possible in 30 seconds. Change partners & repeat.

### Coaching Points
1. Proper passing technique
2. Pass then move - don't watch
3. Communicate with your partner

## Activity 2: Coconut Shy
### Focus: Passing and Receiving

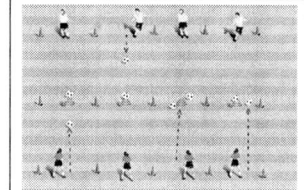

1. Area 30 x 20 yds
2. Ball per player
3. Cones

### Objective
A line of cones 5 yds apart are placed along the center (10 yds) of the rectangle. A ball is placed on top of each cone. 2 Players stand opposite each other 20 yds apart. The objective is to pass the ball from behind the line and hit the ball off the cone. The first pair to reach 5 hits wins.

### Coaching Points
1. For accuracy, pass ball with the inside of the foot
2. Run onto the ball straight
3. Kick through the ball for power

## Activity 3: Squares
### Focus: Passing, Receiving

1. Area 15 x 15 yds
2. Ball per player
3. Cones

### Objective
All players stand inside a square marked with cones. One ball only required per game. Trying to keep the ball on the ground and using the inside or outside of the foot only, the players attempt to eliminate each other until one player remains. The ball is passed around one touch as the coach introduces rules. 1) One touch or you are out. 2) If you kick the ball out of the square (last touch) – out! 3) If you could have stopped the ball from leaving the square – out! 4) If you are 'nutmegged' through the legs – out! 5) If you play the ball in the air and it is caught – out! 6) If you attempt to catch the ball but drop it – out!

### Coaching Points
1. Ball on the ground
2. Quick play
3. No arguments – one adjudicator

## Activity 4: Short Passing for Points
### Focus: Passing, Receiving

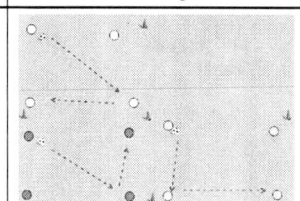

1. Area 20 x 20 yds
2. Balls
3. Cones
4. Training Vests

### Objective
If you have 12 players split them into 3 teams of 4 players. Each team has their own 10 x 10 yds area. One soccer ball per team. The team must pass their ball around their area. Each team has 5 points, every time the balls goes out of bounds or a player stops moving they lose a point.

### Coaching Points
1. Use inside of foot to play short pass
2. Ensure non-kicking foot is next to the ball
3. Follow through towards target
4. Soft receiving touch

**SOCCERPLUS** — THE DICICCO METHOD

soccer interactive.com

# FMS #1 (Plus 1-2)
# Movement Skills

## Activity 1: Agility Race
### Focus: Movement

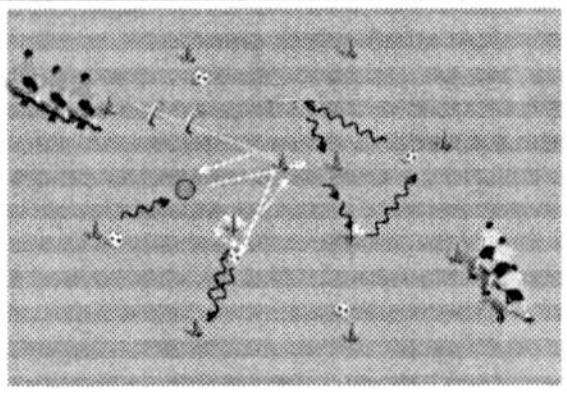

1. Area 40 x 40 yds
2. Balls
3. Cones
4. Training Vests
5. Ladders, hurdles
6. Rings, band & pillows

### Objective
5 mins & 6-36 players. Teams of 3 players. Each team has a home cone (starting point). Sticks, hurdles, ladders, speed bands, cones, rings and wobble pillows placed in area. Coach shouts the order of each activity (ie. hurdle, cone, ring - 1st player sprints out to perform the activity and then returns 'home' for 2nd player to go. Combinations of dribbling the ball and performing without.

### Coaching Points
1. Perform activity with good form
2. Explosive moves
3. Maximum intensity whilst working

## Activity 2: Shapes and Colors
### Focus: Movement

1. Area 20 x 20 yds
2. Flat Markers
3. Colored Cones

### Objective
Players perform different balances and moves in response to the coach's instructions. In the area, place colored markers (or colored objects) on the ground. Instruct the players to follow the coach's commands. For example, "GO A YELLOW MARKER" or "SQUARE". Once the player gets to that object, ask them to perform an exercise – for example - balance alternately on one, two, three, four, and then five body parts. Have them hold each balance for three to five seconds (The players should strive for control when balanced).

### Coaching Points
1. Ask players who perform a skill well to demonstrate
2. Reward creativity – create a points system

## Activity 3: Balancing in Pairs
### Focus: Movement

1. Area 20 x 15 yds
2. 1 Ball per pair
3. 4 Cones

### Objective
Players in pairs, completing various patterns of movement.
1) Throw and catch with two hands. 2) Catch, stretch high, bring into chest and then throw to partner, 3) Catch, stretch high, brush the ground with the ball, bring back to chest and throw to partner, 4) Catch, stretch high, brush the ground with the ball, circle twice around the body, bring into the chest and throw to partner.

### Coaching Points
1. Maintain balance for all movements
2. Two feet on the ground & two hands on the ball
3. Throw chest height

## Activity 4: Four Rings
### Focus: Movement, Defending, Attacking

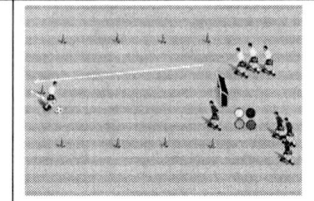

1. Area 20 x 10 yds
2. Ball per player
3. Cones
4. Training Vests
5. Speed rings
6. Small goal

### Objective
In an area 20 x 10 yds the coach places a goal at one end. At the same end as the goal and behind the end line four rings are placed 1 foot apart to form a square. On the command of "GO", one attacking player sprints to the far end to collect a ball and the defender performs an activity in the speed rings.

### Coaching Points
1. Attack - change pace of attack
2. Attack - front foot of defender
3. Attack - use body feints and ball movements to beat defender
4. Defense - close down the space between attacker and goal
5. Defense – force attacker to weaker foot

SOCCERPLUS
THE DICICCO METHOD

soccer interactive.com

# Attacking #1 (Plus 1-2)
# Attacking, Defending

## Activity 1: 1 v 1 to Goal
### Focus: Attacking

1. Area 25 x 25 yds
2. Balls
3. Cones
4. Training Vests

### Objective
Two players start side by side 25 yards from goal. The server (standing to one side of the goal) plays a ball into the area and shouts "GO". Players must turn and compete for the ball and attempt a shot at goal.

### Coaching Points
1. Speed of reaction
2. First touch towards goal but away from defender
3. Awareness of keepers and defenders positions

## Activity 2: Possession 1 v 1
### Focus: Possession

1. Area 20 x 20 yds
2. 1 Ball per pair
3. 4 Cones

### Objective
In pairs - one attacker and one defender. On the command of "GO", the attacker attempts to maintain possession for 20 seconds - preventing the defender from stealing the ball.

### Coaching Points
1. Use body as a barrier to the ball
2. Control and move the ball away from pressure
3. Use body to hold off and push opponent away from the ball

## Activity 3: Attacking Moves - 1 v 1
### Focus: Attacking, Possession

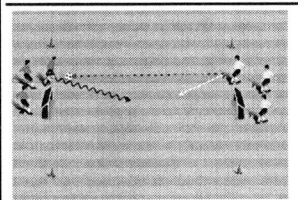

1. Area 30 x 20 yds
2. Several balls
3. Cones
4. Training vests
5. Small Goals

### Objective
3-4 players at each end of the field. First player in each line play 1v1 - defender plays ball to the attacker and attacker performs a take-on move. If backed up, attacker creates space with an escape-move.

### Coaching Points
1. Approach defender at comfortable speed
2. Sell the defender with take on move
3. Create space using escape move

## Activity 4: Winner Stays On
### Focus: Attacking, Shooting, Defending

1. Area 30 x 20 yds
2. Ball per player
3. Cones
4. Training Vests

### Objective
Three teams. Two teams play 3v3 and one team wait on the sideline. Teams attempt to score in two or all four goals. The team scoring first stay on the field and the losing team moves to the sideline – the team on the sideline come on. The new ball is served back in by the coach.

### Coaching Points
1. Get to the ball quickly
2. Look for the goal not protected
3. Move quickly to the goal

**SOCCERPLUS** — THE DICICCO METHOD

soccer interactive.com

# Attacking #2 (Plus 1-2)
# Attacking, Defending

## Activity 1: 1 v 1 to Goal #2
### Focus: Attacking, Defending

1. Area 25 x 25 yds
2. Balls
3. Cones

### Objective
Split the team into two groups - defenders and attackers. The first defender plays a ball to the first attacker and then must run around the cone and chase down the attacker. Attacker must control the pass and quickly dribble at goal to finish.

### Coaching Points
1. Technique of first touch
2. Dribble at speed
3. Dribble to cut off path of defender
4. Shooting technique (side foot, laces)

## Activity 2: One Goal 1 v 1
### Focus: Attacking, Defending

1. Area 10 x 10 yds
2. Ball per player
3. Cones

### Objective
Players are in pairs with a ball. Within a 10 x 10 square players place a goal (cone with ball on top) in the center. Players play for one minute. If a goal is scored, player retains possession, if ball goes out of the square the ball goes to the opponent. Between each game (or every other game), bring player together and make coaching points.

### Coaching Points
1. Attack - change pace of attack
2. Attack - attack the front foot of the defender
3. Attack - use body feints and ball movements to beat defender
4. Defense – force play to weaker foot
5. Defense – keep attacker from goal

## Activity 3: 1 v 1 - 2 goals
### Focus: Two goals

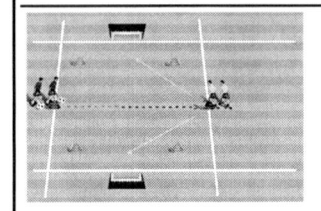

1. Area 20 x 20 yds
2. Balls
3. Cones
4. Training Vests

### Objective
Players in small groups of no more than 4. 1st player passes ball across to the opposite line and immediately defends against the attacker. The attacking player tries to score in either goal set to either side. To score a goal the player has to be beyond the coned shooting line that is about 2-3 yards from goal. If the defender wins the ball they can score a goal. Players change lines each time to ensure everybody defends and attacks.

### Coaching Points
1. Players to use take-on moves to beat the defender
2. Be aware of the open goal to score in
3. Defenders to transition quickly to attackers

## Activity 4: 1st Team to 4
### Focus: Attacking, Defending

1. Area 20 x 20 yds
2. Balls
3. Cones
4. Training Vests

### Objective
Two teams play 4v4 into four small goals with no goalkeepers. The first team to score in all four goals is the winner. This will encourage attackers to move away from defenders as they look for an open goal to score into. Depending on number of players in the session this can be 3v3 or 5v5.

### Coaching Points
1. A positive attitude to scoring by all players
2. Use turns to move away from players to look for an open goal
3. Accuracy of finishing

# Defending #1 (Plus 1-2)
# Defending, Attacking

## Activity 1: 1 v 1 Challenge
## Focus: Defending, Attacking

1. Area 30 x 30 yds
2. Balls
3. Cones
4. Training vests

### Objective
Players work in pairs. One player is the attacker with the ball and one player is the defender. The attacker's objective is to try and dribble through as many of the gates (two cones 2 yds apart) as possible. The defender must try to stop the attacker from scoring. After 45 seconds change roles.

### Coaching Points
1. Defense - try to slow the attacking player
2. Defense - don't be overly concerned with winning the ball
3. Defense - use body strength to force play to one direction
4. Attack - awareness of the open space
5. Attack - keep the ball moving but have control

## Activity 2: Block Tackle
## Focus: Defending

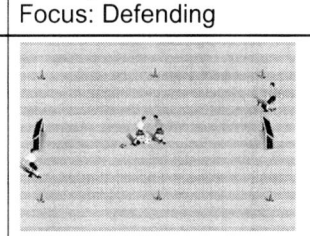

1. Area 20 x 10 yds
2. Ball per player
3. Cones
4. Training Vests
5. Goals

### Objective
Play 1v1 - One goal at each end of the area. Firstly teach the block tackle technique: Players stand face to face with hands on their partners shoulder. One ball between each pair. One player counts to 3 and then the players perform a block tackle - both players tackling at the same time. When the ball is won, the players attempt to score. 4 players to an area, next 2 on when goal is scored.

### Coaching Points
1. Non-kicking foot by the side of the ball
2. Block tackle with inside of foot
3. Lean into challenge with body weight forward
4. Do not kick at the ball

## Activity 3: 1 v 1 - 4 Gates
## Focus: Defending, Attacking

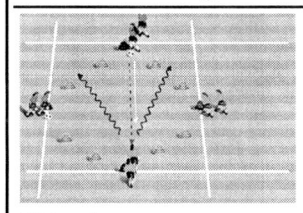

1. Area 20 x 20 yds
2. Balls
3. Cones
4. Training Vests

### Objective
Four pairs positioned on each side of the area. Start by alternating - Play games one after another (two teams opposite each other compete). The server sends a ball across the area to the attacker. The attacker attempts to score by dribbling the ball through either of the two gates either side of the server (defender). If the defender wins the ball they can score through the opposite two gates.

### Coaching Points
1. Defense - close down space quickly
2. Defense - force attacker to their weaker side
3. Defense - win possession when the attacker makes an error
4. Attack - You have to beat a player to score
5. Attack - Realism in the moves

## Activity 4: Defending 3 Goals
## Focus: Defending

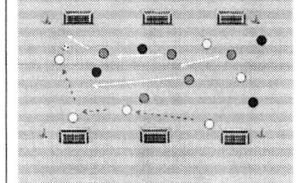

1. Area 60 x 20 yds
2. Balls
3. Cones
4. Training Vests
5. 6 small goals or flags

### Objective
Two teams defend and attack 3 goals each. 3v3 to 5v5. Plus 2 stage of development focus on the individual defender 1v1. For Plus 3-5 introduce the principles of pressure and cover in small teams.

### Coaching Points
1. #1 priority is to protect the goals
2. Position body to stop the shot
3. Shift defense as attack moves across field

# Defending #2 (Plus 1-2)
# Defending, Attacking

## Activity 1: Defending 1 v 1 A
### Focus: Defending

1. Area 10 x 10 yds
2. Ball per pair
3. Cones
4. Training Vests

### Objective
In pairs 10 yds apart. One player (defender) passes the ball to the attacker. The defender follows the pass and closes the space. Coach the players to get into a good staggered position. Walk through to begin with the defenders passive (no tackles). Then allow the players to compete for the ball and attack the other end. The defender then becomes the attacker.

### Coaching Points
1. Close space quickly
2. Staggered stance and low center of gravity
3. Stop opponent scoring – then win possession (patience)
4. Get tight to attacker if their back is to goal – no turns
5. Focus on the ball and not on body feints

## Activity 2: Defending 1 v 1 B
### Focus: Defending

1. Area 20 x 10 yds
2. Ball per player
3. Cones
4. Training Vests
5. Goals

### Objective
Play 1v1 - One goal at each end of the area. From the defensive end of the field, the defender passes the ball firmly along the ground to the attacker. On receipt, the attacker attacks the defender and attempts to score a goal. If the defender wins the ball, he/she can also score in the attacker's goal. 4 players to an area – next defender and attacker start when ball leaves the area or a goal is scored. Gradually introduce coaching points.

### Coaching Points
1. Close space quickly to keep attacker away from goal
2. Staggered stance and low center of gravity
3. Stop opponent scoring - win possession (patience)
4. Get tight to attacker – no turns
5. Focus on the ball and not on body feints

## Activity 3: Defending 1 v 1 Recover
### Focus: Defending, Attacking

1. Area 30 x 30 yds
2. Balls
3. Cones
4. Training Vests

### Objective
Two groups of 3 players. One team starts with the ball and has an unopposed dribble and shot at one of two goals opposite the starting position. The attacker must be in the shooting zone (cones placed 10 yds from the goals to shoot. Immediately after the shot (score or miss) the attacker recovers to become a defender against the first attacker from the opposite line. The other team cannot go until the ball is shot.

### Coaching Points
1. Defender must quickly recover to defend after attacking
2. Attacker to go at pace at the defender - minimal time to recover

## Activity 4: 4 v 4 Defending
### Focus: Defending

1. Area 20 x 20 yds
2. Balls
3. Cones
4. Training Vests

### Objective
The defenders have to protect the center of the area (5 x 5 yd). The attackers have a ball each and have to try and beat the defender and dribble into the center. If the defender wins the ball he/she should dribble to the outside of the area to score a point. Switch roles every 1 minute.

### Coaching Points
1. Apply pressure
2. Get into the staggered position
3. Be patient

# Shooting #1 (Plus 1-2)
# Shooting, Attacking

## Activity 1: Driven Pass/Shot
## Focus: Shooting, Passing

1. Area: 10 x 20 yds
2. Ball per person
3. Cones
4. Goal

### Objective
In pairs, 20 yards apart, drive the ball back and forth with the instep (laces). Keep balls on the ground and strike through the middle of the ball – minimizing rotation of the ball.

Open the area to 20 yards and drive the ball to each other.

### Coaching Points
1. Strike the ball with the laces
2. Approach the ball from the front
3. Drive through the ball for power

## Activity 2: Creating Space 1 v 1
## Focus: Shooting, Attacking, Defending

1. Area 20 x 20 yds
2. 8 balls
3. Cones
4. Training Vests

### Objective
Place 8 balls 15-20 yards from goal. Start with 2 Defenders and Attackers on the goal line. On the command of "GO" the attackers sprint to collect any ball. The defender is partnered with one attacker and must prevent the attacker from scoring. The attacker must attempt to create space to create a scoring opportunity. Start without a goal keeper and then add one in. When all the balls have been used, change the attackers and defenders.

### Coaching Points
1. Attack - move quickly to the ball
2. Attack - use escape and take on moves to beat the defender
3. Attack - shoot at every opportunity
4. Defend - restrict attackers space
5. Defend - don't dive into a tackle

## Activity 3: Hot Shot 1
## Focus: Shooting

1. Area 20 x 20 yds
2. Ball per player
3. Flat markers (or cones)
4. Training Vests
5. Goal

### Objective
Split into two teams. One team is shooting against the clock and the other is collecting the balls. Team A shoots first. The starting position for all players is next to the left post. On the call of "GO", the first player sprints to a cone on the 18 yard line, then back to a small 2 x 2 yds shooting box where the ball is laid off for the shot. Player 1 shoots at goal first time and player 2 follows the path of player 1 – player 3 passes to 2 etc.

### Coaching Points
1. Strike with laces
2. Place ball low in the corners
3. Don't stand admiring pass or shot

## Activity 4: Numbers Hot Shot
## Focus: Shooting, Attacking, Defending

1. Area 30 x 20 yds
2. Ball per player
3. Cones
4. Training Vests
5. Goal

### Objective
Players separated into 4 teams and each team stands between two cones, equal distance from goal on each corner of the area. At one end this is a goal and at the other end are 4 cones with 4 balls balanced on them. When a number is called, the player runs to compete for the ball. A goal = 1pt, dislodge their teams ball off the cone = 2pts, knock off another team's ball = 2pts to other team.

### Coaching Points
1. Quick sprint to the ball
2. Use a turn to change direction
3. Dribble and shoot with laces

# Shooting #2 (Plus 1-2)
# Shooting, Attacking

## Activity 1: Striker Breakaway
Focus: Dribbling and shooting

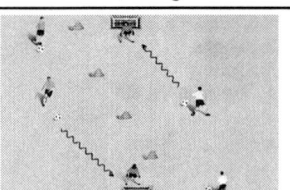

1. Area 10 x 30 yds
2. 10-12 balls
3. Cones
4. Training Vest

### Objective
Three pairs compete. Two teams start from either end of the area and the other pair are the goal keepers. The first person from each pair dribbles the ball towards the opposite goal (simultaneously). A time limit of 5 seconds to score. Once the ball is dead (scored a goal, saved by the goal keeper etc), the attacker moves out of the way and joins the opposite line. The next player then goes. Give each team 5 attacks each player and then change the goalkeepers.

### Coaching Points
1. Attack at pace - get the ball out of the feet
2. Lift your head as you decide what type of shot to take
3. Be ready for a rebound and a second opportunity to score

## Activity 2: World Cup
Focus: Shooting, Attacking

1. Area 20 x 20 yds
2. Ball per player
3. Cones
4. Training Vests
5. Goal

### Objective
World Cup singles is each player for himself/herself! World Cup Doubles is played in pairs. Game starts with 1 goalkeeper and all the other players in the area. Create a nogo area 5 yds from goal to protect the goalkeeper (flat markers are perfect). Depending on the numbers, the objective is to play three rounds – eliminating 1-2 or 3 individuals/teams per round. If a player/team scores they are through to the next round. Last touch counts to encourage predatory instincts around goal. Players/Teams eliminated have a drink and collect the balls. The final is between the two individuals/teams and is first to two goals.

### Coaching Points
1. Take every opportunity to score
2. Be ready for rebounds
3. Strike low with laces

## Activity 3: Hot Shot 2
Focus: Shooting

1. Area 30 x 10 yds
2. Balls - 2 for every player
3. Cones
4. Training Vests
5. Goals

### Objective
The team is separated into two – team A lines up 5 yards outside the penalty area to the left and right 25 yds from goal. A server kneels facing away from goal with all the balls. The other team provides two players for each post and the remaining players collect the balls missing the goal. A cone is placed 5 yards along the goal line outside of each post and the two post players stand next to the cone. On the command of "GO" the server feeds a ball to the left for the first attacker to run onto – they must strike the ball before a line 5 yds inside the penalty box. Every 2-3 sec the server feeds another ball – alternating between sides. The goalkeeper has to react very quickly to save the rapid fire shots. A post player on each side assists the GK – each time a goal is scored, a new post player enters (they must start on the cone). After a minute the teams change over.

### Coaching Points

## Activity 4: Numbers Turn
Focus: Shooting, Attacking

1. Area 30 x 20 yds
2. Ball per player
3. Cones
4. Training Vests
5. Goal

### Objective
Players are separated into 2, 3 or 4 teams and each team stands between two cones. A square, 5 x 5 yds is created between the players and the goal. Place a cone for each team 10 yards behind the teams. When a number is called the players run out to the center square, collect one of the balls and dribble around the cone behind their team. Once around the cone, the players go for goal and attempt to be the first team to score. 1pt for each goal - first team to 5 points wins the game.

### Coaching Points
1. Quick sprint to the ball
2. Use a turn to change direction
3. Dribble and shoot with laces

**SOCCERPLUS** — THE DICICCO METHOD

soccer interactive.com

# Heading # 1 (Plus 1-2)
# Heading

## Activity 1: Heading Basics
### Focus: Heading

1. Area 10 x 10 yds
2. 1 Ball between 2

### Objective
In pairs, one player performs the heading (A) and the other serves the ball (B). 1) Player A lies on his/her stomach and rests on the elbows. Kneeling and 2 yds apart from Player A, Player B feeds the ball with two hands. Using the back and abdominal muscles, Player A heads the ball back to B. 2) A gets into a 'crab' position and this time uses the neck muscles to generate power to head the ball back.

### Coaching Points
1. Contact with the forehead
2. Keep eyes open and watch the ball
3. Use knees, back and neck to generate power

## Activity 2: Heading 1 v 1
### Focus: Heading

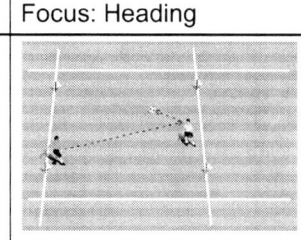

1. Area 10 x 10 yds
2. Ball per player
3. Cones
4. Training Vests
5. Coaching sticks

### Objective
In pairs, players stand 10 yards apart in an 8 yds wide goal, marked with coaching sticks. Player A throws a two handed underarm throw to Player B at head height. Player B attempts to head the ball at the goal defended by Player A. A goal counts as one point. Alternate the serve. First to 3 or 5 points wins the game.

### Coaching Points
1. Reiterate basic technique
2. Set up header using a cushion header
3. Attacking header should be headed down and in the corners

## Activity 3: Heading 1 v 1 v 1 v 1
### Focus: Heading

1. Area 10 x 10 yds
2. Ball per player
3. Cones
4. Training Vests
5. Coaching sticks

### Objective
Four players play against each other to score 5 headed goals. Place 4 coaching sticks in the corner to form a 10 x 10 yds square with 4 goals. One of the four players start with the ball (A). Player A serves to the person directly opposite (B). Player B can head for any of the 3 goals defended by players A, C and D. The play is dead if a goal is scored, the ball is saved or the ball hits the post. The next server is the player to the right of the first server (rotate around). First player to score 3 goals wins.

### Coaching Points
1. Reiterate basic technique
2. Set up header is a cushion header
3. Attacking header should be headed down and in the corners

## Activity 4: 10 Continuous Attacks
### Focus: Attacking, Defending

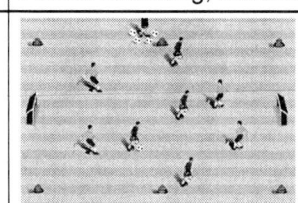

1. Area 40 x 30 yds
2. Balls
3. Cones
4. Goals
5. Training Vests

### Objective
4v4. 4 attacking players start the game on the centre line and the 4 players on the defending team are separated into two pairs - each defending one half of the field. The defending teams cannot enter into the opposing half of the field. The coach starts each attack by feeding the ball into the attackers. The 4 attackers attack one end of the field creating a 4 v 2 situation. If the defenders win the ball they must clear the ball off the field. The attackers have 10 continuous attacks to score as many goals as possible. Attacks must alternate from one end to the other (i.e. 5 attacks at each end).

### Coaching Points
1. Positive attitude towards attacking by all attackers
2. Look to go past a defender at every opportunity
3. Shoot when the opportunity presents itself

# Cooperation Games (Plus 1-2)
# Fun Activities

## Activity 1: Cooperation Games 1
Focus: Movement and team work

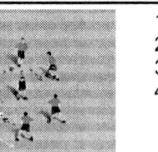

1. Area 20 x 20 yds
2. Ball per player
3. Cones
4. Training Vests

### Objective
Caterpillar Sit – split the group in two – 4-8 players in each - players are seated on the floor with their legs stretched flat out in front of them. One player behind the other, in a line similar to a train or caterpillar. Players have to move in close enough to each other so that each player can place their feet just below the hips/quadriceps of the player in front. The group has to work together to reach a target (end line). No hands are permitted to touch the floor, except the hands of the last person in the group. Add obstacles (cones) to increase difficulty. Once the players have had a chance to practice the activity, you can organize relays between the groups.

### Coaching Points
1. Encourage good technique for sprinting, catching and hopping etc
2. Add pressure by applying times and competition
3. Intersperse between skill activities

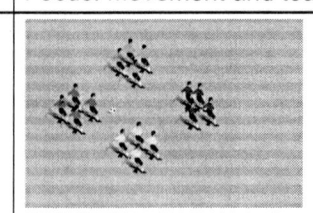

## Activity 2: Cooperation Games 2
Focus: Movement and team work

1. Area 20 x 20 yds
2. Ball per player
3. Cones
4. Training Vests

### Objective
Follow the leader juggling in pairs – 'A' starts performing one juggle – B follows. B then leads with two juggles – A follows.
No hands – see how many ways players can get the ball into the air – no hands allowed.
Around the body – juggle the ball from the right foot to right thigh to right shoulder to head to left shoulder to left thigh to left foot - all with one touch on each surface.

### Coaching Points
1. Add pressure by applying times and competition
2. Intersperse between skill activities

## Activity 3: Cooperation Games 3
Focus: Movement and team work

1. Area 20 x 20 yds
2. Ball per player
3. Cones
4. Training Vests

### Objective
Straight line passing – In pairs 5 yards apart – one ball. 'A' passes the ball from the right hand – 'B' catches with two hands and passes to A with the right hand. Change direction.
Straight line passing with feet. In pairs 5 yards apart – one ball. A passes the ball along ground using the right foot – B controls the ball and passes to A with right foot. Change direction.

### Coaching Points
1. Communicate with each other to coordinate release
2. Start slow and increase pace and intensity
3. Get a rhythm going

## Activity 4: Cooperation Games 4
Focus: Movement, Team Work

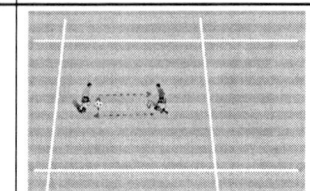

1. Area 20 x 20 yds
2. Ball per player
3. Cones
4. Training Vests

### Objective
2 ball rebound throw– players attempt to coordinate the throw so the balls rebound off each other in mid air – how many in a row? 2 ball rebound pass with feet – players attempt to coordinate the pass so the balls rebound off each other along the ground. Start 3 yards apart and increase distance. 2 ball over under throw – one player throws the ball over and the other ball is a chest pass. 2 ball over under with feet – one player chips a ball that is played along the ground.

### Coaching Points
1. Communicate with each other to coordinate release
2. Start slow and increase pace and intensity
3. Get a rhythm going

PLUS 2 COACHING FOR DEVELOPMENT

## **Plus 2 - Mid to Late Stage Activities**

| Activities | Theme | Page |
|---|---|---|
| 2 v 1 Countdown to Goal | Attacking, Defending | pg. 158 |
| 2 v 2 + 2 Support | Passing, Receiving | pg. 159 |
| 3 v 1 Exchange | Defending, Passing | pg. 160 |
| 3 v 1 Numbers Game | Attacking, Defending | pg. 161 |
| 3 v 1 to Goal | Attacking, Defending | pg. 162 |
| 3 v 3 Moving Goal | Passing, Receiving | pg. 163 |
| 3 v 3 Scrimmage | Attacking, Defending | pg. 164 |
| 3 v 3 Take On & Escape | Attacking, Creating Space | pg. 165 |
| 3 v 3 to Wide Goals | Defending | pg. 166 |
| 3 v 3 with Targets | Passing, Receiving | pg. 167 |
| 4 Box Possession | Passing, Receiving, Possession | pg. 168 |
| Attacking Heading 2 v 2 | Heading | pg. 169 |
| Back to Goal 1 v 1 | Attacking, Creating Space | pg. 170 |
| Back to Goal Series | Attacking, Creating Space | pg. 171 |
| Catch me | Defending | pg. 172 |
| Defending in Pairs | Defending | pg. 173 |
| Defending Recovery | Defending | pg. 174 |
| Escape Game with Gates | Dribbling, Creating Space | pg. 175 |
| Escape Move - Cruyff Turn | Dribbling, Creating Space | pg. 176 |
| Escape Moves - The 'V' | Dribbling, Creating Space | pg. 177 |
| Goals for Points | Shooting | pg. 178 |
| Handball with Volleys | Shooting | pg. 179 |
| Head Catch - 3 v 3 | Heading | pg. 180 |
| Heading to Goal | Heading | pg. 181 |
| Know your Number | Passing, Receiving | pg. 182 |
| Match 3 v 3 | Game | pg. 183 |

# SOCCER COACHING ACTIVITIES, SESSION PLANS AND ASSESSMENT

| | | |
|---|---|---|
| Milan Passing Game | Passing, Receiving | pg. 184 |
| Moving Net | Heading | pg. 185 |
| One up – One down | Attacking, Defending, Creating Space | pg. 186 |
| One vs All | Attacking, Defending | pg. 187 |
| Passing & Moving | Passing, Receiving | pg. 188 |
| Passing Competition | Passing, Receiving | pg. 189 |
| Poke Tackle | Defending | pg. 190 |
| Possession 2 Touch | Passing, Receiving, Possession | pg. 191 |
| Receiving Technique | Passing, Receiving | pg. 192 |
| Shoot, Save, Score | Shooting | pg. 193 |
| Shooting in Fours | Shooting | pg. 194 |
| Squares | Passing, Receiving | pg. 195 |
| Take On - Hesitation | Dribbling, Creating Space | pg. 196 |
| Take On - The Scissors | Dribbling, Creating Space | pg. 197 |
| Take On with Gates | Dribbling, Creating Space | pg. 198 |
| Target | Passing, Receiving | pg. 199 |
| Transition Attack | Attacking, Defending | pg. 200 |
| Turn or Go | Dribbling | pg. 201 |

© SOCCERPLUS ALL RIGHTS RESERVED

# 2 v 1 Countdown to Goal

**Materials Needed**

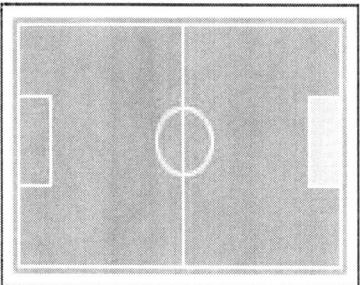

Area 25 x 35 yds
- Balls
- Cones

## 2 v 1 Countdown to Goal (Attacking)

### Description:
Balls are placed 35 yards from goal in a central position. Player A starts on a cone (next to the balls) with a ball. Player A must make a decision on which one of the two support players to pass to (B or C). The support players start on a cone 5 yds closer to the ball than player A and in line with the edge of the 6 yard box. Whichever support player receives the pass, the other player becomes a defender to create a 2v1 situation. The two attackers must combine to score. The two attackers have 8 seconds to score.

### Coaching Points
- Positive touch towards goal
- Movement to support ball carrier
- Shoot when opportunity arises

### Progressions:
Progress by increasing or decreasing the number of players.

# 2 v 2 + 2 Support

**Materials Needed**

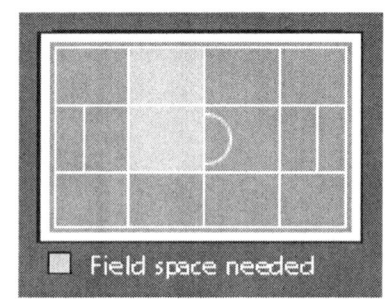

Area 20 x 30 yds
- Balls
- Cones
- Training Vests

## 2 v 2 + 2 Support (Passing, Receiving)

**Description:**
Two neutral players (play for the team in possession of the ball) at either end of the area. The ball starts with one of the neutral players. The ball is played to one of the teams plaing a 2v2 game in between the neutral players. The team in possession have to pass the ball to the other neutral player without losing possession to the other team. The two defenders must try and stop the attackers and if they win the ball they can become the attackers. Each pass to the neutral player counts as a point. The neutral player always passes back to the team that are in possession. If the ball leaves the area, a new ball is played to the other team.

**Coaching Points**
- Movement to create space
- Awareness of defenders
- Don't force the ball forward

**Progressions:**
Add conditions such as both players must touch the ball before passing to a neutral player.

# 3 v 1 Exchange

## Materials Needed

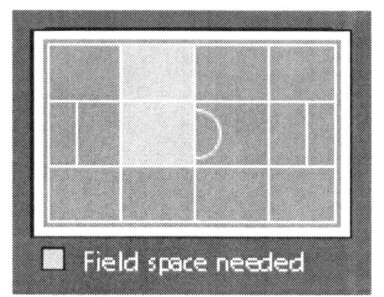

Field space needed

Area 20 x 20 yds
- Balls
- Cones
- Training Vests

## 3 v 1 Exchange (Defending, Passing)

### Description:
Two groups of 4 players. Players keep possession in their own 10 x 10 grid. On the coach's command, each team sends a defender over to break up the opposition's passing sequence. First defender to break up opponent's passing earns point for his/her team. Alternate defenders.

### Coaching Points
- Close down the space quickly
- Force a mistake and perform a poke tackle
- Don't dive into a tackle - be patient

### Progressions:
1) 4v2, 5v2.
2) Increase/decrease area size.

# 3 v 1 Numbers Game

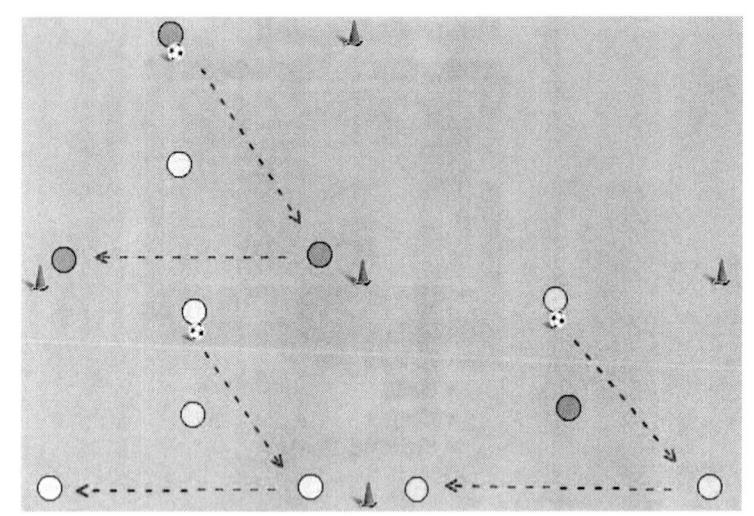

## Materials Needed

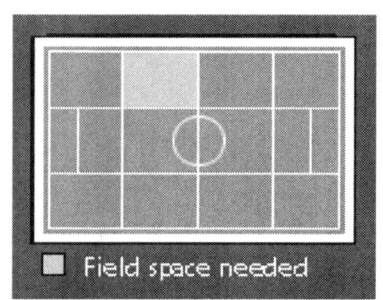

Area 20 x 20 yds
- Balls
- Cones
- Training Vests

## 3 v 1 Numbers Game (Attacking, Defending)

**Description:**
3 groups play a 3v1 game in their own 10 x 10 yds area. Number each player in the team 1-4. When their number is called they must run into the box on the right and try to steal the ball (creating a 3v1 situation). 5 passes equals a point. The first defender to win the ball scores a point for their team.

**Coaching Points**
- Maintain passing shape (Triangle)
- Keep ball moving
- Play ball away from pressure

**Progressions:**
Progress to 2 or 1 touch only.

# 3 v 1 to Goal

**Materials Needed**

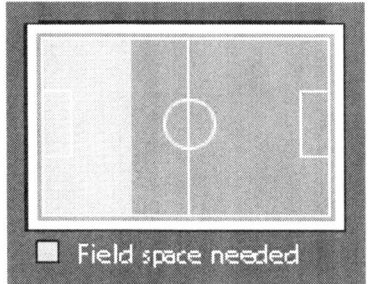

Area 25 x 40 yds
- Balls
- Training Vests
- Goal

## 3 v 1 to Goal (Attacking)

### Description:
Attacking team start 15 yds from goal. 1 defender and a goalkeeper defend the goal. The goalkeeper starts with the ball and distributes it to the attackers - who attack at goal. The objective for the attacking team is to score as many goals in 5 minutes - each attack is started by the goal keeper. Attackers must sprint back to the starting positions after each attack.

### Coaching Points
- Vary attacking runs/patterns
- Attack at speed
- Accurate shooting - follow for rebounds
- Don't allow players to be offside

### Progressions:
1) 3v2.
2) No goalkeeper (for success).

# 3 v 3 Moving Goal

**Materials Needed**

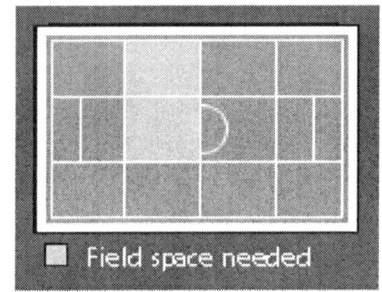

Area 30 x 30 yds
- Balls
- Cones
- Training Vests

## 3 v 3 Moving Goal (Passing, Receiving)

### Description:
2 players hold a training vest between them in one hand and at arms length to form a goal. The goal moves around the field at a walking pace. In the area, two teams of 3 players attempt to combine passes and score a goal by passing through the goal for a teammate to receive on the opposite side.

### Coaching Points
- Maintain team shape
- Awareness of moving goal
- Speed of movement to support

### Progressions:
1) Play three passes before shooting at goal.
2) Add plus players.

# 3 v 3 Scrimmage

**Materials Needed**

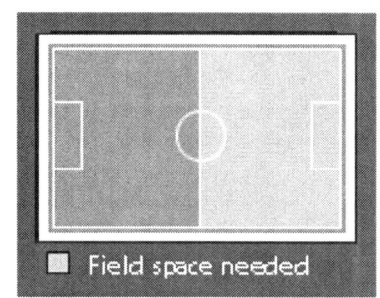

Area 40 x 25 yds
- Balls
- Cones
- Training Vests

## 3 v 3 Scrimmage (Attacking, Defending)

### Description:
Two teams - 3v3 play to 6 goals. Each team has three small goals to score in. Defending the three goals is a goalkeeper. The attacking team must try to attack the open goal before the keeper can recover.

### Coaching Points
- Maintain width and depth
- Move ball away from presssure
- Attack any spaces that open up

### Progressions:
Allow the keeper to join in to create a 4v3 situation.

# 3 v 3 Take On & Escape

**Materials Needed**

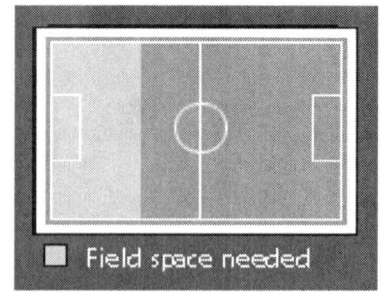

Area 25 x 35 yds
- Several balls
- Cones
- Training Vests

## 3 v 3 Take On & Escape (Attacking, Creating Space)

### Description:
Play 3v3 to begin. Teams must attempt to score points during a 5 minute game. Points are scored by performing a take on or escape move (1pt each). The attacking team can score 2pts for a goal and the defending team can score 2pts for dribbling over the coned line 35 yds from goal. Change teams after 5 minutes and repeat. The goal keeper serves the ball to the attackers to start each game.

### Coaching Points
- Approach defender at comfortable speed
- Sell the defender with take on move
- Create space using escape move

### Progressions:
Progress to a small sided game.

# 3 v 3 to Wide Goals

**Materials Needed**

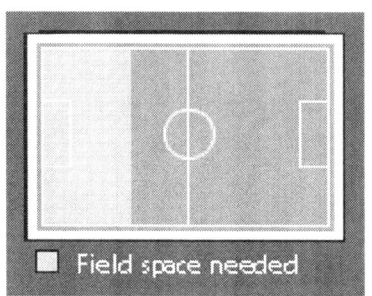

Area 30 x 30 yds
- Balls
- Cones
- Training Vests

## 3 v 3 to Wide Goals (Defending as a Unit)

### Description:
Play a scrimmage in a typical manner, but instead of one central goal, played to two wide goals.

### Coaching Points
- 1st defender provides pressure to the ball
- 2nd defender provides cover for the 1st defender
- 3rd defender provides balance, covering the 2nd defender

### Progressions:
1) Add touch restriction (two touch, one touch).
2) Add 'plus' player(s).

# 3 v 3 with Targets

**Materials Needed**

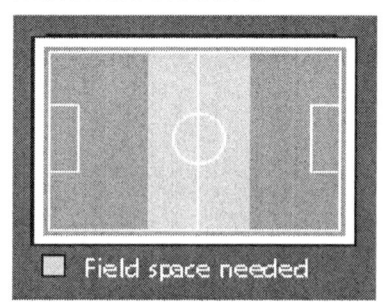

Area 40 x 20 yds
- Balls
- Cones
- Training Vests

## 3 v 3 with Targets (Passing, Receiving)

### Description:
3v3 play in the central zone 20 x 20 yds. The team with the ball attempt to possess the ball until there is an opportunity to deliver a pass to a target player. One Target Player for each team stand in a 10 x 20 yds end zone at either end of the area. Rotate target players every 3-4 minutes.

### Coaching Points
- Movement to maintain possession in middle zone
- Communication
- Awareness of open target

### Progressions:
5 passes in the middle before delivering a long driven ball to targets.

# 4 Box Possession

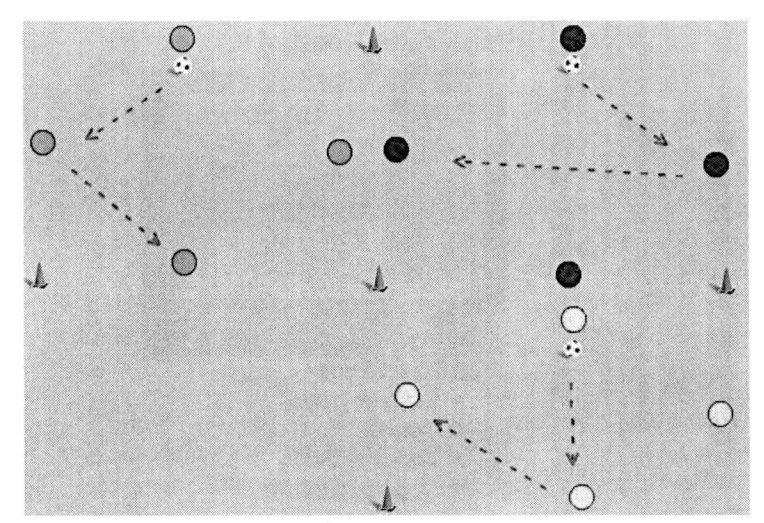

**Materials Needed**

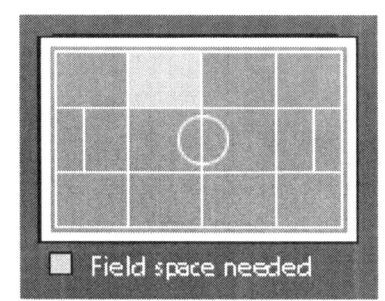

Area 20 x 20 yds
- Balls
- Cones
- Training Vests

## 4 Box Possession (Possession)

**Description:**
Three teams of four start in their own 10 x 10 yds area. Each team has a ball. The team must pass and move around their box without the ball stopping or going out of bounds. After the team has played 10 passes they move into the next box (clockwise). The first team to make it all the way around wins the game.

**Coaching Points**
- Keep ball moving at all times
- Concentrate on the quality of the pass
- Maintain shape
- Communication

**Progressions:**
Progress to 2-touch or 1-touch only.

# Attacking Heading 2 v 2

## Materials Needed

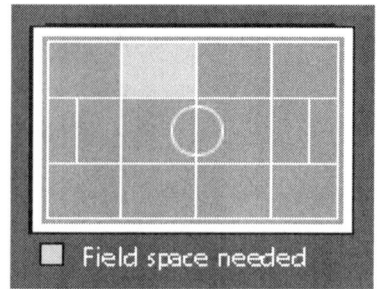

Field space needed

Area 10 x 10 yds
- Ball per player
- Cones
- Training Vests
- Coaching sticks

## Attacking Heading 2 v 2 (Heading)

### Description:
2v2. Each team defends a goal (either coaching sticks or a large mini goal). Standing on the goal line, one player throws a two handed underarm throw to his/her partner who heads the ball in the air to set up an attacking header by the partner. The attacking player attempts to score past one goal keeper in a goal opposite. Cones are placed along the center of the square to represent the border line between both teams. Keep changing positions – first to five wins.

### Coaching Points
- Balanced position for heading - arms out
- Attack the ball using forward momentum for power
- Contact ball with forehead aiming low at the Goalkeeper's feet

### Progressions:

# Back to Goal 1 v 1

## Back to Goal 1 v 1 (Attacking, Creating Space)

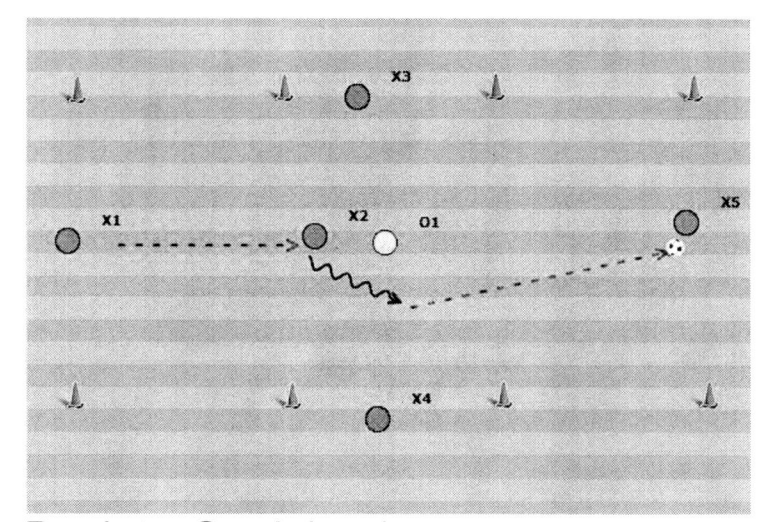

**Materials Needed**

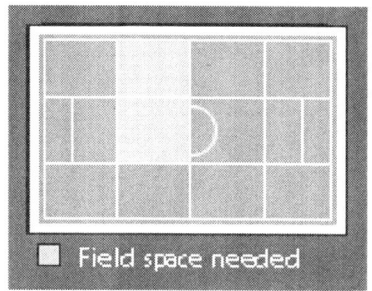

Area 30 x 20 yds
- Balls
- Cones

### Description:
Six players - 1 server (X1), 1 attacker (X2), 1 defender (O1), 2 support (X3 & X4) and 1 target (X5). X1 plays a firm pass to X2. Using a back to goal move, X2 attempts to play ball to X5. X3 and X4 can be used for support. Five attempts and rotate.

### Coaching Points
- Receive sideways on to create distance from defender
- Use body contact with defender to create separation
- Check away from the defender by accelerating towards the ball

### Progressions:
Forward players spend a high percentage of their play with back to goal - usually with a defender or two breathing down on them. Back to goal play is a true art and needs to be learned by many repetitions in practice. Forwards proficient in back to goal play seem to create separation with ease to create time and space - ofton this requires timing and body contact.

# Back to Goal Series

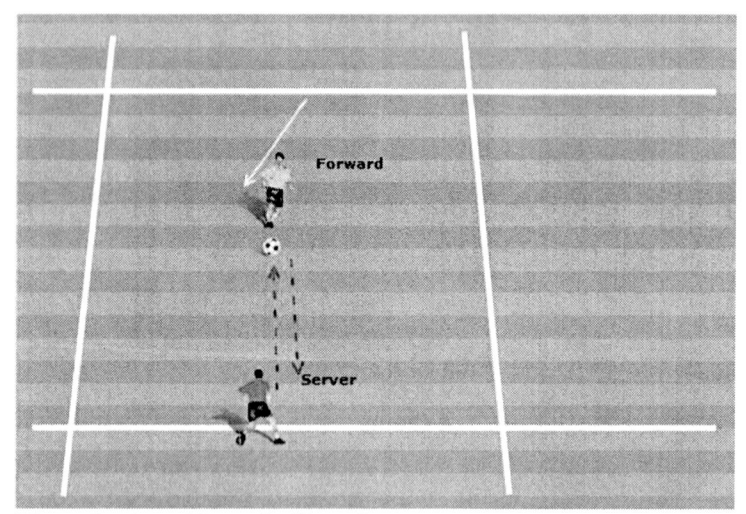

**Materials Needed**

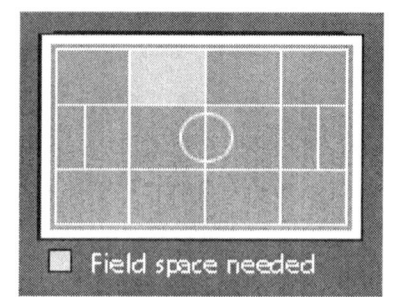

Area 10 x 10 yds
- Balls
- Cones

## Back to Goal Series (Attacking, Creating Space)

### Description:
Two players face each other 10 yards apart. The server initiates all movements by playing a firm pass along the ground to the forward. The forward player has to turn and attack the line behind him/her. Start without a defender and then add a defender into the activity starting behind the forward. There are 5 moves for the forward when receiving the ball - 1) Turn, 2) Self pass (receiving touch plays the ball towards the server approx 5 yards and then a quick turn), 3) Check towards the server at an angle and turn, 4) Check and let the ball run through the legs (dummy) and turn, 5) Check, hesitate (to initate contact with the defender and check to the ball again. 5-10 attempts each and switch.

### Coaching Points
- Receive the ball sideways to create distance from the defender
- Use body contact with defender to create separation
- When checking to the ball accelerate

### Progressions:
Forward players spend a high percentage of their play with back to goal - usually with a defender or two breathing down on them. Back to goal play is a true art and needs to be learned in practice sessions. Forwards proficient in back to goal play seem to create separation with ease to create time and space. This proficiency requires timing and body contact.

# Catch me

**Materials Needed**

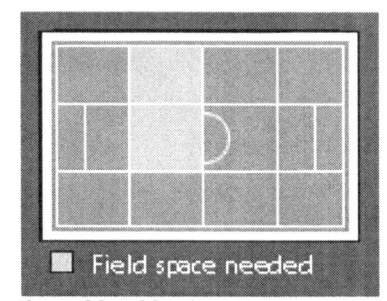

Area 20 x 20 yds
- Balls
- Cones
- Training Vests

## Catch me (Defending)

**Description:**
Players in pairs - 1 attacker and 1 defender. Attacker dribbles the ball in the area and the defender gives chase. When the coach shouts "FREEZE" the defender must try to touch the attacker - if they can they score 1pt. If attacker is out of reach the attacker scores a point. Switch roles.

**Coaching Points**
- Keep pressure on the ball and attacker
- React quickly to a change in direction

**Progressions:**
Progress to a game of knock out.

# Defending in Pairs

**Materials Needed**

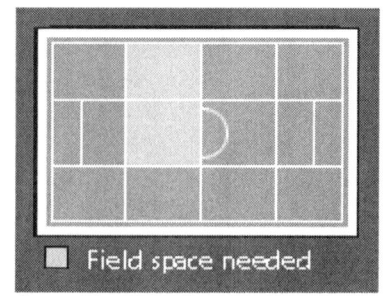

Area 10 x 10 yds
- Ball per player
- Cones
- Training Vests

## Defending in Pairs (Defending)

**Description:**
In a 10 x 10 yds area, two attackers (X1 & X2) stand opposite two defenders (O1 & O2). The attackers pass the ball back and forth on a 3-touch rhythm. On the 3rd pass, the defender opposite the receiver applies pressure and the 2nd defender provides cover - game is now live and the attackers attempt to get to the end line. Defenders try to win possession and attack the attackers end line.

**Coaching Points**
- Communicate with your defensive partner
- Decide support or cover
- Patience
- Slow the attack and force play back
- Force a mistake
- Balanced on the balls-of-feet

**Progressions:**

As the ball is played between the attackers the defenders should move forward and back to apply pressure and cover.

# Defending Recovery

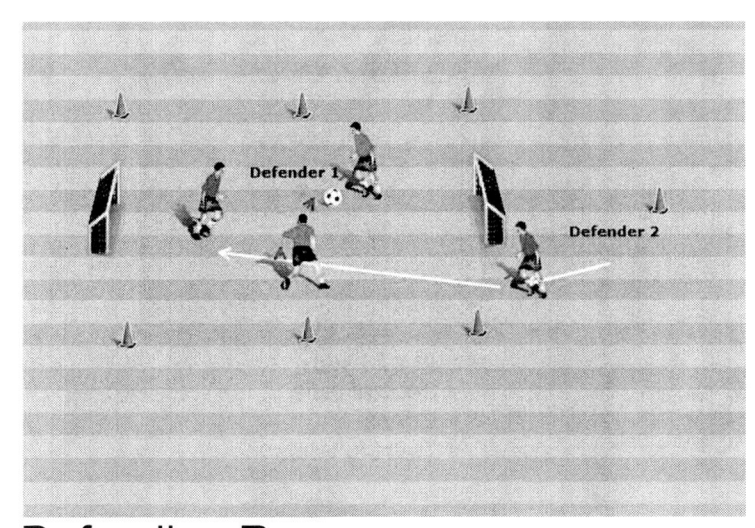

## Materials Needed

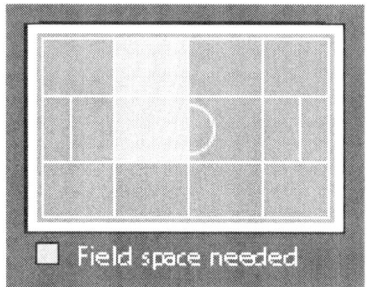

Area 20 x 10 yds
- Ball per player
- Cones
- Training Vests
- Goals

## Defending Recovery (Defending)

**Description:**
Play 2 attackers v 2 defenders - One goal at the defensive end and one at the attacking end of the area. From the defensive end of the field 1 defender passes the ball firmly along the ground to 1 of the 2 attackers standing in the opposite corners. On receipt, the attackers attack the defender and attempt to score. The recovery defender sprints to help.

**Coaching Points**
- Communicate with your defensive partner
- Decide support or cover
- Patience
- Slow the attack and force play back
- Force a mistake
- Balance on the balls-of-feet

**Progressions:**

The recovering player sprints into a goal side position and then provides pressure, support or cover (the first objective must be to get back quickly to a central position to protect the goal). If the defenders win the ball, they can coorc. 8 players to an area – 4 defenders and 4 attackers - next two defenders and two attackers start when ball leaves the area or a goal is scored.

# Escape Game with Gates

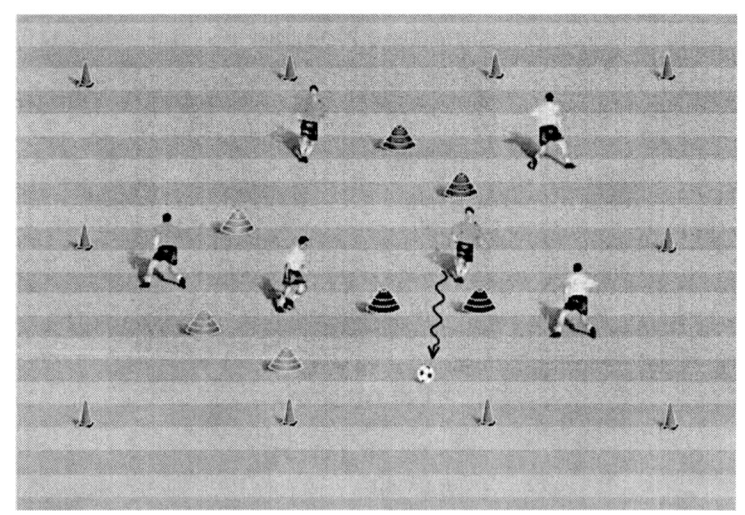

**Materials Needed**

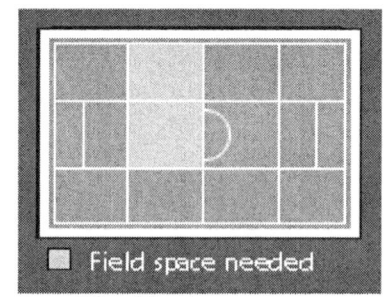

Area 30 x 20 yds
- Several balls
- Cones
- Training Vests

## Escape Game with Gates (Dribbling, Creating Space)

**Description:**
Two teams of players 3v3 to 5v5 attempt to score points by dribbling through gates (cones 2 yards apart). 1 point for going through a gate and 2pts for an escape move.

**Coaching Points**
- Encourage players to try and try again
- Be aware of the space - 360° vision
- Add points for an escape move

**Progressions:**
The freedom to experiment and practice 'escape' skills against an opponent is critical to their development. The more proficient a player becomes in dribbling and creating space as a young player, the more confident they will become in a game situation and the more likely they are to perform the skill. Repetition is very important, but ensuring the technique is correct (the players are able to 'sell' the opponent and escape) to essential. This activity is a good warm-up with the ball. In this activity, players must be encouraged to practice escape moves - additional points should be awarded for escape moves. Progress from the escape activities (sole drag, 'V' and step over) into a 3v3. Increase the size of the area, number of players and the number of gates once players perform 3v3 well.

# Escape Move - Cruyff Turn

## Materials Needed

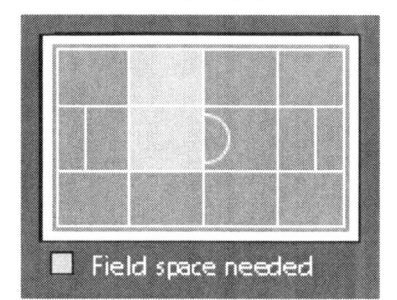

Field space needed

Area 30 x 20 yds
- Ball per player
- Cones

## Escape Move - Cruyff Turn (Dribbling, Creating Space)

### Description:
One ball per player in an open grid to begin. Isolate the skill by performing on-the-spot. The Cruyff Turn is performed by faking to kick/or dribble the ball in one direction and then playing the ball between the legs. Using the toe end of the shoe, the ball is flicked through the legs and the attacker pivots on the other leg to the outside. Accelerate away with pace. Progress to 1) performing the skill on the move, 2) 1v1 passive defending, 3) 1v1 active defending 4) Game with gates, 5) Small sided game.

### Coaching Points
- Start in stationary position - not a dribble
- Fake to pass and quick turn
- Accelerate away leaving defender behind

### Progressions:
The freedom to experiment and practice 'escape' skills against an opponent is critical to their development. The more proficient a player becomes in dribbling and creating space as a young player, the more confident they will become in a game situation and the more likely they are to perform the skill. Repetition is very important, but ensuring the technique is correct (the players are able to 'sell' the opponent and escape) to essential. This activity is a good warm-up with the ball. To emphasize the skill in a small sided game award points/goals to a player who escapes a defender.

# Escape Moves - The 'V'

**Materials Needed**

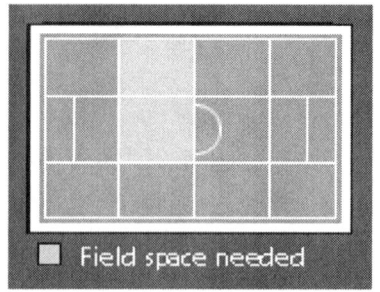

Field space needed

Area 30 x 20 yds
- Ball per player
- Cones

## Escape Moves - The 'V' (Dribbling, Creating Space)

### Description:
One ball per player in an open grid to begin. Isolate the skill by performing on-the-spot. The 'V' is performed by dragging the ball away from a defender with the sole of the foot (back towards the attacker) and then pushing the ball forward past the defender on the other side. The movement pattern 'draws' a V in the grass. Progress to: 1) Performing the skill on the move, 2) 1v1 passive defending, 3) 1v1 active defending 4) Game with gates, 5) Small sided game.

### Coaching Points
- Start in stationary position - not a dribble
- Quick transfer of the ball from one foot to the other
- Accelerate away leaving defender behind

### Progressions:
The freedom to experiment and practice 'escape' skills against an opponent is critical to their development. The more proficient a player becomes in dribbling and creating space as a young player, the more confident they will become in a game situation and the more likely they are to perform the skill. Repetition is very important, but ensuring the technique is correct is essential (the players are able to 'sell' the opponent and escape). This activity is a good warm-up with the ball. The starting point will depend on the players proficiency - the skill can be progressed from performing on one spot, to a small sided game. To emphasize the skill in a small sided game award points/goals to a player who escapes a defender.

# Goals for Points

**Materials Needed**

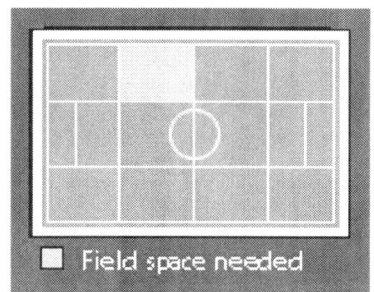

Area 25 x 25 yds
- Ball per player
- Cones
- Training Vests
- Goal

## Goals for Points (Shooting, creating space, passing)

**Description:**
Players are separated into teams of two or three players, with a goal keeper. Two games can occur simultaneously on two different areas. Whichever team brings (passes or dribbles) the ball into the penalty box can score. The other teams must win possession and reset the game by taking the ball outside. Points are scored in the following way – 3pts for a long range shot (coach decides on the distance), 2pts for an inside shot, and 2pts for a header. However, to convert the points, the scorer must convert a penalty.

**Coaching Points**
- Provide a good angle for support
- Take every goal scoring opportunity
- Be alive in front of goal for 'poacher' finishing

**Progressions:**
Add a rebound only zone – 3-6 yards from goal – only rounds from saves or posts can be scored – 2pts.

# Handball with Volleys

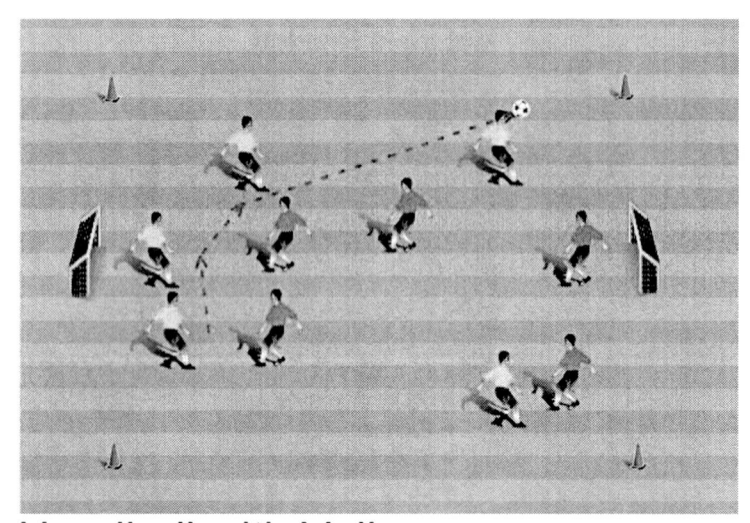

**Materials Needed**

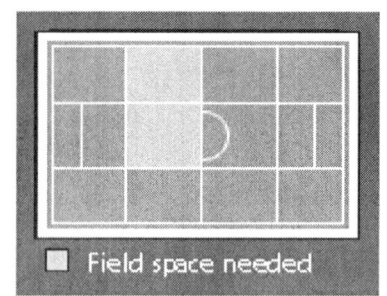

Area 30 x 20 yds
- Ball per player
- Cones
- Training Vests
- Goals - full

## Handball with Volleys (Shooting)

### Description:
Two teams of 5 players and 2 plus players playing for the team in possession. The ball is passed with the hands and the attacker is only allowed 3 steps with ball. Score one point by scoring a volley or half volley. First to 5 points wins.

### Coaching Points
- Find space - stretch the distance the defender needs to cover
- Strike volley and half volley with laces
- Attacking - creating space and keeping possession
- Defending - goal side, zone and man for man defense

### Progressions:
1) If a team can accomplish a head-head-head combination they win the game.
2) Add two large goals with goal keepers - teams attempt to finish a move with a headed goal.
3) See 'Transition' game and instead of using feet, players use their head.
Note: to get more goal mouth action reduce the size of the area.

# Head Catch - 3 v 3

**Materials Needed**

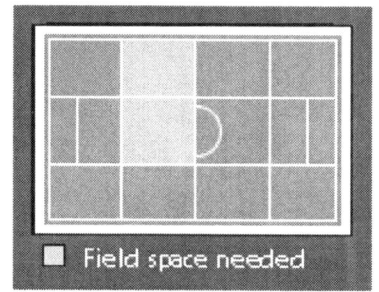

Area 30 x 20 yds
- Ball per player
- Cones
- Training Vests
- Goals - mini

## Head Catch - 3 v 3 (Warm-up, Heading and Movement Skills)

### Description:
The area is split into two with cones down the center. In one half, play 3v1 – the 3 attacking players have the ball and attempt for a head-catch-head-catch-head-catch combination to win 1 point. If the ball hits the ground or the defender wins the ball, possession transfers to the other half – one attacker enters the other half and defends.

### Coaching Points
- Find space - stretch the distance the defender needs to cover
- Introduce different headers - glance, flick, power, cushion etc
- Open the body to provide direction to the headers

### Progressions:
If a team can accomplish a head-head-head combination they win the game. Add goals in the corners – after a throw-head-catch combination a team can score – in all 4 goals or just 2.

# Heading to Goal

**Materials Needed**

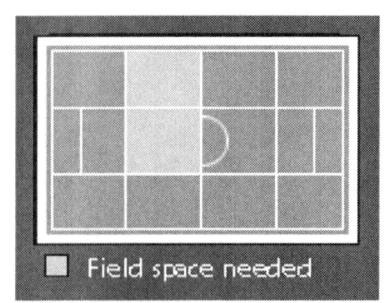

Balls
- Cones
- Training Vest
- 10x10

## Heading to Goal (Heading)

**Description:**
This is an excellent fun competition. Two teams stand either side of the goal about 8 yards away. The coach acts as the server who starts by serving into the Greens to head at goal. After the header they must replace the keeper and the coach serves to the other team.

**Coaching Points**
- Keep eyes on the ball
- Make contact with forehead
- Head down towards the ground

**Progressions:**
This is a fun game that builds confidence in heading

# Know your Number

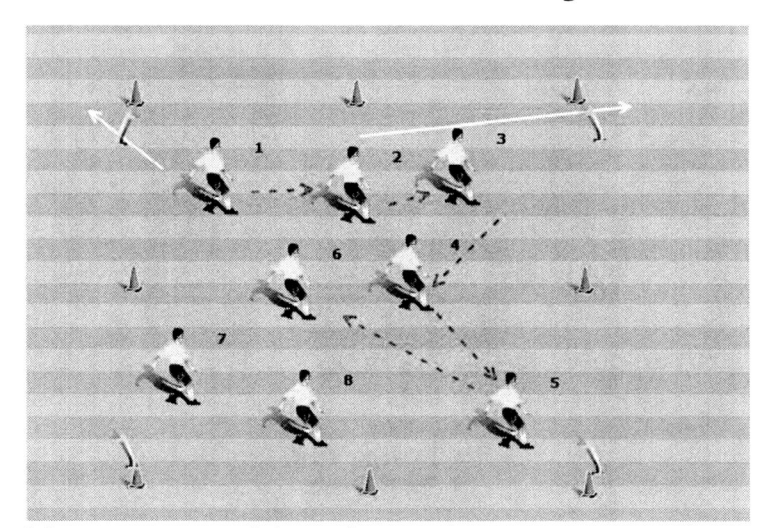

**Materials Needed**

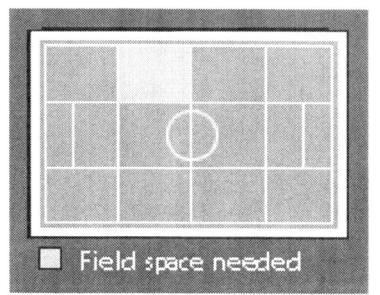

Field space needed

Area 30 x 30 yds
- Balls 2-3
- Cones
- Speed equipment

## Know your Number (Passing, Receiving)

**Description:**
Give every player a number. In the area the players pass the ball to each other 1 to 2, 2 to 3, 3 to 4 etc. The last numbered player plays back to 1. Once the ball has passed through the team once or twice, instruct the players to jog to a corner of the square, jump over the hurdle (or around a cone) and return to receive the next pass.

**Coaching Points**
- Communicate to your team mate
- Work hard to get in a good receiving position
- Firm and accurate passing – keep the tempo

**Progressions:**
Progressions for this activity are endless – a few include 1) Add in more than one ball, 2) Players sprint to the corner and jog back, 3) Before receiving the ball the player performs a move and then calls for the ball, 4) On receipt, the player dribbles into a space before passing, 5) One touch, 6) On receipt the player turns, 7) To receive the ball the player has to be in front of the ball 8) Ball is thrown in the air – must not bounce etc.

# Match 3 v 3

**Materials Needed**

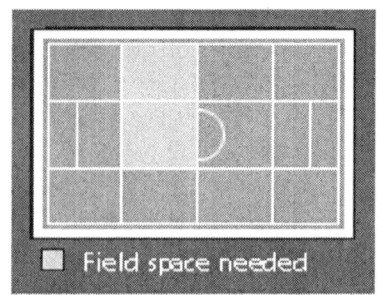

Area 30 x 15 yds
- Balls
- Cones
- Training Vests
- Small Goals

## Match 3 v 3 (Game)

### Description:
A small sided game 3v3 is a good way to finish a practice session. Use the opportunity to emphasize the theme of the session - award points for a particular move in addition to scoring a goal. Let the players play with little or no coaching - 15-20 minutes at the end of the session.

### Coaching Points
- Little or no coaching
- Encourage players to try skills practiced during the session

### Progressions:
The final activity of most practice sessions should focus on the theme of the session. Conditions can be added by the coach to emphasize the theme. For example, the coach can award a point (goal) if a player performs a turn learned during the session. Other conditions/progressions include: 1 or 2 touches, 1 touch finish, All players must touch the ball before scoring, Add a plus player (an extra player for the team in possession of the ball), 3 goals - one scored with the right foot, one with the left foot and one with the head (or any surface).

# Milan Passing Game

## Materials Needed

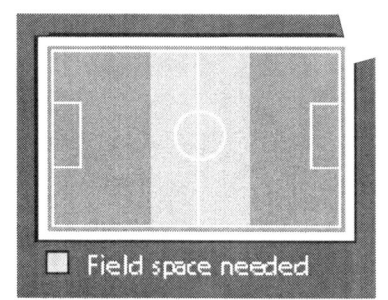

Area 15 x 15 yds
- Balls
- Cones
- Training Vests

## Milan Passing Game (Passing)

### Description:
Create a circle (or use center circle) and position 5-6 players on the edge of the circle. The perimeter players are restricted to moving between the perimeter cones. 1 receiver and 3 defenders are inside the circle. The goal is for the 7 players to retain possession of the ball and achieve 10 consecutive passes. If the defenders win the ball they must try and keep the ball away from the center player. When defenders complete 5 passes, they earn a point. Alternate defenders.

### Coaching Points
- Accurate passing
- Awareness of space, teammates, defenders
- Communication with teammates
- First touch when receiving

### Progressions:
1) 2-touch only, 1-touch only.
2) Increase or decrease the number of defenders.

# Moving Net

**Materials Needed**

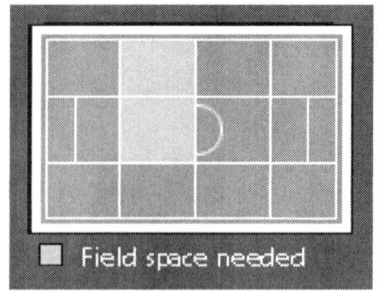

Area 30 x 15 yds
- Ball per player
- Cones
- Training Vests

## Moving Net (Heading)

**Description:**
At each end of the 30 yds grid is a 3 yds end zone stretching the width of 15 yds. To begin the game, players stand either side of an imaginary net the height of the coach. The purpose of the game is to move the net into the opposition half and score points into their end zone. Coach starts the game by serving the ball up for team A to head.

**Coaching Points**
- Use legs to generate power
- Explode into the ball for power and distance
- Use arms to develop momentum and protect face
- Communicate - call a name

**Progressions:**
One player from team A heads high and as long as they can into the oppositions half. If the ball clears the height of the net, team B must attempt to head the ball back over the net within 3 touches (headers). If the ball bounces, the coach moves the net to the point of impact with the ground and the teams shift. If the ball bounces in the end zone, the team wins a point and if the ball does not clear the net, the net moves to the point of the last header. Set the exercise up twice if you have more than 5v5 !

# One up – One down

**Materials Needed**

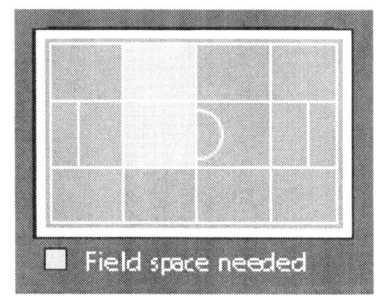

Area 40 x 20 yds
- Ball per player
- Cones
- Training Vests
- Goals

## One up – One down (Attacking, defending, creating space)

### Description:
3v3 – 5v5 – two teams compete as in a normal game. However, each player is matched with a player from the other team and if a goal is scored, the partner of the goal scorer must complete a lap of the field before reentering the game. During this time, the game progresses with uneven teams – if the same team scores before the first player arrives, the first player has to complete another lap, and the second player also completes a lap. Players learn to create attacking and defending strategies for when they have superior and inferior numbers.

### Coaching Points
- Attacking with superior numbers – quick movement
- Defending with inferior numbers – consolidate around the goal (zonal)
- Communicate effectively with teammates

### Progressions:
Add conditions such as one touch finish and two touches everywhere else.

# One vs All

## Materials Needed

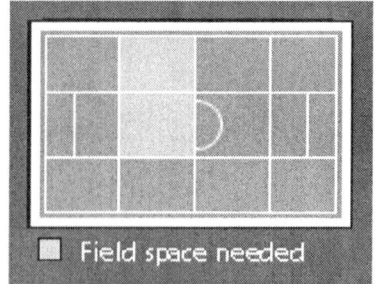

Area 20 x 10 yds
- Ball per player
- Cones
- Training Vests
- Goals
- Clip board

## One vs All (Attacking, defending)

### Description:
Players play together in small teams of 1v1 to 3v3. Games are 2 minutes in length. Although the teams play against each other, the scoring is recorded by indvidual player. Start by writing the names of all the players on a piece of paper and assign each player a number. 2v2 format: The first game players get into pairs – After 2 minutes bring the pairs back to one location to report the scores. Subsequent games the coach should ensure players are with different partners.

### Coaching Points
- Keep the games high tempo
- Quick re-starts (kick in or throws)
- Provide angles for attacking and defensive support

### Progressions:

Call out the players number and the players respond with a point total (2 pts for a win, 1pt –tie, 0pts – loss & if the theme is attacking award 1pt per goal or if defending, deduct one pt per goal) – i.e. #1 – 2pts, #2 – 3pts etc - this should be quick fire responses. Instruct the players to pair with a partner they have not played with – each game they have to partner with a different player. Repeat the play-report-play-report sequence. Don't stop the games to coach – make points between games. This is a great game for fitness – particularly 1v1.

# Passing & Moving

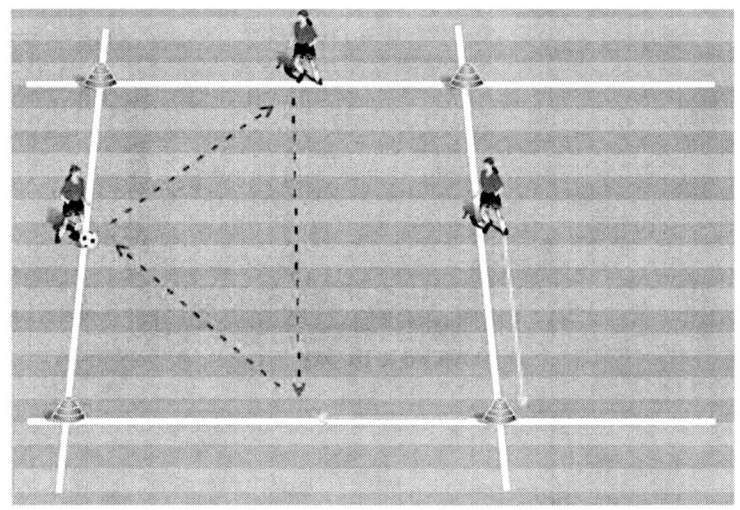

**Materials Needed**

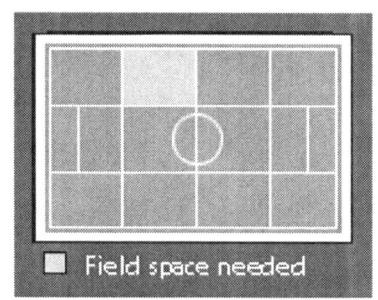

Area 20 x 20 yds
- Balls
- Cones

## Passing & Moving (Passing, Receiving)

**Description:**
3 players (A, B & C) must remain on the perimeter of a 10 x 10 yds square. The player can only move along the lines between the cones. Player A passes to either B or C. The receiving player must take 2 touches to control and pass the ball. Once the ball is passed, the 2 other players should support the receiver by creating an angle of support - a triangle.

**Coaching Points**
- Quick footwork to move around the square in support
- Alertness and understanding of supporting angles
- Move laterally keeping the body open to receive a pass
- Passing into the feet of the receiver
- Receiving touch should set up the next pass
- Communicate between the players

**Progressions:**
Add a defender to create a 3 attackers v 1 defender scenario

# Passing Competition

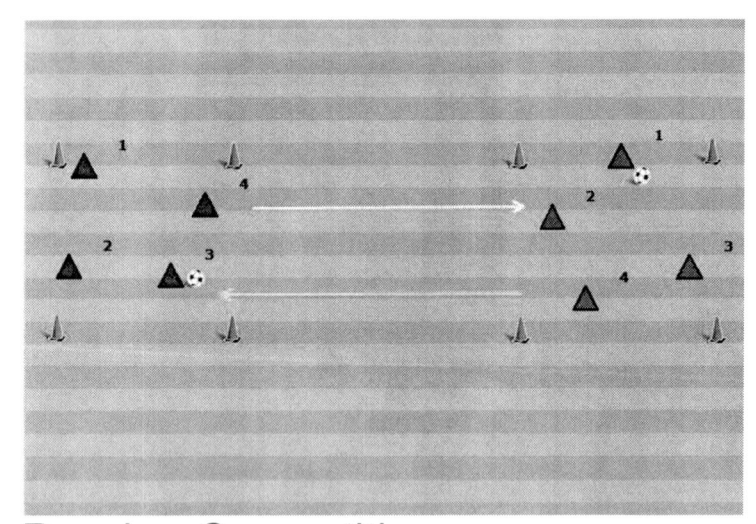

**Materials Needed**

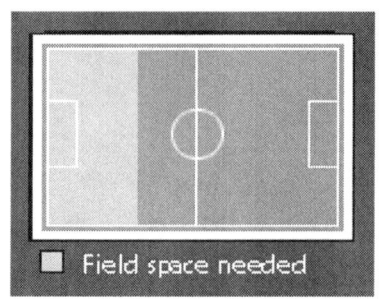

Area 30 x 10 yds
- Balls
- Cones

## Passing Competition (Passing, Receiving)

### Description:
2 Teams of four are each in a 10 x 10 yds square - 10 yds between the sqaures. Each team player is numbered 1-4. Both teams have a ball and start to pass and move. The coach shouts a number and that player becomes a defender. The defender sprints to the other square to create a 3v1 situation. The first team to make 6 consecutive passes get 1pt - the first team to 5 points wins.

### Coaching Points
- Movement off the ball to provide support
- Receive the ball in the direction of the next pass
- Accuracy and pace on the ball
- Communication
- Defender - close down quickly

### Progressions:
The defender can gain an extra point if they win possession from the 3 attackers.

# Poke Tackle

**Materials Needed**

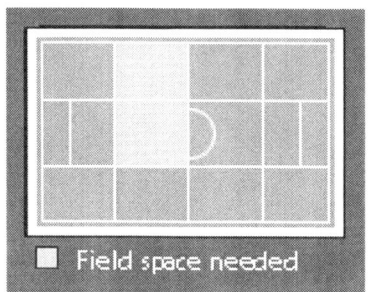

Area 20 x 20 yds
- Balls
- Cones

## Poke Tackle (Defending)

**Description:**
A poke tackle is used when an opponent loses possession of the ball - the defender makes a lunge with either foot to knock the ball away from the attacker. Players have a ball each and dribble around the area. On the coach's command the players react to the instruction. When the coach calls "STAGGER" the defender gets into a staggered position. "SWITCH" - the defender spins to face the other direction. "CHANGE" - change balls with another player. "POKE" poke the ball away from another player.

**Coaching Points**
- Get body side on into staggered position
- Keep low
- Poke the ball away with closest foot

**Progressions:**
Play until the last player is in the area with a ball.

# Possession 2 Touch

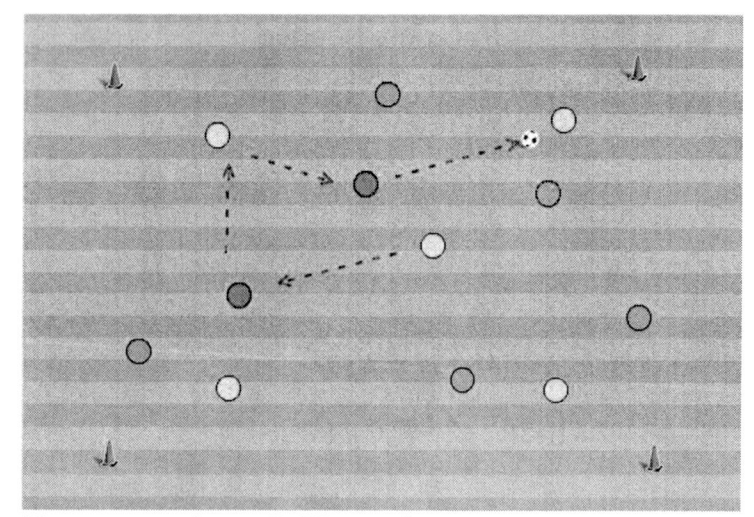

## Materials Needed

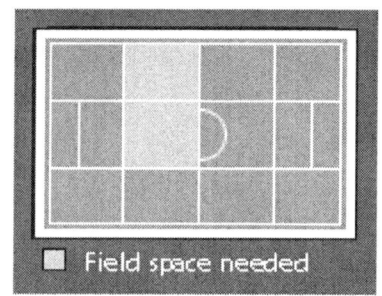

Area 40 x 30 yds
- Balls
- Cones
- Training Vests

## Possession 2 Touch (Passing, receiving, possession)

### Description:
3v3 up to 7v7 + two neutral players playing for the team in possession. First team to 25 total passes wins the game. Restrict to 2 touches only.

### Coaching Points
- 1st touch must create space and time
- Supporting players must provide good angles
- Think ahead - what options are available on receipt of the ball

### Progressions:
This is a non-directional possession game - there are no goals or targets to aim for. This exercise will allow the coach to emphasize decision making, support play, thinking clearly under pressure against opponents and with limited touches. If the coach wants to emphasize the importance of quick restarts from free kicks, the game can be stopped from time to time and the coach can award possession to one team or another. Get to the ball quickly and look for the open player.

# Receiving Technique

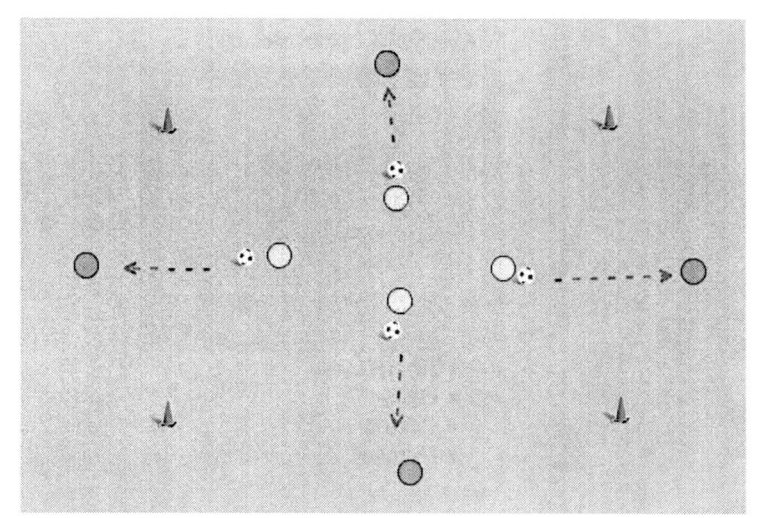

**Materials Needed**

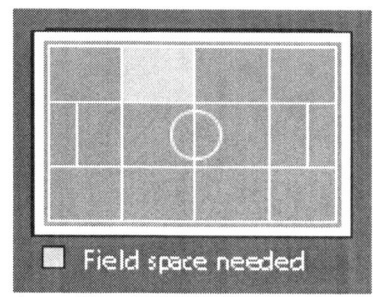

Area 20 x 20 yds
- Balls
- Cones
- Training Vests

## Receiving Technique (Passing, Receiving)

**Description:**
Split players into two groups. 5 players start in the middle of the area with a ball each and 5 on the outside of the area without a ball. Players in the middle dribble to an open player on the outside and when approximately 5 yds apart, the dribbling player passes the ball to the perimeter player. The perimeter player plays the ball back to the dribbling player who then repeats with another open player.

**Coaching Points**
- Be on your toes ready to receive
- Present the receiving surface to the ball
- Cushion ball on first touch and keep ball in front of body
- Open up body to the field to receive

**Progressions:**
Add a competition to see who can go to 5 different perimeter players first. Progress to: The perimeter player plays the ball first touch out of their feet into the middle and dribbles towards another perimeter player.

# Shoot, Save, Score

**Materials Needed**

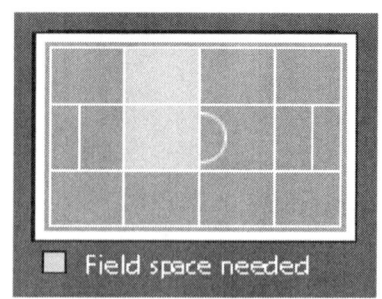

Area 20 x 30 yds
- Balls
- Cones
- Pinnies

## Shoot, Save, Score (Shooting)

**Description:**
Each team has 3 players - 2 attackers and 1 goalkeeper. Players are allowed to use their hands in the defensive zone. 1 point awarded for a shot, 3 points for a shot on target, 5 points for a goal, 1 point for a save. First team to 21 wins.

**Coaching Points**
- Try to shoot at every opportunity
- Shoot low and away from the keeper
- Follow up on rebounds

**Progressions:**
Increase or decrease the number of players.

# Shooting in Fours

**Materials Needed**

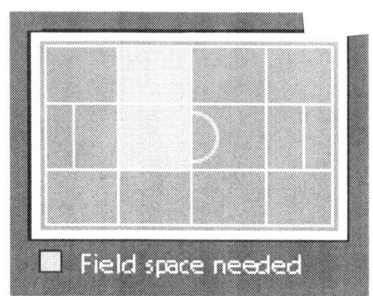

Area 20 x 20 yds
- Balls
- Cones

## Shooting in Fours (Shooting)

**Description:**
4 players work in a group. 1 keeper, two strikers and 1 server. The server plays a ball to Striker 1 who takes a touch before shooting. The server then repeats with Striker 2. Rotate players every 2-3 minutes.

**Coaching Points**
- 1st touch out of your feet
- Lock you ankle
- Strike ball with laces

**Progressions:**
1) Server throws the ball in for a volley or half volley.
2) Attackers have 1 touch to score.

# Squares

**Materials Needed**

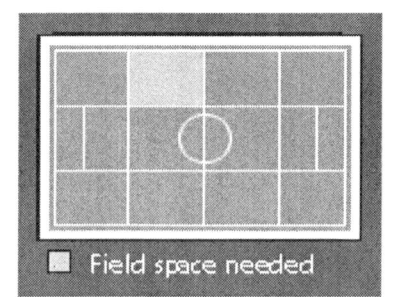

Area 15 x 15 yds
- Ball per player
- Cones

## Squares (Passing, Receiving)

**Description:**
All players stand inside a square marked with cones. One ball only required per game. Trying to keep the ball on the ground and using the inside or outside of the foot only, the players attempt to eliminate each other until one player remains. The ball is passed around one touch as the coach introduces rules: 1) One touch or you are out. 2) If you kick the ball out of the square (last touch) – out! 3) If you could have stopped the ball from leaving the square – out! 4) If you are 'nutmegged' through the legs – out! 5) If you play the ball in the air and it is caught – out! 6) If you attempt to catch the ball but drop it – out!

**Coaching Points**
- Ball on the ground
- Quick play
- No arguments – one adjudicator

**Progressions:**
Eliminated players can form another square – when eliminated from one square join the others – play for 5 minutes (person who changes squares the least wins the game).

# Take On - Hesitation

**Materials Needed**

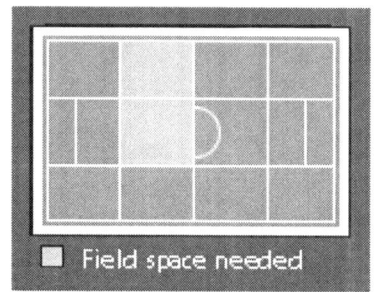

Area 30 x 20 yds
- Ball per player
- Cones

## Take On - Hesitation (Dribbling, Creating Space)

**Description:**
One ball per player in an open grid to begin. Isolate the skill by performing on-the-spot. The hesitation move requires the attacker to momentarily pause in the dribble causing the defender to either overrun or stop. The attacker can then accelerate away. Progress to 1) performing the skill on the move, 2) 1v1 passive defending, 3) 1v1 active defending 4) Game with gates & 5) Small sided game.

**Coaching Points**
- Determine a speed of approach that works for each individual
- Realistic movement to unbalance the defender
- Accelerate away leaving defender behind

**Progressions:**
The freedom to experiment and practice 'take on' skills against an opponent is critical to their development. The more proficient a player becomes in dribbling and creating space as a young player, the more confident they will become in a game situation and the more likely they are to perform the skill. Repetition is very important, but ensuring the technique is correct is essential (the players are able to 'sell' the opponent and escape). This activity is a good warm-up with the ball. The starting point will depend on the players proficiency - the skill can be progressed from performing on one spot, to a small sided game. To emphasize the skill in a small sided game award points/goals to a player who takes on a defender.

# Take On - The Scissors

**Materials Needed**

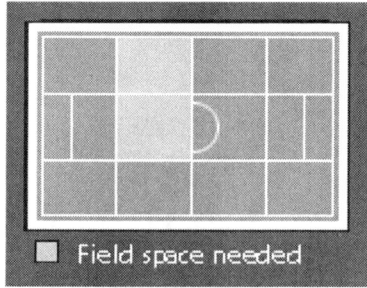

Area 30 x 20 yds
- Ball per player
- Cones

## Take On - The Scissors (Dribbling, Creating Space)

### Description:
One ball per player in an open grid to begin. Isolate the skill by performing on-the-spot. The Scissors move normally starts with a slow approach towards the defender. The attacker then unbalances and creates uncertainty for the defender by kicking over the ball with left and right foot (The move can be multiple scissors). The attacker should also move their body in the direction of the scissors to add to the uncertainty. Once the defender is flat-footed, the attacker can then accelerate away. Progress to 1) Performing the skill on the move, 2) 1v1 passive defending, 3) 1v1 active defending 4) Game with gates 5) Small sided game.

### Coaching Points
- Determine a speed of approach that works for each individual
- Realistic movement to unbalance the defender
- Accelerate away leaving defender behind

### Progressions:
The freedom to experiment and practice 'take on' skills against an opponent is critical to their development. The more proficient a player becomes in dribbling and creating space as a young player, the more confident they will become in a game situation and the more likely they are to perform the skill. Repetition is very important, but ensuring the technique is correct is essential(the players are able to 'sell' the opponent and escape). This activity is a good warm-up with the ball. The starting point will depend on the players proficiency - the skill can be progressed from performing on one spot, to a small sided game. To emphasize the skill in a small sided game award points/goals to a player who takes on a defender.

# Take On with Gates

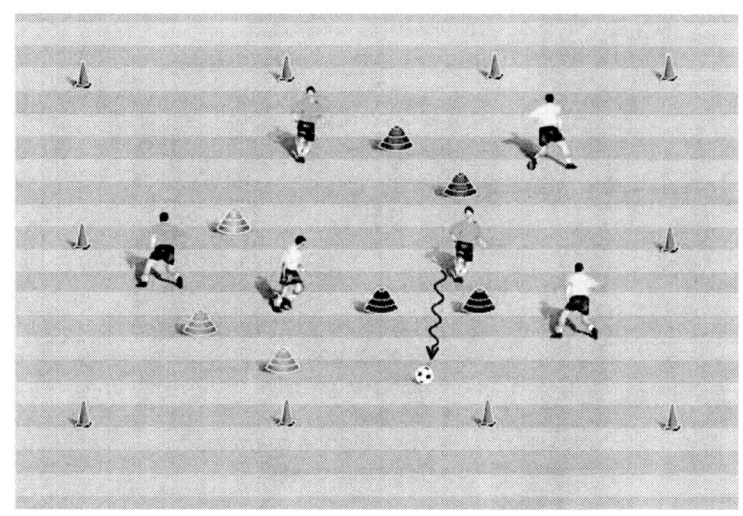

**Materials Needed**

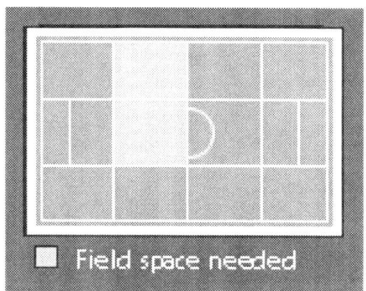

Area 30 x 20 yds
- Several balls
- Cones
- Training Vests

## Take On with Gates (Dribbling, Creating Space)

**Description:**
Two teams of players (3v3 to 5v5) attempt to score points by dribbling through gates (cones 2 yards apart). 1 point for going through a gate and 2pts for a take on move.

**Coaching Points**
- Encourage players to try and try again
- Be aware of the space - 360° vision
- Add points for a take on move

**Progressions:**
The freedom to experiment and practice take on skills against an opponent is critical to their development. The more proficient a player becomes in dribbling and creating space as a young player, the more confident they will become in a game situation and the more likely they are to perform the skill. Repetition is very important, but ensuring the technique is correct is essential (the players are able to 'sell' the opponent and escape). This activity is a good warm-up with the ball. In this activity, players must be encouraged to practice take on moves - additional points should be awarded for take on moves. Progress from the take on activities (scissors, the lunge etc) into a 3v3. Increase the size of the area, number of players and the number of gates once players perform 3v3 well.

# Target

## Materials Needed

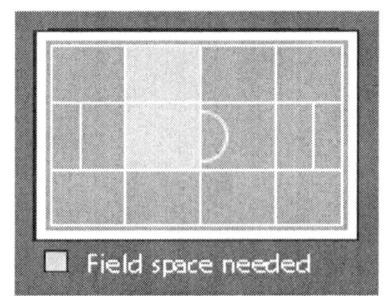

Area 30 x 20 yds
- Ball per player
- Cones
- Hula Hoops or cones
- Training Vests

## Target (Passing, Receiving)

### Description:
Each team has 3 players - Play 2v2 and nominate one target player for each team. First team to score five points wins. Two hoops are placed 5 yards from each end of the rectangle - inside the hoops stand the target players for each team. Keeping inside the area, each team attempts to combine play in an attempt to play the ball to the hands of the target player.

### Coaching Points
- Attack – be creative to beat your opponent
- Attack – after passing the ball support the play – not to lose to create pressure
- Attack – first touch away from pressure or penetrate
- Defense – protect the target
- Defense – communicate with your partner
- Defense – be patient to win possession

### Progressions:

Each successful pass – change the target players. Kick or throw-in each time the ball exits the area. Depending on the proficiency of the players, the game can start using hands (basketball style). Progressions: 1) Target players play for the team in possession increasing point scoring opportunities, 2) Add an additional player to each team 3) Add conditions – limited touches, one touch finish, etc 4) Add a neutral player creating 3v2.

# Transition Attack

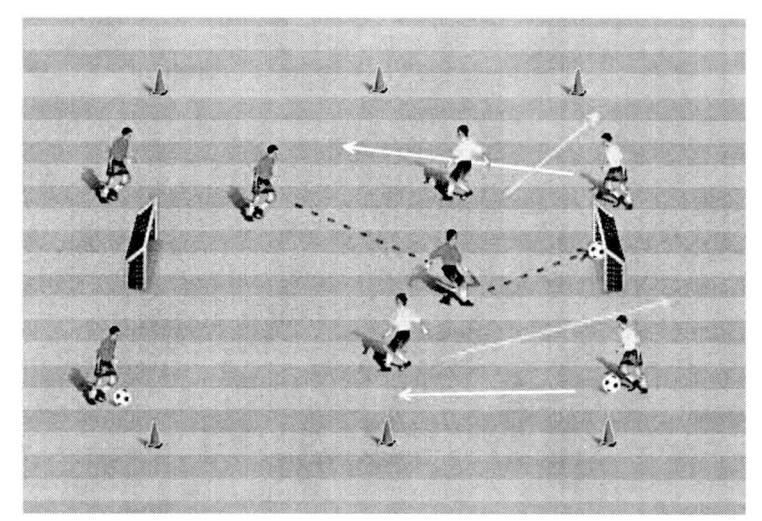

**Materials Needed**

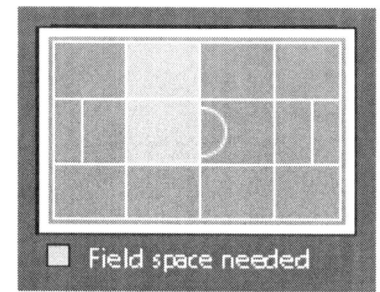

Area 30 x 10 yds
- Ball per player
- Cones
- Training Vests
- Goals

## Transition Attack (Attacking, defending)

**Description:**
Two teams of 4 players. Each team separates into two - 2v2 game. The other players stand behind their defensive end waiting to come onto the field. If a ball goes over the end line (a goal or not), the players behind that goal enter the field with a ball and attack the opposition. The team that is replaced quickly get off the field and get a ball ready to return.

**Coaching Points**
- Transition should be explosive – take advantage
- Bring a new ball from wide positions
- Defensively, retreat quickly to protect the goal

**Progressions:**
4 players: 1v1 in the area and the other player behind the defensive end with a ball, 8 players: 2v2 in the area and 2 players behind each end with a ball, 12 players: 3v3 in the area and 3 players behind each end with a ball

# Turn or Go

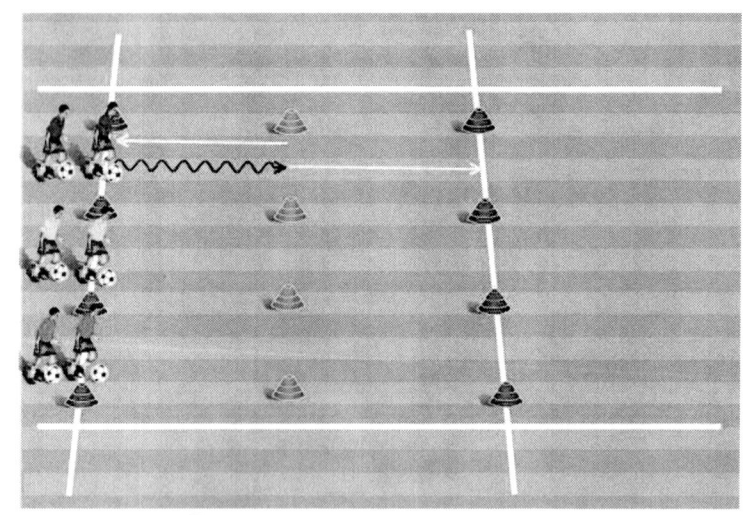

## Materials Needed

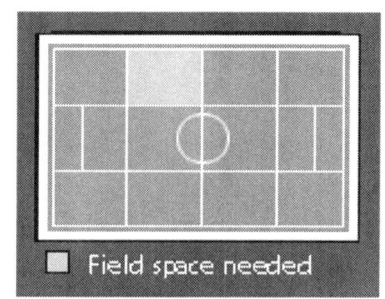

Area 30 x 20 yds
- Balls
- Cones
- Training Vests

## Turn or Go (Dribbling)

### Description:
Players in pairs start on the end line with a ball each. On the coach's signal the first player in each pair jogs without the ball down their channel. If the coach whistles once, they sprint forward to the opposite end line. If the coach whistles twice then they turn and sprint back to the start line. Repeat with the second player in each pair. Progress the movement as follows: 1) Skip, 2) Gallop, 3) Hop. Pairs compete against the other teams - A point is awarded each time for the winner.

### Coaching Points
- Controlled movement or dribble before the whistle(s)
- Run or dribble forward at pace after one whistle but maintain control of the ball
- Turn with minimal touches and accelerate back to the line with the ball under control

### Progressions:
Progress to ball mastery exercises moving forward: 1) Toe Taps, 2) Sole Taps, 3) Lateral ball rolls. One whistle and the players dribble forward and stop the ball on the line. Two whistles they perform a specified turn and dribble back to the starting line. 1) Drag back 2) Step on 3) Inside cut, 4) Coach calls out a specific turn rather than two whistles for change of direction, 5) On one whistle players to leave the ball on the opposite end line, turn and sprint back to the start line without the ball.

PLUS 2 COACHING FOR DEVELOPMENT

## Plus 2 - Mid to Late Stage Sessions

| Sessions | Page |
|---|---|
| 1. Dribbling #6 (Plus 2-3) (Dribbling, Ball Mastery) | pg. 203 |
| 2. Dribbling #7 (Plus 2-3) (Dribbling, Ball Mastery) | pg. 204 |
| 3. Passing #4 (Plus 2-3) (Passing, Receiving) | pg. 205 |
| 4. Passing #5 (Plus 2-3) (Passing, Receiving) | pg. 206 |
| 5. Passing #6 (Plus 2-3) (Passing, Receiving) | pg. 207 |
| 6. Attacking #3 (Plus 2-3) (Attacking, Defending) | pg. 208 |
| 7. Attacking #4 (Plus 2-3) (Attacking, Defending) | pg. 209 |
| 8. Defending #3 (Plus 2-3) (Defending, Attacking) | pg. 210 |
| 9. Defending #4 (Plus 2-3) (Defending, Attacking) | pg. 211 |
| 10. Shooting #3 (Plus 2-3) (Shooting, Attacking) | pg. 212 |
| 11. Heading #2 (Plus 2-3) (Heading) | pg. 213 |

# Dribbling #6 (Plus 2-3)
# Dribbling, Ball Mastery

## Activity 1: Escape Move - Cruyff Turn
Focus: Dribbling, Creating Space

1. Area 30 x 20 yds
2. Ball per player
3. Cones

### Objective
One ball per player in an open grid to begin. Isolate the skill by performing on-the-spot. The Cruyff Turn is performed by faking to kick/or dribble the ball in one direction and then playing the ball between the legs. Using the toe end of the shoe, the ball is flicked through the legs and the attacker pivots on the other leg to the outside. Accelerate away with pace. Progress to 1) performing the skill on the move, 2) 1v1 passive defending, 3) 1v1 active defending 4) Game with gates, 5) Small sided game.

### Coaching Points
1. Start in stationary position - not a dribble
2. Fake to pass and quick turn
3. Accelerate away leaving defender behind

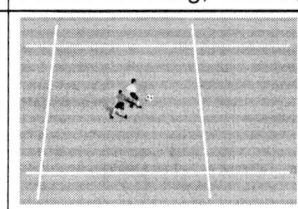

## Activity 2: Escape Moves - The 'V'
Focus: Dribbling, Creating Space

1. Area 30 x 20 yds
2. Ball per player
3. Cones

### Objective
One ball per player in an open grid to begin. Isolate the skill by performing on-the-spot. The 'V' is performed by dragging the ball away from a defender with the sole of the foot (back towards the attacker) and then pushing the ball forward past the defender on the other side. The movement pattern 'draws' a V in the grass. Progress to: 1) Performing the skill on the move, 2) 1v1 passive defending, 3) 1v1 active defending 4) Game with gates, 5) Small sided game.

### Coaching Points
1. Start in stationary position - not a dribble
2. Quick transfer of the ball from one foot to the other
3. Accelerate away leaving defender behind

## Activity 3: Escape Game with Gates
Focus: Dribbling, Creating Space

1. Area 30 x 20 yds
2. Several balls
3. Cones
4. Training Vests

### Objective
Two teams of players 3v3 to 5v5 attempt to score points by dribbling through gates (cones 2 yards apart). 1 point for going through a gate and 2pts for an escape move.

### Coaching Points
1. Encourage players to try and try again
2. Be aware of the space - 360° vision
3. Add points for an escape move

## Activity 4: Match 3 v 3
Focus: Game

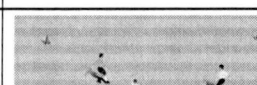

1. Area 30 x 15 yds
2. Balls
3. Cones
4. Training Vests
5. Small Goals

### Objective
A small sided game 3v3 is a good way to finish a practice session. Use the opportunity to emphasize the theme of the session - award points for a particular move in addition to scoring a goal. Let the players play with little or no coaching - 15-20 minutes at the end of the session.

### Coaching Points
1. Little or no coaching
2. Encourage players to try skills practiced during the session

**SOCCERPLUS** THE DICICCO METHOD

soccer interactive.com

# Dribbling #7 (Plus 2-3)
# Dribbling, Ball Mastery

## Activity 1: Take On - Hesitation
### Focus: Dribbling, Creating Space

1. Area 30 x 20 yds
2. Ball per player
3. Cones

### Objective
One ball per player in an open grid to begin. Isolate the skill by performing on-the-spot. The hesitation move requires the attacker to momentarily pause in the dribble causing the defender to either overrun or stop. The attacker can then accelerate away. Progress to 1) performing the skill on the move, 2) 1v1 passive defending, 3) 1v1 active defending 4) Game with gates & 5) Small sided game.

### Coaching Points
1. Determine a speed of approach that works for each individual
2. Realistic movement to unbalance the defender
3. Accelerate away leaving defender behind

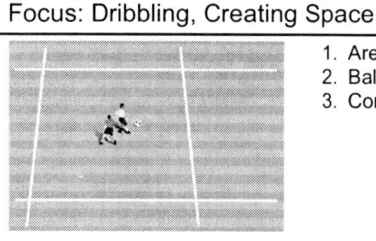

## Activity 2: Take On - The Scissors
### Focus: Dribbling, Creating Space

1. Area 30 x 20 yds
2. Ball per player
3. Cones

### Objective
One ball per player in an open grid to begin. Isolate the skill by performing on-the-spot. The Scissors move normally starts with a slow approach towards the defender. The attacker then unbalances and creates uncertainty for the defender by kicking over the ball with left and right foot (The move can be multiple scissors). The attacker should also move their body in the direction of the scissors to add to the uncertainty. Once the defender is flat-footed, the attacker can then accelerate away. Progress to 1) Performing the skill on the move, 2) 1v1 passive defending, 3) 1v1 active defending 4) Game with gates 5) Small sided game.

### Coaching Points
1. Determine a speed of approach that works for each individual
2. Realistic movement to unbalance the defender
3. Accelerate away leaving defender behind

## Activity 3: Take On with Gates
### Focus: Dribbling, Creating Space

1. Area 30 x 20 yds
2. Several balls
3. Cones
4. Training Vests

### Objective
Two teams of players (3v3 to 5v5) attempt to score points by dribbling through gates (cones 2 yards apart). 1 point for going through a gate and 2pts for a take on move.

### Coaching Points
1. Encourage players to try and try again
2. Be aware of the space - 360° vision
3. Add points for a take on move

## Activity 4: One vs All
### Focus: Attacking, defending

1. Area 20 x 10 yds
2. Ball per player
3. Cones
4. Training Vests
5. Goals
6. Clip board

### Objective
Players play together in small teams of 1v1 to 3v3. Games are 2 minutes in length. Although the teams play against each other, the scoring is recorded by indvidual player. Start by writing the names of all the players on a piece of paper and assign each player a number. 2v2 format: The first game players get into pairs – After 2 minutes bring the pairs back to one location to report the scores. Subsequent games the coach should ensure players are with different partners.

### Coaching Points
1. Keep the games high tempo
2. Quick re-starts (kick in or throws)
3. Provide angles for attacking and defensive support

# Passing #4 (Plus 2-3)
# Passing, Receiving

## Activity 1: Passing & Moving
Focus: Passing, Receiving

1. Area 20 x 20 yds
2. Balls
3. Cones

### Objective
3 players (A, B & C) must remain on the perimeter of a 10 x 10 yds square. The player can only move along the lines between the cones. Player A passes to either B or C. The receiving player must take 2 touches to control and pass the ball. Once the ball is passed, the 2 other players should support the receiver by creating an angle of support - a triangle.

### Coaching Points
1. Quick footwork to move around the square in support
2. Alertness and understanding of supporting angles
3. Move laterally keeping the body open to receive a pass
4. Passing into the feet of the receiver
5. Receiving touch should set up the next pass

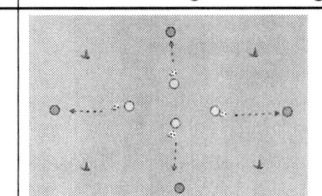

## Activity 2: Receiving Technique
Focus: Passing, Receiving

1. Area 20 x 20 yds
2. Balls
3. Cones
4. Training Vests

### Objective
Split players into two groups. 5 players start in the middle of the area with a ball each and 5 on the outside of the area without a ball. Players in the middle dribble to an open player on the outside and when approximately 5 yds apart, the dribbling player passes the ball to the perimeter player. The perimeter player plays the ball back to the dribbling player who then repeats with another open player.

### Coaching Points
1. Be on your toes ready to receive
2. Present the receiving surface to the ball
3. Cushion ball on first touch and keep ball in front of body
4. Open up body to the field to receive

## Activity 3: Squares
Focus: Passing, Receiving

1. Area 15 x 15 yds
2. Ball per player
3. Cones

### Objective
All players stand inside a square marked with cones. One ball only required per game. Trying to keep the ball on the ground and using the inside or outside of the foot only, the players attempt to eliminate each other until one player remains. The ball is passed around one touch as the coach introduces rules: 1) One touch or you are out. 2) If you kick the ball out of the square (last touch) – out! 3) If you could have stopped the ball from leaving the square – out! 4) If you are 'nutmegged' through the legs – out! 5) If you play the ball in the air and it is caught – out! 6) If you attempt to catch the ball but drop it – out!

### Coaching Points
1. Ball on the ground
2. Quick play
3. No arguments – one adjudicator

## Activity 4: One up – One down
Focus: Attacking, defending, creating space

1. Area 40 x 20 yds
2. Ball per player
3. Cones
4. Training Vests
5. Goals

### Objective
3v3 – 5v5 – two teams compete as in a normal game. However, each player is matched with a player from the other team and if a goal is scored, the partner of the goal scorer must complete a lap of the field before reentering the game. During this time, the game progresses with uneven teams – if the same team scores before the first player arrives, the first player has to complete another lap, and the second player also completes a lap. Players learn to create attacking and defending strategies for when they have superior and inferior numbers.

### Coaching Points
1. Attacking with superior numbers – quick movement
2. Defending with inferior numbers – consolidate around the goal (zonal)
3. Communicate effectively with teammates

**SOCCERPLUS** — THE DICICCO METHOD

soccer interactive.com

# Passing #5 (Plus 2-3)
# Passing, Receiving

## Activity 1: Know your Number
Focus: Passing, Receiving

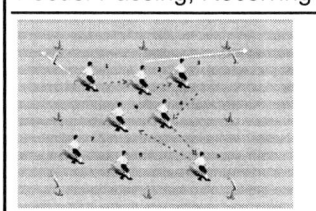

1. Area 30 x 30 yds
2. Balls 2-3
3. Cones
4. Speed equipment

### Objective
Give every player a number. In the area the players pass the ball to each other 1 to 2, 2 to 3, 3 to 4 etc. The last numbered player plays back to 1. Once the ball has passed through the team once or twice, instruct the players to jog to a corner of the square, jump over the hurdle (or around a cone) and return to receive the next pass.

### Coaching Points
1. Communicate to your team mate
2. Work hard to get in a good receiving position
3. Firm and accurate passing – keep the tempo

## Activity 2: 2 v 2 + 2 Support
Focus: Passing, Receiving

1. Area 20 x 30 yds
2. Balls
3. Cones
4. Training Vests

### Objective
Two neutral players (play for the team in possession of the ball) at either end of the area. The ball starts with one of the neutral players. The ball is played to one of the teams plaing a 2v2 game in between the neutral players. The team in possession have to pass the ball to the other neutral player without losing possession to the other team. The two defenders must try and stop the attackers and if they win the ball they can become the attackers. Each pass to the neutral player counts as a point. The neutral player always passes back to the team that are in possession. If the ball leaves the area, a new ball is played to the other team.

### Coaching Points
1. Movement to create space
2. Awareness of defenders
3. Don't force the ball forward

## Activity 3: 4 Box Possession
Focus: Possession

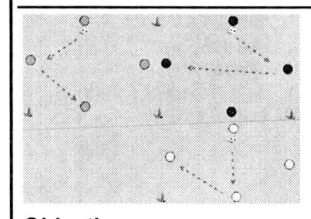

1. Area 20 x 20 yds
2. Balls
3. Cones
4. Training Vests

### Objective
Three teams of four start in their own 10 x 10 yds area. Each team has a ball. The team must pass and move around their box without the ball stopping or going out of bounds. After the team has played 10 passes they move into the next box (clockwise). The first team to make it all the way around wins the game.

### Coaching Points
1. Keep ball moving at all times
2. Concentrate on the quality of the pass
3. Maintain shape
4. Communication

## Activity 4: 3 v 3 Moving Goal
Focus: Passing, Receiving

1. Area 30 x 30 yds
2. Balls
3. Cones
4. Training Vests

### Objective
2 players hold a training vest between them in one hand and at arms length to form a goal. The goal moves around the field at a walking pace. In the area, two teams of 3 players attempt to combine passes and score a goal by passing through the goal for a teammate to receive on the opposite side.

### Coaching Points
1. Maintain team shape
2. Awareness of moving goal
3. Speed of movement to support

# Passing #6 (Plus 2-3)
# Passing, Receiving

## Activity 1: Passing Competition
### Focus: Passing, Receiving

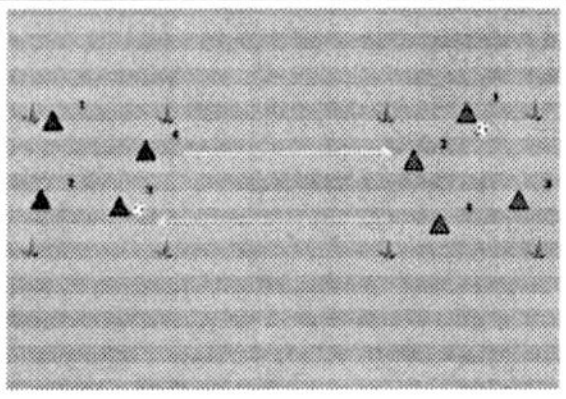

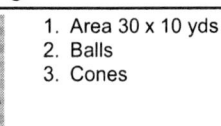

1. Area 30 x 10 yds
2. Balls
3. Cones

### Objective
2 Teams of four are each in a 10 x 10 yds square - 10 yds between the sqaures. Each team player is numbered 1-4. Both teams have a ball and start to pass and move. The coach shouts a number and that player becomes a defender. The defender sprints to the other square to create a 3v1 situation. The first team to make 6 consecutive passes get 1pt - the first team to 5 points wins.

### Coaching Points
1. Movement off the ball to provide support
2. Receive the ball in the direction of the next pass
3. Accuracy and pace on the ball
4. Communication
5. Defender - close down quickly

## Activity 2: Milan Passing Game
### Focus: Passing

1. Area 15 x 15 yds
2. Balls
3. Cones
4. Training Vests

### Objective
Create a circle (or use center circle) and position 5-6 players on the edge of the circle. The perimeter players are restricted to moving between the perimeter cones. 1 receiver and 3 defenders are inside the circle. The goal is for the 7 players to retain possession of the ball and achieve 10 consecutive passes. If the defenders win the ball they must try and keep the ball away from the center player. When defenders complete 5 passes, they earn a point. Alternate defenders.

### Coaching Points
1. Accurate passing
2. Awareness of space, teammates, defenders
3. Communication with teammates
4. First touch when receiving

## Activity 3: 3 v 3 with Targets
### Focus: Passing, Receiving

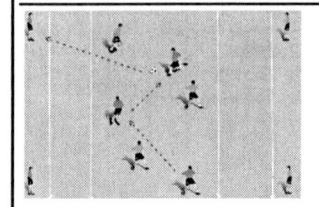

1. Area 40 x 20 yds
2. Balls
3. Cones
4. Training Vests

### Objective
3v3 play in the central zone 20 x 20 yds. The team with the ball attempt to possess the ball until there is an opportunity to deliver a pass to a target player. One Target Player for each team stand in a 10 x 20 yds end zone at either end of the area. Rotate target players every 3-4 minutes.

### Coaching Points
1. Movement to maintain possession in middle zone
2. Communication
3. Awareness of open target

## Activity 4: Target
### Focus: Passing, Receiving

1. Area 30 x 20 yds
2. Ball per player
3. Cones
4. Hula Hoops or cones
5. Training Vests

### Objective
Each team has 3 players - Play 2v2 and nominate one target player for each team. First team to score five points wins. Two hoops are placed 5 yards from each end of the rectangle - inside the hoops stand the target players for each team. Keeping inside the area, each team attempts to combine play in an attempt to play the ball to the hands of the target player.

### Coaching Points
1. Attack – be creative to beat your opponent
2. Attack – after passing the ball support the play – not to lose to create pressure
3. Attack – first touch away from pressure or penetrate
4. Defense – protect the target

# Attacking #3 (Plus 2-3)
# Attacking, Defending

## Activity 1: Back to Goal Series
## Focus: Attacking, Creating Space

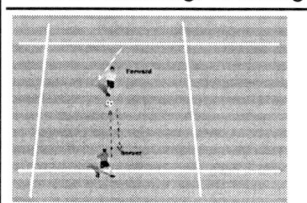

1. Area 10 x 10 yds
2. Balls
3. Cones

### Objective

Two players face each other 10 yards apart. The server initiates all movements by playing a firm pass along the ground to the forward. The forward player has to turn and attack the line behind him/her. Start without a defender and then add a defender into the activity starting behind the forward. There are 5 moves for the forward when receiving the ball - 1) Turn, 2) Self pass (receiving touch plays the ball towards the server approx 5 yards and then a quick turn), 3) Check towards the server at an angle and turn, 4) Check and let the ball run through the legs (dummy) and turn, 5) Check, hesitate (to initate contact with the defender and check to the ball again. 5-10 attempts each and switch.

### Coaching Points

1. Receive the ball sideways to create distance from the defender
2. Use body contact with defender to create separation
3. When checking to the ball accelerate

## Activity 2: 2 v 1 Countdown to Goal
## Focus: Attacking

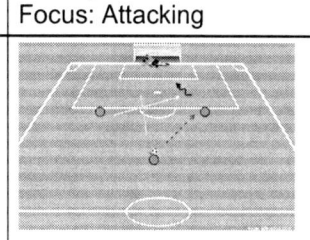

1. Area 25 x 35 yds
2. Balls
3. Cones

### Objective

Balls are placed 35 yards from goal in a central position. Player A starts on a cone (next to the balls) with a ball. Player A must make a decision on which one of the two support players to pass to (B or C). The support players start on a cone 5 yds closer to the ball than player A and in line with the edge of the 6 yard box. Whichever support player receives the pass, the other player becomes a defender to create a 2v1 situation. The two attackers must combine to score. The two attackers have 8 seconds to score.

### Coaching Points

1. Positive touch towards goal
2. Movement to support ball carrier
3. Shoot when opportunity arises

## Activity 3: Back to Goal 1 v 1
## Focus: Attacking, Creating Space

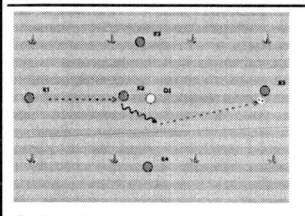

1. Area 30 x 20 yds
2. Balls
3. Cones

### Objective

Six players - 1 server (X1), 1 attacker (X2), 1 defender (O1), 2 support (X3 & X4) and 1 target (X5). X1 plays a firm pass to X2. Using a back to goal move, X2 attempts to play ball to X5. X3 and X4 can be used for support. Five attempts and rotate.

### Coaching Points

1. Receive sideways on to create distance from defender
2. Use body contact with defender to create separation
3. Check away from the defender by accelerating towards the ball

## Activity 4: 3 v 3 Scrimmage
## Focus: Attacking, Defending

1. Area 40 x 25 yds
2. Balls
3. Cones
4. Training Vests

### Objective

Two teams - 3v3 play to 6 goals. Each team has three small goals to score in. Defending the three goals is a goalkeeper. The attacking team must try to attack the open goal before the keeper can recover.

### Coaching Points

1. Maintain width and depth
2. Move ball away from presssure
3. Attack any spaces that open up

# Attacking #4 (Plus 2-3)
# Attacking, Defending

## Activity 1: 3 v 1 to Goal
Focus: Attacking

1. Area 25 x 40 yds
2. Balls
3. Training Vests
4. Goal

### Objective
Attacking team start 15 yds from goal. 1 defender and a goalkeeper defend the goal. The goalkeeper starts with the ball and distributes it to the attackers - who attack at goal. The objective for the attacking team is to score as many goals in 5 minutes - each attack is started by the goal keeper. Attackers must sprint back to the starting positions after each attack.

### Coaching Points
1. Vary attacking runs/patterns
2. Attack at speed
3. Accurate shooting - follow for rebounds
4. Don't allow players to be offside

## Activity 2: 3 v 1 Numbers Game
Focus: Attacking, Defending

1. Area 20 x 20 yds
2. Balls
3. Cones
4. Training Vests

### Objective
3 groups play a 3v1 game in their own 10 x 10 yds area. Number each player in the team 1-4. When their number is called they must run into the box on the right and try to steal the ball (creating a 3v1 situation). 5 passes equals a point. The first defender to win the ball scores a point for their team.

### Coaching Points
1. Maintain passing shape (Triangle)
2. Keep ball moving
3. Play ball away from pressure

## Activity 3: 3 v 3 Take On & Escape
Focus: Attacking, Creating Space

1. Area 25 x 35 yds
2. Several balls
3. Cones
4. Training Vests

### Objective
Play 3v3 to begin. Teams must attempt to score points during a 5 minute game. Points are scored by performing a take on or escape move (1pt each). The attacking team can score 2pts for a goal and the defending team can score 2pts for dribbling over the coned line 35 yds from goal. Change teams after 5 minutes and repeat. The goal keeper serves the ball to the attackers to start each game.

### Coaching Points
1. Approach defender at comfortable speed
2. Sell the defender with take on move
3. Create space using escape move

## Activity 4: Possession 2 Touch
Focus: Passing, receiving, possession

1. Area 40 x 30 yds
2. Balls
3. Cones
4. Training Vests

### Objective
3v3 up to 7v7 + two neutral players playing for the team in possession. First team to 25 total passes wins the game. Restrict to 2 touches only.

### Coaching Points
1. 1st touch must create space and time
2. Supporting players must provide good angles
3. Think ahead - what options are available on receipt of the ball

# Defending #3 (Plus 2-3)
# Defending, Attacking

## Activity 1: Turn or Go
## Focus: Dribbling

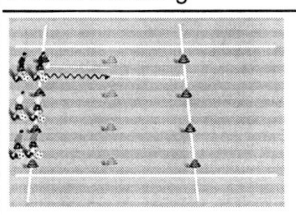

1. Area 30 x 20 yds
2. Balls
3. Cones
4. Training Vests

### Objective

Players in pairs start on the end line with a ball each. On the coach's signal the first player in each pair jogs without the ball down their channel. If the coach whistles once, they sprint forward to the opposite end line. If the coach whistles twice then they turn and sprint back to the start line. Repeat with the second player in each pair. Progress the movement as follows: 1) Skip, 2) Gallop, 3) Hop. Pairs compete against the other teams - A point is awarded each time for the winner.

### Coaching Points

1. Controlled movement or dribble before the whistle(s)
2. Run or dribble forward at pace after one whistle but maintain control of the ball
3. Turn with minimal touches and accelerate back to the line with the ball under control

## Activity 2: Poke Tackle
## Focus: Defending

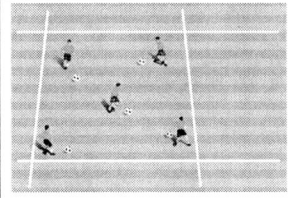

1. Area 20 x 20 yds
2. Balls
3. Cones

### Objective

A poke tackle is used when an opponent loses possession of the ball - the defender makes a lunge with either foot to knock the ball away from the attacker. Players have a ball each and dribble around the area. On the coach's command the players react to the instruction. When the coach calls "STAGGER" the defender gets into a staggered position. "SWITCH" - the defender spins to face the other direction. "CHANGE" - change balls with another player. "POKE" poke the ball away from another player.

### Coaching Points

1. Get body side on into staggered position
2. Keep low
3. Poke the ball away with closest foot

## Activity 3: Catch me
## Focus: Defending

1. Area 20 x 20 yds
2. Balls
3. Cones
4. Training Vests

### Objective

Players in pairs - 1 attacker and 1 defender. Attacker dribbles the ball in the area and the defender gives chase. When the coach shouts "FREEZE" the defender must try to touch the attacker - if they can they score 1pt. If attacker is out of reach the attacker scores a point. Switch roles.

### Coaching Points

1. Keep pressure on the ball and attacker
2. React quickly to a change in direction

## Activity 4: 3 v 1 Exchange
## Focus: Defending, Passing

1. Area 20 x 20 yds
2. Balls
3. Cones
4. Training Vests

### Objective

Two groups of 4 players. Players keep possession in their own 10 x 10 grid. On the coach's command, each team sends a defender over to break up the opposition's passing sequence. First defender to break up opponent's passing earns point for his/her team. Alternate defenders.

### Coaching Points

1. Close down the space quickly
2. Force a mistake and perform a poke tackle
3. Don't dive into a tackle - be patient

# Defending #4 (Plus 2-3)
# Defending, Attacking

## Activity 1: Defending in Pairs
## Focus: Defending

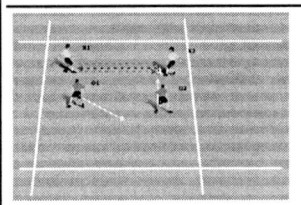

1. Area 10 x 10 yds
2. Ball per player
3. Cones
4. Training Vests

### Objective
In a 10 x 10 yds area, two attackers (X1 & X2) stand opposite two defenders (O1 & O2). The attackers pass the ball back and forth on a 3-touch rhythm. On the 3rd pass, the defender opposite the receiver applies pressure and the 2nd defender provides cover - game is now live and the attackers attempt to get to the end line. Defenders try to win possession and attack the attackers end line.

### Coaching Points
1. Communicate with your defensive partner
2. Decide support or cover
3. Patience
4. Slow the attack and force play back
5. Force a mistake

## Activity 2: Defending Recovery
## Focus: Defending

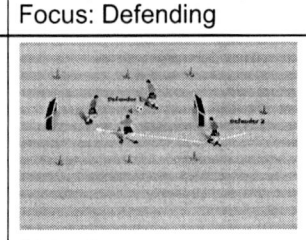

1. Area 20 x 10 yds
2. Ball per player
3. Cones
4. Training Vests
5. Goals

### Objective
Play 2 attackers v 2 defenders - One goal at the defensive end and one at the attacking end of the area. From the defensive end of the field 1 defender passes the ball firmly along the ground to 1 of the 2 attackers standing in the opposite corners. On receipt, the attackers attack the defender and attempt to score. The recovery defender sprints to help.

### Coaching Points
1. Communicate with your defensive partner
2. Decide support or cover
3. Patience
4. Slow the attack and force play back
5. Force a mistake

## Activity 3: 3 v 3 to Wide Goals
## Focus: Defending as a Unit

1. Area 30 x 30 yds
2. Balls
3. Cones
4. Training Vests

### Objective
Play a scrimmage in a typical manner, but instead of one central goal, played to two wide goals.

### Coaching Points
1. 1st defender provides pressure to the ball
2. 2nd defender provides cover for the 1st defender
3. 3rd defender provides balance, covering the 2nd defender

## Activity 4: Transition Attack
## Focus: Attacking, defending

1. Area 30 x 10 yds
2. Ball per player
3. Cones
4. Training Vests
5. Goals

### Objective
Two teams of 4 players. Each team separates into two - 2v2 game. The other players stand behind their defensive end waiting to come onto the field. If a ball goes over the end line (a goal or not), the players behind that goal enter the field with a ball and attack the opposition. The team that is replaced quickly get off the field and get a ball ready to return.

### Coaching Points
1. Transition should be explosive – take advantage
2. Bring a new ball from wide positions
3. Defensively, retreat quickly to protect the goal

# Shooting #3 (Plus 2-3)
# Shooting, Attacking

## Activity 1: Handball with Volleys
### Focus: Shooting

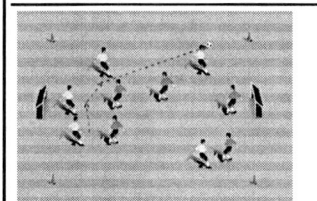

1. Area 30 x 20 yds
2. Ball per player
3. Cones
4. Training Vests
5. Goals - full

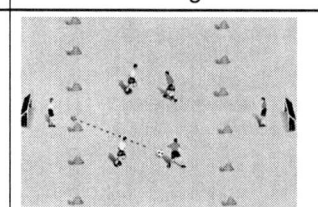

### Objective
Two teams of 5 players and 2 plus players playing for the team in possession. The ball is passed with the hands and the attacker is only allowed 3 steps with ball. Score one point by scoring a volley or half volley. First to 5 points wins.

### Coaching Points
1. Find space - stretch the distance the defender needs to cover
2. Strike volley and half volley with laces
3. Attacking - creating space and keeping possession
4. Defending - goal side, zone and man for man defense

## Activity 2: Shoot, Save, Score
### Focus: Shooting

1. Area 20 x 30 yds
2. Balls
3. Cones
4. Pinnies

### Objective
Each team has 3 players - 2 attackers and 1 goalkeeper. Players are allowed to use their hands in the defensive zone. 1 point awarded for a shot, 3 points for a shot on target, 5 points for a goal, 1 point for a save. First team to 21 wins.

### Coaching Points
1. Try to shoot at every opportunity
2. Shoot low and away from the keeper
3. Follow up on rebounds

## Activity 3: Shooting in Fours
### Focus: Shooting

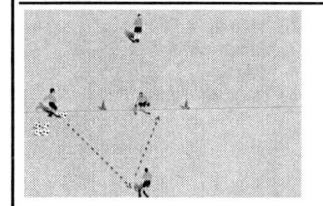

1. Area 20 x 20 yds
2. Balls
3. Cones

### Objective
4 players work in a group. 1 keeper, two strikers and 1 server. The server plays a ball to Striker 1 who takes a touch before shooting. The server then repeats with Striker 2. Rotate players every 2-3 minutes.

### Coaching Points
1. 1st touch out of your feet
2. Lock you ankle
3. Strike ball with laces

## Activity 4: Goals for Points
### Focus: Shooting, creating space, passing

1. Area 25 x 25 yds
2. Ball per player
3. Cones
4. Training Vests
5. Goal

### Objective
Players are separated into teams of two or three players, with a goal keeper. Two games can occur simultaneously on two different areas. Whichever team brings (passes or dribbles) the ball into the penalty box can score. The other teams must win possession and reset the game by taking the ball outside. Points are scored in the following way – 3pts for a long range shot (coach decides on the distance), 2pts for an inside shot, and 2pts for a header. However, to convert the points, the scorer must convert a penalty.

### Coaching Points
1. Provide a good angle for support
2. Take every goal scoring opportunity
3. Be alive in front of goal for 'poacher' finishing

SOCCERPLUS — THE DICICCO METHOD

soccer interactive.com

# Heading #2 (Plus 2-3)
## Heading

### Activity 1: Head Catch - 3 v 3
Focus: Warm-up, Heading and Movement Skills

1. Area 30 x 20 yds
2. Ball per player
3. Cones
4. Training Vests
5. Goals - mini

#### Objective
The area is split into two with cones down the center. In one half, play 3v1 – the 3 attacking players have the ball and attempt for a head-catch-head-catch-head-catch combination to win 1 point. If the ball hits the ground or the defender wins the ball, possession transfers to the other half – one attacker enters the other half and defends.

#### Coaching Points
1. Find space - stretch the distance the defender needs to cover
2. Introduce different headers - glance, flick, power, cushion etc
3. Open the body to provide direction to the headers

### Activity 2: Heading to Goal
Focus: Heading

1. Balls
2. Cones
3. Training Vest
4. 10x10

#### Objective
This is an excellent fun competition. Two teams stand either side of the goal about 8 yards away. The coach acts as the server who starts by serving into the Greens to head at goal. After the header they must replace the keeper and the coach serves to the other team.

#### Coaching Points
1. Keep eyes on the ball
2. Make contact with forehead
3. Head down towards the ground

### Activity 3: Attacking Heading 2 v 2
Focus: Heading

1. Area 10 x 10 yds
2. Ball per player
3. Cones
4. Training Vests
5. Coaching sticks

#### Objective
2v2. Each team defends a goal (either coaching sticks or a large mini goal). Standing on the goal line, one player throws a two handed underarm throw to his/her partner who heads the ball in the air to set up an attacking header by the partner. The attacking player attempts to score past one goal keeper in a goal opposite. Cones are placed along the center of the square to represent the border line between both teams. Keep changing positions – first to five wins.

#### Coaching Points
1. Balanced position for heading - arms out
2. Attack the ball using forward momentum for power
3. Contact ball with forehead aiming low at the Goalkeeper's feet

### Activity 4: Moving Net
Focus: Heading

1. Area 30 x 15 yds
2. Ball per player
3. Cones
4. Training Vests

#### Objective
At each end of the 30 yds grid is a 3 yds end zone stretching the width of 15 yds. To begin the game, players stand either side of an imaginary net the height of the coach. The purpose of the game is to move the net into the opposition half and score points into their end zone. Coach starts the game by serving the ball up for team A to head.

#### Coaching Points
1. Use legs to generate power
2. Explode into the ball for power and distance
3. Use arms to develop momentum and protect face
4. Communicate - call a name

# Chapter 6
# Player Assessment

# PLUS 2 COACHING FOR DEVELOPMENT
## Player Assessment

### Player Assessment

Assessment should form an integral component of the Player Development Curriculum. Although assessment processes can have negative connotations and outcomes (such as cutting players, overly focusing on weaknesses or the basis for firing coaches), the correct use of assessment methodologies offer significant benefits to players, teams, coaches and parents. Some of the purposes and benefits of assessment include:

- Correlate player performance with end of stage expectations – determine if the player is at, below or above expectations.
- Align program practices with program standards.
- Determine progress in skill acquisition and performance.
- Enable individual plans and goals to be created for each player, team and coach.
- Evaluate the success of a particular approach to coaching and learning.
- Create and implement education programs to enhance strengths and address weaknesses.
- Validate the curriculum.
- Identify issues in assessment and develop corrective actions.
- Communicate progress to players and parents.
- Provide evidence and to promote and support program improvement.
- Document and celebrate program effectiveness.
- Provide information allowing duplication of effective programs. Effective programs that meet the intended outcomes or program standards are worthy of replication.

### Performance Standards and Assessment Matrix

SoccerPlus Performance Standards and Assessment Matrix have been created with the aforementioned benefits of evaluation in mind. Benchmarks for performance are provided at the end of each stage of development. The assessment program measures the players 'competence' – the relationship between skill; the selection and application of skills, tactics; strategies and ideas; and the readiness of the body and mind to cope with the activity.

# SOCCER COACHING ACTIVITIES, SESSION PLANS AND ASSESSMENT

The following three measurement levels are used for player assessment and are mapped against standards expected at the end of each stage of development:

- Exceeds expectation: correlates to a score 70-100% - suggests the player has reached a high performance standard in a particular skill. Often an indication that the player can progress to the next level of complexity.
- Meets expectation: correlates to a score of 50-69% - suggests a player has achieved a level of competency consistent with the expectation for this stage in their development. The player is ready to move on to the next level but further reinforcement of the original skill will be required.
- Below expectation: correlates to a score of 0-49% - suggests additional focus on the skill and effort required to raise performance. Unlikely the player can move forward to a more complex skill with success. Ongoing reinforcement of original skill required.

Player performance expectations and the scoring mechanism are based on the following assumptions:

- Final evaluation is based on anticipated performance at the end of the Plus 2 stage.
- Players have been participating in soccer for at least 5 years prior to the final assessment.
- Players have received adequate training
    - 2 seasons per year for 5 years
    - 16 sessions per season = 160 sessions (5 yr total)
- Coaches have followed the progressions as outlined in the activity manual
- Activities were appropriate for the stage of development
- Sessions were focused on Plus 2 competencies.
- Corrective measures were addressed by the coach with the players.

It is anticipated that players exceeding performance expectations are showing additional interest in soccer outside of the training sessions. This may include playing with friends or family members at home, watching soccer, participating in supplementary soccer training opportunities (i.e. winter training) and participating in other sports.

There are eight activities for assessing player competency for Plus 2 players.

PLUS 2 COACHING FOR DEVELOPMENT

## **Plus 2 Assessment Activities**

| Activities | Page |
|---|---|
| Plus 2 Assessment #1 ( Dribbling, Ball Mastery ) | pg. 218 |
| Plus 2 Assessment #2 ( Ball Mastery ) | pg. 219 |
| Plus 2 Assessment #3 ( Passing & Receiving ) | pg. 220 |
| Plus 2 Assessment #4 ( Running with the Ball ) | pg. 221 |
| Plus 2 Assessment #5 ( Shooting ) | pg. 222 |
| Plus 2 Assessment #6 ( Attacking ) | pg. 223 |
| Plus 2 Assessment #7 ( Defending ) | pg. 224 |
| Plus 2 Assessment #8 ( Locomotor - Run & Hop ) | pg. 225 |

# Plus 2 Assessment #1

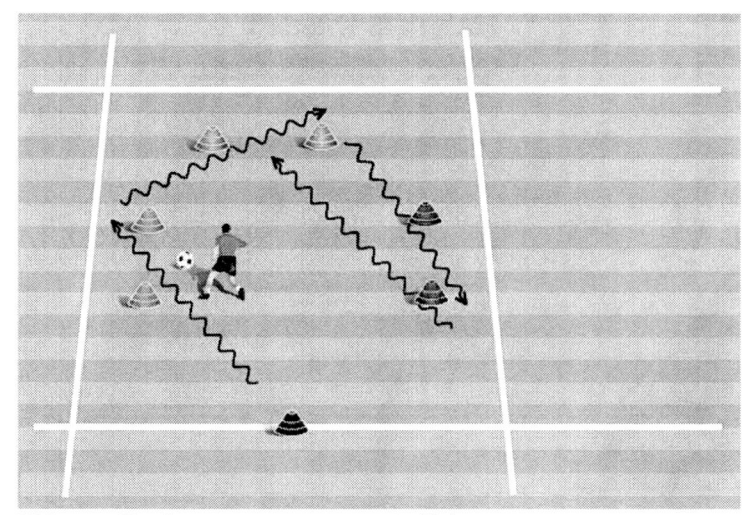

**Materials Needed**

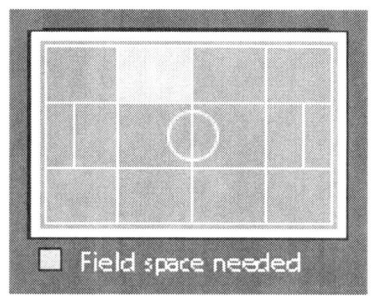

Area 10 x 10 yds
- 1 Ball
- 6 Cones (3 colors)

## Plus 2 Assessment #1 (Dribbling, Ball Mastery)

### Description:
This activity evaluates a player's ability to dribble, change direction and avoid obstacles. This assessment activity also evaluates a player's visual awareness. See activity plan for detailed instructions.

### Coaching Points
- Assessor can offer encouragement during the activity without telling the player what to do.

### Progressions:
#### Through the gates
A square measuring 10x10 yards has three gates marked with colored cones. The first gate (2 cones of the same color) measures 1 yard between the cones and is set 2 yards from one side of the square. The two remaining gates are set central to two of the three remaining sides of the square. A starting point (cone) is created on the remaining side without a gate.

1. On the command of "GO", the player has 30 seconds to dribble between as many gates as possible.
2. 1 point is awarded for each gate the player dribbles through.
3. Player can enter the gate from either side, but must go through another gate before entering the same gate a cocond timc.
4. There is no sequence required – just enter as many gates as possible in 30 seconds.
5. If the ball hits a gate (cone) no points are awarded, but the player can go back through the gate.
6. If the ball goes out of the square the player must bring the ball back in and continue (no penalty).

The assessor should demonstrate the skill, dribbling between 3 gates prior to the player's attempt. Allow the player to have two attempts and record the best score.

**Scoring:** 0-4 pts below expectation; 5-8 pts at expectation; 9+ pts above expectation

# Plus 2 Assessment #2

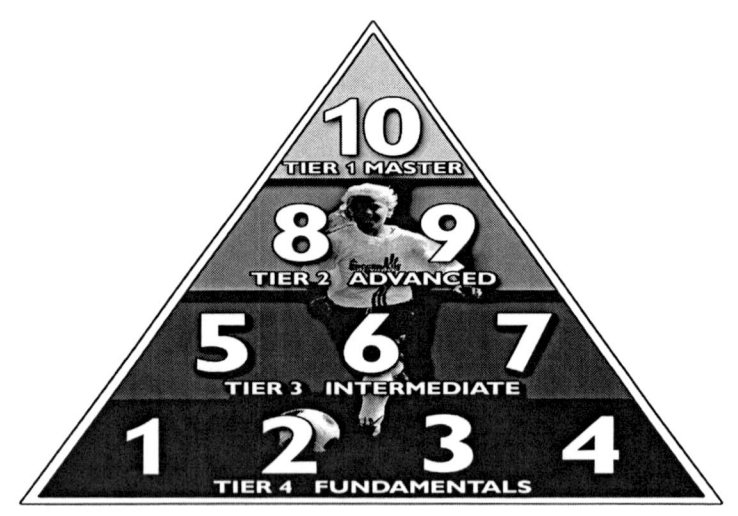

## Materials Needed

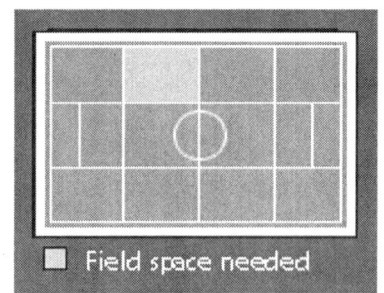

Area 10 x 10 yds
- 1 Ball

## Plus 2 Assessment #2 (Ball Mastery)

### Description:
Player stands in the center of the square and the assessor asks the player to perform the 1st activity. Once the assessor is satisfied the player has mastered the skill move on to the next activity. If the player does not recall the skill, the assessor can provide one demonstration at slow speed and one at game speed. Continue until the player performs an activity below expectation and then terminate the assessment.

### Coaching Points
- Assessor can offer encouragement during the activity without telling the player what to do.

### Progressions:
**Skill Challenge Pyramid:** Activities are numbered 1-10. Activity number 1 is regarded as the easiest skill to learn in the Pyramid and number 10 is regarded as the most difficult.
**Tier 4** - 1. Inside cut, 2. Ball rolls, 3. Outside cut, 4. Take on dribble (outside of foot).
**Tier 3** - 5. Single cut dribble, 6. Forward drag rolls, 7. Step-pivot turn.
**Tier 2** - 8. Flick turn, 9. Double tap and dribble.
**Tier 1** - 10. Double cut dribble.
A simple evaluation system is incorporated for each activity:
<u>Below expectation</u> – movements are awkward and uneven, there is little consistency between two or more attempts and the skill is performed below game speed. <u>At expectation</u> – At least 50% or more of the attempts are completed in one smooth movement, are at game speed and appear to be natural (second nature and free flowing). <u>Above expectation</u> – At least 90% or more of the attempts are completed in one smooth movement, are at game speed and appear to be natural (second nature and free flowing).

# Plus 2 Assessment #3

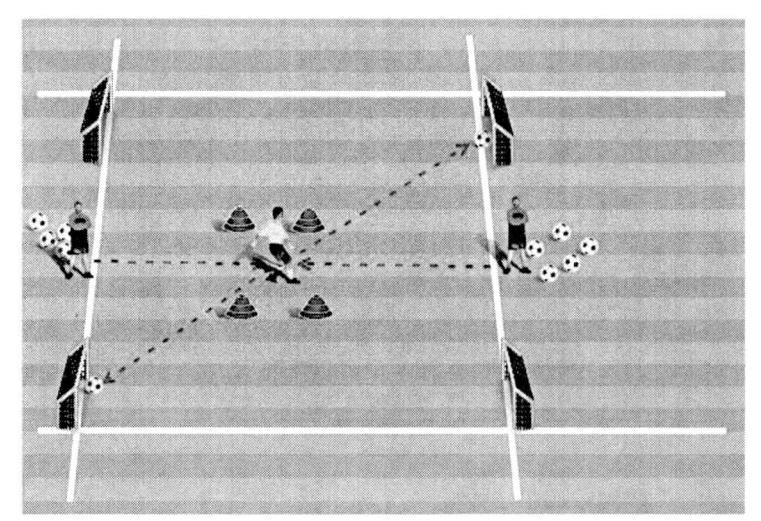

## Materials Needed

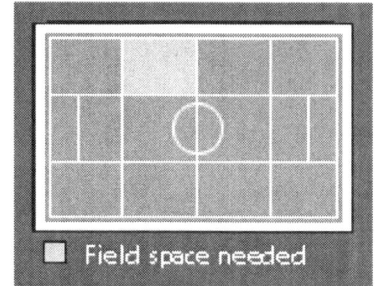

Area 10 x 10 yds
- 10-15 Balls
- 12 Cones
- Small goals/targets

## Plus 2 Assessment #3 (Passing & Receiving)

**Description:**
The player stands in the center of a small square (4 x 4 yds) that is situated in the center of a large square (20 x 20). At opposite ends of the square are two servers (adults) with at least 5 balls each. To either side of each server are two targets/goals measuring 2 yards wide and adjacent to the sides of the square. On the command of "GO", Server 1 rolls the ball along the ground to the player. The player attempts to receive the first ball with the inside of either foot and then with the second touch play the ball to the side of the server into either goal. The player then spins around 180 degrees and repeats the activity with the other server.

**Coaching Points**
- Assessor can offer encouragement during the activity without telling the player what to do.

**Progressions:**

There is no time limit, but there is a limit to the number of attempts:
1). Ground ball received with foot - 4 attempts (2 from each end); 2). Bouncing ball (1 bounce before player) received with foot - 4 attempts (2 from each end); 3). Aerial ball (no bounce) received with foot - 4 attempts (2 from each end); 4). Aerial ball (no bounce) received with thigh - 4 attempts (2 from each end); 5). Aerial ball (no bounce) received with chest - 4 attempts (2 from each end); 6). Aerial ball (no bounce) received with head - 4 attempts (2 from each end). Player is allowed 1 touch to receive and 1 to pass for activities 1-3 and 2 touches to receive and 1 to pass for activities 4-6. The player must play the passing touch from inside the 4x4 square. Player is rewarded 1 point for receiving the ball inside the square within the permitted touches and 1 point to an accurate pass. Bad service - serve again.
Max score: 48. Below expectation 0-11, At expectation 12-20, Above expectation 21+

# Plus 2 Assessment #4

**Materials Needed**

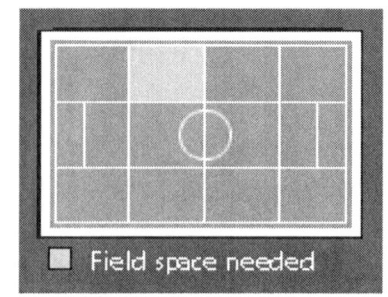

Area 30 x 5 yds
- 10 Balls
- Cones

## Plus 2 Assessment #4 (Running with the Ball)

**Description:**
Players have 1 minute to perform as many attempts as they can running with the ball. The player starts at one end of a 30 yd long and 5 yd wide channel with one ball. On the command of "GO", the player pushes the ball forward with their feet and attempts to cover the 30 yard distance as quickly as possible - maintaining control of the ball. When the player reaches the other end of the channel there is a 5 yd 'turning area'. The player must turn inside this area quickly and return with the ball to the other end - where the player must turn inside the turning area and repeat.

**Coaching Points**
- Assessor can offer encouragement during the activity without telling the player what to do.

**Progressions:**

**Scoring:**
2pts for every successful attempt in one direction. 1pt for a turn performed inside the 'turning area'. - (minus) 1pt for the ball leaving the channel. - (minus) 1pt for not performing the turn inside the 'turning area'.
Scoring: Below expectation 0-7, At expectation 8-12, Above expectation 13+
Note: Place extra balls along the channel at 10 yd intervals on both sides and place an extra ball at each end. If the ball goes outside, the player should resume with the nearest ball.

# Plus 2 Assessment #5

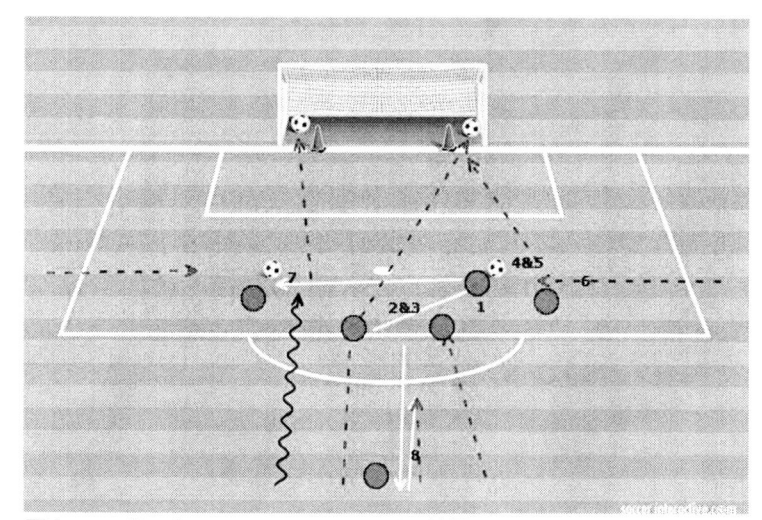

## Materials Needed

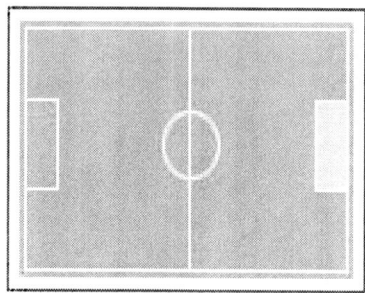

Area 20 x 20 yds
- 16 Balls
- Cones
- Goal (appropriate)

## Plus 2 Assessment #5 (Shooting)

### Description:
In this activity the player will be assessed on their shooting performance in a variety of different scenarios. A shooting circuit is created to enable 8 different shots: 1) Starting 25 yds from goal, on the command of "GO" the player dribbles the ball towards the goal. The player must shoot the ball before a line (marked with cones) 15 yards from goal, 2) Player turns to face the starting cone and a ball is rolled by the server into the player who must turn and shoot (a maximum 2 touches), 3) Repeat 2 but turn to the other side, 4) Once the shot has been taken the player must run and take a first time shot of a stationary ball 15 yards from goal and opposite the goal post on either side of the goal 5) Next shot is the stationary ball on the other side. 6) A server rolls the ball to the center of the square from the side for a first time shot. 7) Player spins to receive a ball from the other side for a first time shot. 8) Player runs to the starting cone and the server throws a bouncing ball towards the goal and the player must shoot first time (volley/half volley) before reaching the 15 yd line. Repeat twice for one complete assessment.

### Coaching Points
- Assessor can offer encouragement during the activity without telling the player what to do.

### Progressions:

### Scoring:
1pt for each goal scored. 1pt extra scored for each shot entering the goal within 1 yd of the goal post (marked on each side with cones). Max score: 32 (16 goals and 16 accuracy points). Below expectation 0-10, At expectation 11-18, Above expectation 19+.

# Plus 2 Assessment #6

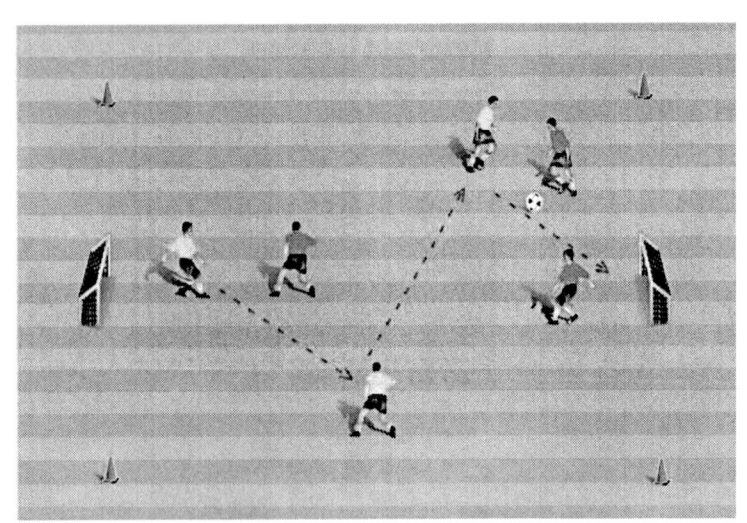

**Materials Needed**

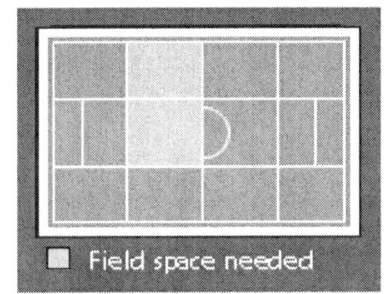

Area 30 x 15 yds
- 5-10 Balls
- Cones
- Goals

## Plus 2 Assessment #6 (Attacking)

**Description:**
Attacking game evaluation:
Evaluating players in a game environment is somewhat subjective, but is often the best way to assess a player's true performance. This assessment focuses on individual attacking. Two teams play 3v3 in an area 30 x 15 yards. The game is two 5 minute periods.

**Coaching Points**
- Assessor can offer encouragement during the activity without telling the player what to do.

**Progressions:**
Below expectation: Player invariably 'kicks' the ball forward aimlessly, rarely dribbles the ball, tends to stay in one position (defensively), rarely supports the attack and when attempting to control the ball normally needs 2+ touches. At expectation: The player tries to bring the ball under control before passing or dribbling, passes more than dribbles to beat an opponent, will join in attacking sequences and attempts skills learned in practice. Above expectation: When receiving the ball the players first instinct is to beat an opponent, often starts attacking sequences, tries to get in a threatening position in every move, rarely gives possession away, is creative with the ball and is not discouraged if a skill is not successful.

# Plus 2 Assessment #7

**Materials Needed**

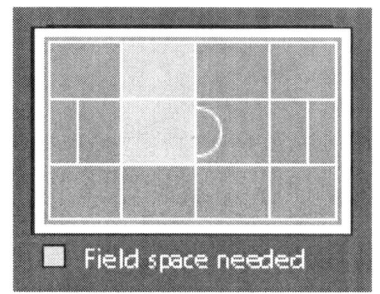

☐ Field space needed

Area 30 x 15 yds
- 5-10 Balls
- Cones
- Goals

## Plus 2 Assessment #7 (Defending)

**Description:**
Defending game evaluation:
Evaluating players in a game environment is somewhat subjective, but is often the best way to assess a player's true performance. This assessment focuses on individual defending. Two teams play 3v3 in an area 30 x 15 yards. The game is two 5 minute periods.

**Coaching Points**
- Assessor can offer encouragement during the activity without telling the player what to do.

**Progressions:**

Below expectation: Player seems reactive to situations – getting the wrong side of the attacker and chasing to get back in position, mentally disengages when attack breaks down – first instinct not to defend, tends to be off balance and easy to pass, and attempts to tackle awkwardly with the wrong foot. At expectation: Tends to be a little impatient and in so doing tries to win the ball every challenge, has a good starting defensive position, has difficulty with attackers with the ball at pace, recovers well to a goal-side position and knows how to force a player away from goal. Above expectation: Seems to have 'timo' when defending, exerts pressure when necessary, in 1v1 situations forces attackers away from goal, excellent positional play (knows where the goal is) and when committed to a challenge invariably wins the ball.

# Plus 2 Assessment #8

**Materials Needed**

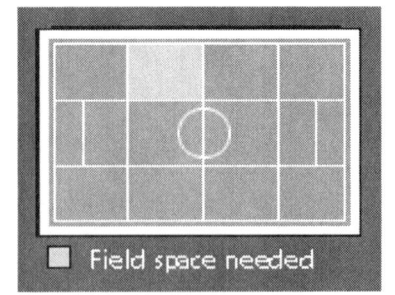

☐ Field space needed

Area 20 x 5 yds
- Tape Measure

## Plus 2 Assessment #8 (Locomotor - Run & Hop)

**Description:**
These activities assess the ability of the player to perform a number of essential locomotor activities requiring coordination of thought and movement.

**Coaching Points**
- Assessor can offer encouragement during the activity.

**Progressions:**
**Run- assesses running pattern: Below expectation** - Running flat-footed with wide base of support, hold arms bent at or above waist height, with feet shoulder-width or wider apart and take awkward, short, flat-footed strides with legs slightly bent. **At expectation** - Running with arm opposition and short strides, swings arms in opposition below waist but runs with a shorter than normal heel-to-toe stride, with legs bent awkwardly at about a 90-degree angle. **Above expectation** - Running with arm opposition and long strides, swings arms in opposition, and runs with long strides, placing feet in a heel-to-toe pattern, bending the lead leg at about a 90-degree angle.
**Hop - assesses the ability to hop forward on one foot while holding the other foot suspended. Below expectation** - Hopping with slight knee bend, minimal balance, suspended knee is bent at less than a 90-degree angle, balance is poor, and the arms move excessively and awkwardly. **At expectation** - Hopping with full knee bend, exaggerated arm swing, suspended knee is bent at a 90-degree angle, balance is maintained, but the arms swing upward in a slightly awkward manner while hopping. **Above expectation** - hopping with full knee bend, coordinated arm movements, knee is bent at a 90-degree angle, elbows are bent at the sides, and the arms swing slightly at the sides. The assessor should demonstrate the skill each time prior to the player's attempt. Allow the player to have two attempts and record the best score. **Scoring:** Below expectation; At expectation; Above expectation.

# Appendix

PLUS 2 COACHING FOR DEVELOPMENT

## SoccerPlus Big Picture of Curriculum

**1. What is the purpose of the curriculum?**

| Aims | Equality of Opportunity | Est. Standards | Continuity & Coherence | Promotes Understanding | Pathway (U5 - U18+) |
|---|---|---|---|---|---|
| Outcomes | Achieve Soccer Standards | Achieve academic, social & health aims | Commitment to learning | Confident learners | Individual & Team Success |
| Focus | | Skill Development Individual and Team | Knowledge and understanding e.g. Identifying visual cues, tactical awareness | Attitudes and attributes e.g. sportsmanship, respect, confidence | |

**2. How is the curriculum structured?**

| Content | Fundamental Movement Skills | Tactical Awareness & Understanding | Physical & mental preparation | Academic & social responsibility | Fundamental Soccer Skills |
|---|---|---|---|---|---|
| Methodology | Practical and theory | Individual and Team Assessment | Guided practice | Self-discovery | Directed & Modeling |
| Supporting knowledge | Cognitive Development Mental acumen | Biological Development Growth and Maturation | Emotional Development Confidence, self esteem etc | Nutrition Balanced diet and hydration | Physical fitness Speed, agility, balance & coordination |
| Learning Environment | Team practices, positional instruction & optional sessions | 'Street Soccer' and un-structured practice | Competition e.g. 11 v 11 and small sided games | Tournaments & Festivals | Indoor training and games |

**3. Are the aims being achieved?**

| Evaluation | Skill acquisition Against performance standards | Team selections Tryout process combined with regular seasonal assessments | Talent Identification Planning for exceptional talent | Knowledge and Understanding Decision making & tactical awareness | 360° Review Parents, players, coaches and administrators |
|---|---|---|---|---|---|

227

© SOCCERPLUS ALL RIGHTS RESERVED

# SOCCER COACHING ACTIVITIES, SESSION PLANS AND ASSESSMENT

## SoccerPlus Player Development Model

| Chronological Age | 0, 1, 3 | 4 5 | 6 7 8 | 9 10 11 | 12 13 14 15 | 16 17 18 |
|---|---|---|---|---|---|---|
| Balyi LTAD Model | | Active Start | Fundamentals | Learning to Train | Training to Train | Training to Compete |
| SoccerPlus FC Stages | | +PLUS 1 | +PLUS 2 | +PLUS 3 | +PLUS 4 | +PLUS 5 |
| Age Group | | U5 - U6 | U7 - U9 | U10 - U12 | U13 - U15 | U16 - U18 |
| Soccer Age (Developmental) | | 2 years +/- | 2 years +/- | 2 years +/- | 2 years +/- | 2 years +/- |
| Coaching Time Annually | | 40 - 90 hours | 100 - 200 hours | 150 - 320 hours | 150 - 360 hours | 150 - 540 hours |
| Developmental Focus | | 1. Social<br>2. Physical<br>3. Technical<br>4. Psychological<br>5. Tactical | 1. Technical<br>2. Social<br>3. Physical<br>4. Tactical<br>5. Psychological | 1. Technical<br>2. Physical<br>3. Tactical<br>4. Psychological<br>5. Social | 1. Technical<br>2. Tactical<br>3. Physical<br>4. Psychological<br>5. Social | 1. Tactical<br>2. Psychological<br>3. Technical<br>4. Physical<br>5. Social |
| Specialist Training | | General | All Positions | Specific Positions | Groups & Units | Whole Team |
| Players Per Session | | 12 | 12 to 15 | 15 to 18 | 18 | 22 |
| Length of Session | | 45-60 min | 60-75 min | 60-90 min | 75-90 min | 75-90 min |
| Ratio Training to Games | | Training | 4:1 | 3:1 | 3:1 | 2:1 |
| Training Format | | 1v1 to 3v3 | 1v1 to 5v5 | 4v4 to 8v8 | 4v4 to 11v11 | 4v4 to 11v11 |
| Game Format | | N/A | 4v4 or 5v5 | 6v6 to 8v8 | 7v7 to 11v11 | 11v11 |
| Goalkeepers in games | | No | 5v5 only | Yes | Yes | Yes |
| Player Assessment | | 2 per year | 3 per year | 4 per year | 6 per year | 8 per year |
| Coach Assessment | | 2 per year | 2 per year | 2 per year | 2 per year | 2 per year |
| Coach Certification | | Youth Module | Youth Module | E License | D License | C License |

PLUS 2 COACHING FOR DEVELOPMENT

## SoccerPlus Y-SAT Club Assessment

The Y-SAT is a proprietary tool developed by SoccerPlus FC for the purpose of assessing a youth soccer program in four areas:

1. Coaching.
2. Curriculum.
3. Player Development including talent Identification and Assessment.
4. Administration including facilities and equipment.

The primary purpose of the assessment is to identify the strengths and weaknesses that currently exist and to inform recommendations aimed at enhancing the program.

### Common Issues Addressed in the Assessment

SoccerPlus FC has provided solutions to recreation and town programs resulting from the Y-SAT:

1. Creating a pathway for players from U5 to U18.
2. Implementing a curriculum for players and coaches.
3. Supporting and mentoring volunteer coaches.
4. Ensuring all players receive equal opportunity to be successful.
5. Creating a strategic plan for long term growth and development of the program.
6. Assessing and selecting players to teams.
7. How to keep town players in town programs.

To learn how your youth soccer program can receive a Y-SAT Assessment, contact David Newbery – dave@soccerplus.org

SOCCER COACHING ACTIVITIES, SESSION PLANS AND ASSESSMENT

## Facts about SoccerPlus FC

*SoccerPlus FC* was formed in response to issues identified during extensive research into town and recreation soccer programs. For over 30 years youth organizations have been advised by professional coaching organizations to hire trainers and provide summer camps. Unfortunately, this approach has not solved issues of attracting volunteers, developing coaching talent from within, the significant attrition of young players from the game or engaging parents. *SoccerPlus FC* provides a unique approach in developing systems, procedures and programs providing the infrastructure to ensure long-term growth and success. One tangible outcome is to remove the dependency of the organization on professional coaching.

One of the greatest endorsements a company can receive is partnership with some of the most recognizable names in the industry. Our commercial partners offer extra special service and expertise to guide and support SoccerPlus FC club partners.

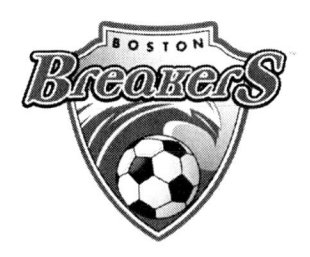

CPSIA information can be obtained at www.ICGtesting.com
Printed in the USA
LVOW032151150812

294559LV00001B/11/P

9 781453 746363